THE BONNIE PRINCE

THE BONNIE PRINCE

Charlie Cooke – My Football Life

Charlie Cooke
with Martin Knight

MAINSTREAM
PUBLISHING

EDINBURGH AND LONDON

First published in Great Britain in 2006 by
MAINSTREAM PUBLISHING COMPANY
(EDINBURGH) LTD
7 Albany Street
Edinburgh EH1 3UG

ISBN 9781845962272

A catalogue record for this book is available
from the British Library

Typeset in Palatino

Printed in Great Britain by
Cox and Wyman Ltd, Reading

Acknowledgements

There are many people I must thank for their help in compiling this book: Martin Knight, my co-author, for his professional skills, without which it would never have seen the light of day; Claire Rose at Mainstream for her endless hours of advice and attention to the copy; my friend Alan Sharp for his excellent foreword – I count it a great honour that he wrote it; old friends Valerie and Len Lee, who provided valuable memories and cuttings of my early days at Chelsea; My pal Tommy Baldwin, with whom I spent many a good time during the great years at Chelsea, and who reminded me of some hilarious ones I'd forgotten; Gabrielle Crawford, who shared many happy times with Diane and me, and has been a close family friend and supporter ever since; old friends Chris Matthews and Theresa Connelly for their friendship and hospitality to Diane and me when we are back in London and for their memories of the old days at Chelsea; old Greenock High School pals Jack Glennie and Jim Geddes, who filled in the details of some old school stories and my early days as a pro; John Adam, my old team manager, for his enthusiastic recollections of my juvenile football days with Port Glasgow Rovers; Desmond Herron, who started his pro football career in the same game as me, against Ayr United at Pittodrie at the start of the 1960 season, when we were both 17-year-old wannabes at Aberdeen, for his old stories and jokes; Dave Forbes, who helped me piece together many of the details of my time at Dundee; Tony Taylor in Canada for his reminiscences of my time at Crystal Palace; Tommy Docherty for his terrific hospitality to Diane and me in Manchester and his frank and funny memories of our days at Chelsea; Paddy Mulligan for his reminiscences of our time at Chelsea and Palace; Terrence Gurney, an ex-Chelsea youth player from my home town, who reminded me how it was way back in the day both at Stamford Bridge and on the Greenock fields; Alfred Galustian, my associate in Coerver® Coaching for his advice and support not only in the writing of this book but throughout our 25-plus years of working together; My sister, Myra, her son, Nicolaus, and my brother, Ian, for their research, advice and reminiscences about the old days and about our parents, Agnes and Charlie Sr. And finally, above all, thanks to my wife, Diane, and my son, Chas, for their unfailing patience and support throughout the writing of this book. Without their encouragement, it would never have been written. To them all, a very sincere thank you.

Martin Knight would like to thank David Johnstone and Ron Hockings for their help in preparing this book. Thanks to Roddy Doyle for permission to quote from 'Heroes and Villains'.

Contents

Foreword

It has been famously said of Charlie Cooke that he was a great player trying hard to be a good one. Perhaps it's just a fondness for paradox on my part, but I have always thought this observation an illuminating one. It touches on the distinction between artist and artisan given such contemptuous expression in Eric Cantona's put-down of Didier Deschamps as a mere water-carrier.

This is a remark Charlie would never have made, despite his undeniable claim to be, in the sense that it applies to footballers, an artist. For he recognised from his earliest days that his especial genius was a gift, a gift that must constantly be girded by application, industry and the discipline of sometimes sublimating individual brilliance to team effort. The origins of this lifelong attitude are to be found in his upbringing and culture, the Scottish working-class ethic, with its Calvinist underpinnings. An ingrained suspicion of exhibitionism was suspended with regard to football in order to accommodate the attribute 'gallus', a flashy, cheeky arrogance that had its fullest flowering in one of Charlie's contemporaries, Jim Baxter.

Charlie was never gallus in the full sense of the term. This was not due to any lack of spectacular skills or a reluctance to occupy centre stage. He was a showman, but not a show-off. Something in his nature, 'humility' might be too strong a word, but certainly a self-questioning bent, held him back from the indulgence of simply doing the thing that came naturally. From within himself, and from those around him, particularly his parents, he drew on the conviction, perhaps compulsion, that without work, hard work, talent alone could not achieve the highest level, the fullest realisation of potential.

It's a striking quality in anyone and for a top-flight athlete an uncommon one, perhaps more so in Charlie's young days than now. Someone of his gifts – marvellous balance, sleight of foot and devastating pace – might well have been expected to play to his strengths, and the gallery, to be the rapier thrust into the bowels of defences (many of which were moved mightily at the prospect), and to leave the hustling and harrying to the water-carriers. But even in his glory days, Charlie embraced the ideal of putting in a shift, and it is this sensibility and its expression throughout a wonderful career that lies behind the opening description: a great player trying to be a good one.

The extent to which he reconciled these contrasting qualities is a matter for debate, and Charlie does discuss in the pages that follow the tensions within himself which resulted as he tried to meet the sometimes contradictory demands they made on him. We, who were admirers, have our favourite images of Charlie the player, and I doubt if many of us would choose one of him slogging it out in midfield, getting in his interceptions, tracking back and all that goes, then as now, with being a good team player. We'd prefer to enshrine the wondrous rhythm of his running, with its hint of speed-skater in the thigh thrusts, the slaloming glide through defenders, drawn against their will and judgement into the premature tackle. Mine is from a game against West Ham at the Bridge when I saw no less an authority than Bobby Moore sucked forward by that mesmerising approach, into that most exposed of situations, the one-on-one, him-or-me schoolyard confrontation. I don't remember the score, but I won't forget the moment, and those of us who saw him all have similar epiphanies in our possession. But Charlie himself thought highly of his efforts in the trenches; perhaps, in his quirky, contrary fashion, more so than of that which came instinctively to him.

One of the pleasures of this book is to hear his distinctive voice, unabashed in its assessment of his own qualities, unsparing yet not malicious in its assessment of clubs, coaches and contemporaries. It gives us a vivid picture of the beautiful game during a period of transition, when the grip of clubs over players was beginning to slacken and the cult of football players as celebrities was a-borning. The Bosman Ruling had not yet rent the fabric of the national game, and Scotsmen were most English clubs' idea of an exotic import. In this world, Charlie Cooke was a nonpareil and one of the few figures from the era you can be assured would have been as remarkable today as he was then. But to read the account of his first steps into the professional game is to be reminded of how much has changed, and not all of it for the best. No less engrossing are his days with Chelsea, and students of that period will be enlivened by the wry yet romantic account of the side of the '70s.

In closing this brief introduction, I should address a word to those of you who, through no fault of your own (i.e. being born too late), have never seen Charlie Cooke play. Imagine Arjen Robben as a more powerful runner, not so much an eluder of tackles as a defier of them, but with altogether more of an engine, and you'll be in the ballpark. It won't entirely convey the way he could cause the game to slow down around him, as if everyone else was operating under a slightly different set of physical laws. You'd have to have been there for that. There are never, at any given time, many such players. Charlie Cooke was one of them, and we'll be lucky if we see his like again.

Alan Sharp

1

Clowns to the Left of Me

Just after midnight on 7 May 1941, German reconnaissance planes avoided anti-aircraft artillery along the River Clyde in south-west Scotland and circled my home town of Greenock, a shipbuilding, torpedo and munitions factory community 20 miles west and downriver from Glasgow and a key target for Hitler's planners. They marked the town with incendiary bombs to the north by the river and to the south by its water supply, Loch Thom. Then, shortly after 2.15 a.m., their following pack of 300 Luftwaffe warplanes and bombers crossed the Clyde from north to south and pounded the town all night long, in wave after thundering wave, on the second night of the town's Second World War blitz.

Tragically for the townspeople, flying across the river and not along it made targeting more difficult for the Führer's swarms, and their deadly cargoes hardly hit the yards or ships they were intended for. Instead, they inflicted catastrophic damage on the business and residential districts of the town, smashing 10,000 of Greenock's 18,000 homes and demolishing 1,000 of them completely. Despite the early-warning sirens and crowded air-raid shelters, 1,250 residents were injured and 280 died. It was collateral damage of the worst kind, which scarred the town and its families physically and emotionally for decades to come.

The Cooke family home in Morton Terrace, near Cappielow Park, where Greenock Morton played football, was a casualty that night. A house across the street was flattened with a single hit, and the blast blew out the side of ours, thankfully not killing or injuring anyone. It forced my father, Charlie Sr, and my mother, Agnes, with my 10-year-old brother, Ian, and 6-week-old sister, Myra, to evacuate and squeeze in with my Uncle Richard and Aunt Margaret Cooke and their young family in nearby Belville Street. Not long after, with the war still raging, Agnes evacuated again with Myra and Ian, to her old family home in St Monance on the east coast of Scotland. And that is how, on 14 October 1942, I came to be born a Fifer in a tiny, sleepy fishing village, where the most threatening things in the sky weren't Hitler's bombers but flocks of cantankerous seagulls.

Although I only lived in St Monance until the end of the war, when I was three years old, I am as proud of my east-coast roots as I am of my west-coast pedigree. I was born there, I holidayed there throughout my childhood, and, of course, it was home to my mother's family – the Smalls – for generations. Located midway between Anstruther and Elie, about five miles from each, it's believed to have been named in the sixth century after a religious recluse from a monastery in neighbouring Pittenweem. You can see the spot where he lived, St Monan's Cell, or Cave, near the path from the church to the shore at the west end of the village.

By the 1700s, St Monance was one of the main fishing ports on the east coast of Scotland – line fishing for white fish in the summer and herring fishing in the winter. The town also developed a small boat-building industry, which peaked in the nineteenth century and declined as wood-structured vessels gave way to steel. The largest boatyard now lies derelict and the old distinctive town sights and smells of sawdust and caulking are no more. But St Monance adapted, and today it is principally a tourist destination and has retained all the charm that I remember it for. The climate is officially mild, but the winter and spring seasons bring violent gales from the south-east that lash the coast for days. They wash ashore huge quantities of seaweed, which in the past was harvested by the village farmers and used as manure on the estates of the local landowners, like the Earl of Balcaskie. Today, it just floats in the harbour and along the seashore, brown, bulbous and ominous, as if a sea monster could rise from within it at any time.

My mother, Agnes, was one of five Small sisters, who all one way or another went into service, as was the way then. The phrase 'in service' may have been coined by working-class women themselves to add some gravitas to their menial duties as maids or servants in the homes of the rich. The employment alternatives for poorer girls from rural backgrounds were limited then, and their days in service often ended only when they married and had a family. This was the case with Agnes when she met Charles Cooke, a shipyard engineer from Greenock.

Agnes was a typical Fifer if being tidy, thrifty and a great cook qualifies her. She enjoyed getting her greying hair done in a blue-rinse perm as she got older but was still a fusser about the smallest details even then. Rationing was never far from her memory and lips, even when it was long past, and she always insisted we finish our meals and leave nothing to waste. Her shortbread and cakes were to die for, and her fresh battered fish and chips, every midweek, have never been bettered. To this day, I can hear the crackling fat, smell the burning gas stove and taste the hot, fresh salted chips that she made in our tiny Thom Street kitchen.

Agnes was a Presbyterian churchgoer and always insisted in our early days at Thom Street on the west side of town, where we finally settled when we returned from St Monance after the war, that Myra and I accompany her to Mount Pleasant Church of Scotland, only five minutes through Murdieston Park, where Reverend Young's sermons went straight over my head and left me scuffing my shoes and counting the panes on the stained-glass windows. After a while, my whining paid off, and I got the answer to my prayers (although not the prayers Reverend Young was urging me to say) and was allowed to miss church and the Sunday school following and instead did my praying while searching for good 'cheggies' (chestnuts) up the Bow Road in the nearby Greenock Cemetery. Sometimes, on nice summer days, I kept walking on through to the other side of the graveyard to watch Greenock Cricket Club play in their posh west-end fields, marvelling at the perfectly mowed turf and wondering what they liked about such a seemingly dull game.

My father was from a line of famous circus folk who toured the United Kingdom, America and beyond for many years as Cooke's Circus, Cooke's Royal Circus, Cooke's Hippodromes and so on. The name Cooke and the circus were synonymous, and in the nineteenth century, the Cookes were as famous as P.T. Barnum was in America or Bertram Mills and the Chipperfields would later be in Britain. It was a Thomas Cooke who started it all. He was born in the mid-eighteenth century in Scotland, and my line can be traced back directly to him. His large family had extraordinarily large families of their own, featuring circus performers of all skills, aptitudes and abilities. Within two generations, there were circus Cookes all over Europe and America. In fact, Cooke's Circus sailed from my home town of Greenock to New York on a ship called the *Roger Stewart* in 1836. It was the Cookes who brought back to England the big top and the whole concept of tented circuses. Thomas's son, Thomas Taplin Cooke, became famous in his day and died a rich man. He was born in 1782 and by 1836 employed 136 staff – 40 of them Cookes. By 1900, there were over 200 T.T. Cooke descendants, and nearly all of them were circus artistes or employees.

T.T. himself was not afraid of getting his hands dirty and was an accomplished leaping horseman, as well as doubling up as a strongman and tightrope walker. He died in 1866 and is buried in Kensal Green Cemetery. His son Henry (1814–1901) worked in the circus but had aspirations and some success as a serious actor. His son Charles was born in the early 1830s in Brighton, where the circus gave a performance for the Royal Family and thereafter took the name Cooke's Royal Circus. However, he too gravitated away from the family business as he got older, and he became an actor, a comedian and, latterly, a photographer. One of Charles's sons was Richard, and he was my grandfather. By this generation we were not part of the Big Top, Richard having moved to Greenock from Glasgow to take work in the shipyards in 1897. My father Charles had been born in 1895.

One of T.T. Cooke's other sons, William, became renowned for William Cooke's Hippodrome, which entertained audiences on both sides of the Atlantic with equestrian shows. For these he mounted battle scenes, hunting chases and even Shakespeare plays, as this contemporary newspaper extract recounts:

When, in the summer of 1843, William Cooke advertised his 'Royal Circus' to the people of Greenock, Scotland, one of the featured performers was his son Alfred. Standing on a horse's back and circling the ring at a slow canter, Alfred entered costumed as Shakespeare's Falstaff leading his ragged recruits to slaughter at the Battle of Shrewsbury. From this position Alfred recited Falstaff's soliloquy about the follies and limitations of honour and then, still standing on his horse's back, shed the Falstaff costume to reveal a second dress, that of Shakespeare's Shylock, complete with prop knife and scales with which to extract his pound of flesh from Antonio's bosom. In the character of Shylock and declaiming a mixture of lines from several scenes of *The Merchant of Venice*, Cooke continued his circling canter. For a second time he shed his costume, revealing beneath the Shylock robe the battle attire of Richard III and in his final equestrian circles of the ring Alfred Cooke shouted out his desire to exchange his kingdom for a horse. As the

Royal Circus playbill promised, 'So far as can be portrayed on Horseback, Mr Alfred Cooke will delineate the varied and conflicting feelings which moved the breasts of Jocund Falstaff, the usurious and relentless Jew, and the ambitious and cruel Richard.'

William died in 1886, having attained a great age. He was said to have made his fortune with his pantomime *The Battle of Waterloo*, but there wasn't much wealth around a generation later – not in my branch of the tree, at least. William himself, as a young man, was no mean juggler, performing whilst standing on a high wire, and the business of running circuses was also a juggling act, it appears, as proprietors seem to have gained and lost fortunes several times in their lives. William was forced back from America when he lost two circus buildings to fire, one in Philadelphia and one in Baltimore. A statue of William's son Alfred sitting astride a horse stands in Highgate Cemetery.

Charles Dickens, no less, mentions the family in one of his essays. The Cooke mark remains not only in the thousands of Cooke descendants who walk around today with the circus running in their blood, knowingly and unknowingly, but also in our buildings. In Britain and America, there are a number of large sites that were formerly Cooke's Circus amphitheatres and other structures. The Royal Court Theatre in Liverpool, for example, was originally built by a John Cooke in 1826 and was Cooke's Royal Amphitheatre of Arts before the building was redesigned by Henry Sumner and became the Royal Court.

Another John Cooke walked his way into the American

history books by successfully crossing a high wire pulled taut between Cliff House and Seal Rocks in San Francisco in 1865. The feat was revered to the extent that Bret Harte, a literary rival of Mark Twain, wrote a poem called 'The Ballad of Mr Cooke' that begins:

> Where the sturdy ocean breeze
> Drives the spray of roaring seas,
> That the Cliff House balconies overlook:
> There, in spite of rain that balked,
> With his sandals duly chalked,
> Once upon a tight-rope walked Mr. Cooke.

Uncovering my circus ancestry has been fun and surprising, and has given me a new perspective on my own life. It would be nice to say that the family circus profession, the skills it required – balance, juggling, conditioning, public performing – and even my attraction to America were in my Cooke genes and contributed to my football career, but I think that might be pushing it. That said, I have to admit I was a bit obsessive and secretive about my juggling records as a kid and took unreal pleasure in every improvement in my personal keepie-uppie best, with no wish or need to tell anybody about it. Although I've mentioned only the more famous Cookes who ran circuses, the bulk of my ancestors worked in them and intermarried with the large array of performers that the circuses employed. Italian clowns, Red Indian horsemen, Russian acrobats, midgets, strongmen and who knows what else form my blood-line. One Cooke woman married Henry Adams, who was a famous clown and one of many who used the celebrated Grimaldi clown name. So I reckon I'm not only Scottish, as I had always assumed, but probably have the blood of several races in me, people who lived on the road, made their living from providing thrills and spills, and drew their satisfaction from their audience's pleasure. So maybe genetics have more to answer for than I've ever realised. But when I informed my best pal and Chelsea colleague Tommy Baldwin about my newly discovered circus ancestry, he confirmed it in no uncertain terms. Looking at me over his glasses, with the inevitable beer in his hand at a function recently, he said, 'I always thought you were a clown.' He was laughing. Well, I think he was smiling a bit.

Charlie Sr, my father, was never a showman in the vaudevillian sense, although there was maybe some connection to the old equestrian family life, as he served in the Horse Artillery in the First World War. The only remaining photograph we have of him as a young man is an old brown-and-white image of him standing shirt-sleeved in the stable with his beloved horse Sherry. Both were injured in the war, leaving Charlie with a large scar on his back and left leg. Many years later, Ian and I watched incredulously as he calmly picked and eased a piece of shrapnel from his knee, and which Ian kept in a matchbox as a souvenir.

Charlie Sr was quiet and an easy guy to be around. He was a smoker, who rolled his own Digger's Shag cigarettes, which always looked crumpled, no matter how carefully he licked and rolled them. He wasn't teetotal, but one or two beers, or a sherry or a Scotch on Hogmanay, was usually more than enough for him, a trait that would surely have made my own adult life simpler had I inherited it. He seldom raised his voice about anything and was what I can only describe as a hard-working father and husband. He worked five days Monday to Friday in the yards and would take three nights and a Sunday overtime when it was available, and, like clockwork, always quietly deposited his pay packet on the kitchen table at dinner-time on Friday evening. It was a staple of our family life, no big deal – something that couldn't be said for every household in Clydeside, where Friday pay night was infamous for closing-time fights and family squabbles over spent wages.

My father was a short, wiry guy with a narrow, bony face. He always walked to work, maybe a mile, the same route around the dam, through Murdieston Park, down past the Orangefield café and the West Station to Hasties, where he worked on ships' steering gear. In the summer evenings while we were playing football, we'd see him walking the path home through the park and around the dam, past the swans and ducks and fishermen, slightly bent forward with his hands clasped behind his back. This was the way he always walked, like he was thinking deeply, with his silver hair parted and combed back flat on his head. In the winter, he'd wear a tan oil-stained raincoat and, on very few occasions and only in the worst weather, a flat cap.

In the winter evenings after work, when he wasn't on overtime, he'd settle into an easy chair by the fireside in the living-room and have a well-earned sleep, with his legs outstretched and his oil-stained fingers clasped on his lap, while Scottish country-dance music played on the radio, as it always did just after teatime. This was followed later by maybe an episode of *Dick Barton: Special Agent* or a *Riders of the Range* Western with what we'd surely now think were primitive galloping noises and sound effects. He'd still be in his working togs, with his sleeves rolled up and his braces unbuttoned, and I used to marvel at the black hair on his muscular forearms and in his nostrils that contrasted with the silver hair on his head and at how soundly he seemed to sleep on those evenings, with his eyes closed and his head laid back against the headrest.

In the small amount of time he had to himself outside of work and watching Morton at Cappielow Park with me every other Saturday, his hobby was growing chrysanthemums in a tiny hothouse he built in our small garden out back at Thom Street. Charlie Sr grew rhubarb, potatoes and tomatoes, like many Clydeside gardeners, but his flowers were unusual. He occasionally had visitors coming around to see his better blooms, and he even exhibited them at local shows once or twice. But if he was proud of them, he hid it well, and it seemed he showed them genuinely more out of interest and pleasure in his hobby than any particular wish for the glory of winning prizes. It was a quiet, single-minded quality he had, which I always admired and wanted to have for myself, but as we can see, writing this book no less, I'm still chasing it.

Ian, at ten years older than me, was always a bit out of my orbit during both my school years and my teens, when he was mostly away at sea. He served for three years in the Scots Guard, red tunic and black bearskin and all, and later went to sea as a second engineer. He's the one with the best memory in the family, recalling details that have escaped the rest of us. He always reminds me of the gaucho boots he brought back to me from one of his sea trips to South America and how the next time he was home I'd kicked the toes out of them playing football. After the sea, he became a fitter in the yards, and today he lives in Greenock in the house we grew up in. He still takes a keen interest in the weekly football news and scores, just like he always did.

Myra, my sister, two years older than me and a baby during the blitz, is the caring one of the family and the one we all go to when we need to get things done. Her husband and my good friend, Bill Lawrie, died suddenly of a heart attack following an operation, leaving Myra with a 13-year-old son, Nicolaus. I'm proud to say that, in her 50s, Myra returned to college to get her Masters in English Literature and today enjoys a lively retirement, living in Berkhamsted with Nicolaus but regularly travelling back to Greenock to see Ian and coming over to the US to visit me, my wife, Diane, and our son, Chas, in Cincinnati. She's not done it yet but she keeps threatening to move back up to Scotland, to Dunoon or Tighnabruaich.

When we came back to Greenock after the war, the contrast couldn't have been greater. From the stone cottages rising from the sleepy harbour in St Monance, we moved back to a bustling Greenock in the midst of rebuilding and resettlement. At first, we moved to Cedar Crescent. Our new home was a brown timber two-storey semi-detached council house in Gibshill, next to the crowded tenements and closes of Bell Street and the rest of 'the Gibby', overlooking the Inchgreen harbour and railway depot, with its tugs and dredgers and dockside machinery and rail cars that brought the coal that heated Greenock's homes in those days. The house was new and in perfect shape, with not a stick out of place. But the homes on Fir Street, only a single narrow street behind, were bombsite rubble and stark testimony, if any was needed, to the devastation Hitler's bombs had inflicted. Ironically, we kids shot and blew one another up in our war games among the debris, oblivious to the real stories of human tragedy the rubble silently held.

The Inchgreen dry dock, a huge, cavernous basin, was where the *Queen Elizabeth* liner was originally fitted out, and it's easy to visualise the ant-like activity of the painters, carpenters, electricians and interior designers that must have gone on there in that great ship and many like it. Today, the dock sits walled off to the passing traffic, deserted and unused, like an empty giant's tomb. First Street, a tenement row street just next to Cedar Crescent across Gibshill Road, was where Tommy Bryceland, a well-known professional footballer, was brought up. He was a few years older than me and achieved Greenock immortality by scoring the first goal in the 1959 Scottish Cup final for St Mirren. He later went on to have a long career with Norwich City in England. In my teens, I counted it an honour to play a few times with his younger brother Hughie at Renfrew Juniors.

After the war, we were still in the days of ration books and coal fires and daily milk delivery. The coalmen's pink lips and white eyes peered from their dusty black faces under shiny leather caps as they toted the bags, in their reinforced shoulder-padded jackets, and dumped them noisily into the coal bin, with no apologies for the copious dross they contained – something that exercised Agnes's thrifty nature no end. The coalmen just shrugged off the complaints, blaming it on their rail deliveries as they folded the bags and piled them neatly on the flatbed of the lorry.

'Loch Fyne fresh herring,' barked an old fish pedlar

who came around every week, leading his skin-and-bones pony pulling a flat rickety cart with the fish in yellow pine boxes next to brass scales and wax wrapping paper and newspapers held down with stones. He usually stopped at the bend in Cedar Crescent, and Agnes always inspected the fish closely before paying and asking about future deliveries so she could plan ahead. He came even in midwinter with the poor pony that resembled an anatomical diagram, with almost every bone, tendon and muscle visible. In its steel shoes, it would slip and slide on the ice patches in white-eyed terror, but the old guy would just hold on to the bridle and keep talking and pulling till it got a footing and then move on like it was no big deal.

The milk lorries stopped and started every morning in all the Gibshill streets, and it was the biggest thrill to get a ride amidst the smell of souring spilt milk and petrol fumes, if only for a couple of stops. I remember, after watching the more gallus kids speak up and get their rides on previous days, I finally plucked up my courage and asked, 'Mister, can I get a ride on yer lorry?'

'Aye, sure – get up, then,' came the reply. I jumped aboard and rode along among the glass bottles jangling in the steel crates to the end of Cedar Crescent. I felt chuffed no end, like the kid in *Shane* riding into town alongside Alan Ladd, and was made up for days. Oh, the simple pleasures of childhood!

2

Oh, Greenock's No a Bonnie Toon

As the first line of the town song 'The Green Oak Tree'
says – 'Oh, Greenock's no a bonnie toon' – it isn't pretty
downtown, and being typical Scots with imagined John
Calvin rebukes echoing in our heads ('Admit your flaws
and all will be forgiven, my sons'), we Greenockians have
made a virtue of acknowledging the town's plainness. At
least, I have. But, as with so many things, if you're willing
to open your eyes, you will see a different side to it. You
can hike the moors behind the town or climb the Lyle Hill
in the west end and look down on the Tail of the Bank, the
mouth of the Clyde at Gourock, where the river widens
towards Rothesay and the Isle of Bute, and be stunned
by the beauty of it all. From either vantage point, you can
look directly across the river to the green hills rising behind
small towns like Dunoon, Helensburgh and Kilcreggan,
with snow-capped peaks beyond them in the winter, and
realise how blind you've been and that some of the world's
finest scenery is right there on the doorstep.

The name Greenock is thought to come from the Gaelic *grianaig* meaning 'sunny' and has been interpreted as 'sunny place' or 'sunny knoll', which is kind of funny, for if you ask anybody who has ever lived there, Greenock is wet. The opening verse of 'The Green Oak Tree' says it all:

> 'Oh, Greenock's no a bonnie toon,'
> Ye'll hear some folks complain,
> For when ye come tae Greenock
> You'll find nothing else but rain.

'Rain, rain go to Spain and never, never come back again,' we used to chant as kids. It turned the Parklea fields in Port Glasgow into mud heaps when we played football there as teenagers on winter days, forcing us to wash off the mud under the single cold-water tap that served as the shower in the old Parklea barn. But that was 'nae bother' to us teenagers in those 'fitbaw'-crazy post-war days. Summer or winter, no matter the season, the rain seemed to zero in on us. It rumbled off the North Atlantic, paused over the Inner Hebrides and Tighnabruaich (pronounced Tin-a-broo-ach), then gathered over Dunoon to the west and dumped on us, leaving us like 'droont rats'. Regularly.

The town's position on the Clyde – it's the nearest port on the west coast to the United States, with easy access to Glasgow and the Lowlands – made it a natural for fishing and trading. After the Act of Union in 1707 it became the biggest port on the west coast, importing tobacco and sugar from the Americas and the Caribbean while exporting emigrants in their thousands. The latter explains in good part the astonishingly high incidence of Scottish names in the early history of Canada and the US. The large number of Scottish Highland Games and Celtic music festivals held across North America today are testimony to their continuing influence. By the end of the nineteenth century, around 400 ships a year were transporting sugar from Caribbean holdings into Greenock's 14 refineries and filling up with emigrants for the journey out. The closure of the Tate & Lyle plant in 1997 marked the end of the town's 150-year-old connections with sugar manufacturing.

Shipbuilding was an important employer from early in the town's history. The first Greenock pier was built early in the seventeenth century, and Scott's, the oldest shipbuilders in the world, was established in 1711 and prospered as it picked up numerous orders from the Royal Navy at a time when Britain was using the sea to expand its empire and protect its interests. In their heyday, Clydeside yards made famous ships such as the *Queen Elizabeth* and the *Mauretania* and warships like the *Prince of Wales*. The words 'Clyde Built' were recognised worldwide as a stamp of quality, a matter of great pride for the town and the whole of Clydeside. In 1969, after more than 250 years of building ships, Scott's was nationalised and merged with rival firm Lithgow's to form Scott Lithgow. But even government intervention couldn't stop the decline of an industry faced with Japanese and South Korean competition that was every bit as damaging to Greenock and its economy as the Jerry bombs of 30 years earlier. During the 1970s and 1980s, Scott Lithgow, along with other firms like Kincaid's and yards like Cartsburn, Cartsdyke and Klondyke, shut down. Three hundred years of industrial history decimated in less than twenty. Today the town has almost completely shed its shipbuilding and heavy engineering industries and become host to IBM and National Semiconducter and similar high-tech and light manufacturing plants. And surprisingly to me, with my smokestack boyhood memories, it has become a friendly base in the west of Scotland for tourists to the Highlands and even a scenic attraction of sorts. It may be a sign of progress, but it's still mildly shocking to this old Greenockian to see a T-Mobile call centre and a Holiday Inn Express on the site by the river that used to be Scott's.

The river was the town's lifeblood, and as 'The Song of the Clyde' says, 'It thrilled us and filled us with pride.' The lyrics have been sung all over the world by Clydesiders drunk and sober, and they paint a terrific picture of the river even today, except of course for the 'hammer ding-dong' references to the shipbuilding that's now a fading memory.

The River Clyde

I sing of a river I'm happy beside,
The song that I sing is the song of the Clyde.
Of all Scottish rivers it's dearest to me,
It flows all the way from Leadhills to the sea.

It borders the orchards of Lanark so fair,
Meanders through meadows with sheep grazing there,
But from Glasgow to Greenock, in towns on each side,
The hammer ding-dong is the song of the Clyde.

(Chorus)
Oh, the River Clyde, the wonderful Clyde,
The name of it thrills me and fills me with pride,
And I'm satisfied, whate'er may betide,
The sweetest of songs is the song of the Clyde.

Immediately after the war, the town had been all about rationing, rebuilding and resettlement. Later, when food shortages were a thing of the past and the displaced families like ours had been resettled, the town reverted as best it could to its old ways. The dredgers kept the narrow upper channels of the Clyde navigable to small ships, while the tugs saw that the heavier downriver traffic flowed; the yards provided Charlie Sr and his fellow workmates with work, a living and strong social ties if they wanted them; and the pubs did a roaring trade on Friday and Saturday nights, and almost as well on the other four nights (Sunday being a dry day under the licensing laws then). But as a teenager growing up there during the '40s and '50s, to my young eyes it was all just damp and grime, and I couldn't wait to get out of it. If you rode a red double-decker bus downtown along the Port Glasgow Road and the river, it was all shipyard cranes and smokestacks and docks filled with tugs and dredgers and lines of more red double-decker buses waiting for the shipyard workers at quitting time, usually in the rain. I couldn't for the life of me see what connection the river and its yards and the jobs they offered had to the future I was dreaming about. The only job I wanted was playin' fitbaw.

Agnes had other things in mind. While Charlie Sr and Ian worked in the yards, she penny-pinched and prayed that I'd pass the 11-plus, get my Highers, go on to university and become a chartered accountant or an architect or whatever made us more respectable. I did pass my 11-plus and I did get my Highers, but there my mother's career aspirations for me ended. But that was all in the future.

After five years in the Gibby in the east end, we moved to Thom Street by the Cowdenknowes Dam, one of two small dams smack dab in the middle of council housing developments on the west side of town, near Greenock High School. The house in Thom Street remains our family home today. Model-yacht clubbers competed on the upper dam at weekends, working out of their red-brick boathouse at one corner, which had a shallow sloping bank in front of it for easy launching. They were big yachts, maybe four to six feet long, and their owners would stride out in their waders to receive their billowing spinnakers and shining hulls as they barrelled in towards the banks. They'd reset the sails and steering gears, then aim the bows and plop the sterns back into the water and follow their models like anxious parents to their next landfalls to make more adjustments before following them between the marker flags to the finish.

Our house in Thom Street was close by the lower dam, not 25 yards from the water, with only the narrow street and a dirt path that ran around the dam between them. On summer evenings, swarms of gnats and moths hovered over the calm surface, and trout would jump clear out of the water while others broke the surface all around them.

Fly-fishermen cast for trout or a decent perch, while we kids used jam jars on strings to catch 'baggie minnows'. When we got older, we made bamboo rods and hand-wrapped the eyelets and cork floats. We caught mostly six-inch perch, which we tossed to protect the trout population, so we thought, and put back the same sized trout when we were lucky enough to get one. I never ever caught a bigger trout there, although occasionally we saw the fly-fishermen get one around 12 or 15 inches long as they aimed their flies among the ripples in the late summer evenings.

The swans were a natural part of the dam life. Often, we'd watch them, no more than 50 yards from our second-floor living-room window, water-skiing in to land from a flight. They nested near the path alongside the dam, and they'd hiss and flex their wings and bend their white necks in S shapes when approached during the nesting period. We kids used to terrify ourselves with tales of how they could break an arm or leg with one swipe of their wings, and we were careful to keep our distance. We fed them bread, fetched adult help when they got entangled in fishing hooks or telephone lines, and kept local dogs from bothering them when they were nesting and hatching. We watched the cygnets grow, take their first flights and leave as winter set in, to return the next year. Some years, they stayed through it all.

In winter, the dam often froze but seldom solid enough to allow us to skate or slide further than a few feet from the bank. The swans, if they were still there, were a good gauge, as you could tell the thickness of the ice out in the deep if they made channels for themselves, like icebreakers. When it froze solid all the way across, we made slides across the narrowest points, no more than 30 yards, and wondered how the fish, if they were still there, could survive such cold.

Happily, in all the years, the dams have never been used as a refuse pit for old prams and bikes and similar hard-to-get-rid-of junk, and they are still attractive local landmarks and wildlife refuges, despite their age and the development around them.

The dam was fed by a small burn that ran into it only 50 yards from our house. This was an underground stream, which was in turn fed by the Cut, a six- or eight-yard-wide man-made stream, so named because it was cut into the moors up behind the town. The Cut started at the far west end of Loch Thom and meandered along the moors, a path running alongside it, towards the Whinhill golf course and into the Long Dam, where it fed into pipes that eventually served the Tate & Lyle sugar refinery on Drumfrochar Road.

The red-brick Tate & Lyle building towered next to the Gourock Ropeworks, overlooking the town. It's gone now, but as kids we used to think of it as Dr Frankenstein's castle, dark and forbidding, and imagined that the burn from the Cut that provided it with water was filled with newts like alligators, rats as big as Alsatians and other unimaginably ugly creepy-crawlies.

Whinhill golf course started where the Cut flowed into the Long Dam. It was a public course carved out of the moors behind the town. It was convenient, and cheap enough for my pal Jim Keenan and me to play as teenagers. The course has fantastic views of the river, the Tail of the Bank at Gourock and the landscape across the river, although we were always too engrossed in our games to appreciate them. The course itself was cut out of gorse, heather rough and a few scrub trees. A barbed-wire fence, a stone dyke and the occasional whin bush bordered the sixth and tenth holes along the road to Loch Thom on the otherwise barren moors, where the only visible life was occasional sheep grazing in the distance and maybe a sole gliding hawk. It was designed around a small loch, with water hazards on several holes, especially the first two, which used to be my nemeses. If I could get around the first four, one of which was a par three, in under twenty, I was happy.

Being working-class kids, we were always skint and hunting for lost balls in the rough and the water hazards. We checked the clubhouse bin for discarded clubs or bags or anything that might be an improvement on what we had. Sometimes we'd find a leather grip or maybe a good iron with a splitting wood shaft that we'd glue and bind with gut and wrap in black insulating tape. And putters. We had putters out the wazoo. Our bags and clubs never amounted to much. No matched irons or sets of woods or fancy covers or trolleys. But our clubs were polished and cared for like precious gems. Come summer, we were almost as crazy about our golf as our football. During the summer holiday when I was 13, Jim and I got season passes and lockers, and we sometimes played three rounds a day. We'd go up to the course in the morning and play a round, come home for lunch then go back up with a sandwich for dinner and play another in the afternoon and another in the evening. By the time we got back at dusk we were dead-beat. We did it quite a few times that summer – not that it helped my game much. I scored in the mid to high 80s. Jim was light years ahead of me; his chipping and putting were particularly good, and he used to finish in the mid to high 70s. I've lost touch with him since those days, but I understand he went on to become the Whinhill men's champion not too many years later. So, belated congratulations to you, Jim, if you read this.

We were just kids from working families finishing a round and desperate to get home for some grub, and we never had time for sightseeing. Today, when I go back, I'm knocked out by the view. Looking north across the river, Dumbarton Rock sits to the right on the opposite bank, like a giant toad guarding the sandbanks beside it and the upper river towards Renfrew and Glasgow. A couple of giant steel cranes remain along the Port Glasgow Road through the town below to remind us of the many others that stood alongside them and the smokestacks and yards that once marked the end of the shipbuilding area of the river. Downriver to our left, the scenic Firth of Clyde opens up, with green hills rising above the water on the opposite bank.

Another pursuit for us in those dreamy days that never seemed to end was fishing from Gourock Pier. The pier was the end of the British Rail line from Glasgow, which fed the car ferries that provided the link with those towns on the other side of the water. First, we'd dig sandworms for bait at Battery Park when the tide was out, shovelling the wet sand and then delving through it with our fingers for these revolting, grey, hairy sandworms with moving tentacles, which gave me the creeps. We'd throw our lines out from the pier and just sit there on bollards, watching the black-and-white car ferries alternately churning and calming the water as their captains manoeuvred them in and scrunched them against the timber pilings to dock. Ropes were thrown and tied, and the wooden gangways and steel loading plates clattered down to allow the passengers and cars to disembark and new ones to load.

Then the process would be reversed, and, in a chorus of whistles and bells, the ferry would chug away in a churning white wake towards Kilcreggan, Dunoon or Rothesay.

Sometimes we'd study the odd cargo ship or tanker that would break the usual rhythm, or we might even see a fleet of navy ships. But the sighting of one of the American nuclear submarines from the Gair Loch, where they were stationed under a controversial Anglo-American treaty, was a real bonus. It was a bit like *Jaws*, really – did we see them mysteriously raising their periscopes out of the depths or was it the product of suggestible boyhood imaginations? At the end of the day, we'd set off home with our catch of flounder and small cod, but, it being a fairly long way back and us kids being highly susceptible to diversionary activities on the route, the fish rarely made it home to the family kitchen. If they did, Agnes would sniff, pull a face and launch them straight into the dustbin.

We walked the Cut many a time in the summer holidays, to fish it or to go hiking in Shielhill Glen towards Inverkip. When hiking to the glen, we'd spot the Cut's small trout darting for cover under the weeds or the ledge of the stone embankment, and we were always on the lookout for a big one we might stop for and try to 'guddle'. This was when we felt under the ledge, attempted to keep the fish calm until we had our hands around it and then grabbed it, which didn't happen often at all. We'd raise the occasional grouse from the heather on the moors, while curlews circled and squawked to lure us away from their nests in the fields behind the new council-house developments. We camped all day in the glen, looking for birds' eggs, for good wood to make staves and spears, and for fern cover to build lean-tos. We made fires, toasted bread on sticks and heated tins of baked beans like cowboys did in Western movies. We checked the pools for frogs and fish, and their banks for birds' nests. It's only now, looking back, that I realise how natural and terrific it all was.

It had its less idyllic moments, too. One day we were whacking our way through dense and thorny undergrowth down in a part of the glen we didn't know when suddenly we were surrounded by a buzzing mass of wasps. We had smashed a nest. We ran screaming like big girls back the way we'd come as quick as our stumbling feet would take us, ducking and falling and swiping at every sting and sighting. We ended up with a couple of dozen stings between us, as well as bunches of bruises and lots of thorn scratches, and an hour later they were sore and hot, and we were still slapping and freaking out when even a midgie came near. Needless to say, we were extra careful about where we whacked with our poles for a long time afterwards.

On another hike, Angus Stormonth, a neighbour and football and track star a couple of years ahead of us at Greenock High School, came along and brought his aptly named black mongrel, Glen. He had a grand time all day, outward bound along the Cut, chasing birds and animals and sniffing cow patties, and in the heather, exploring holes and raising birds. But on the way home, halfway along the Cut, Glen cramped up or was too tired or had a heart attack or something similar. He just lay down silently and wouldn't or couldn't move. A worried Angus carried him all of the last mile or so home in the growing summer dusk. Glen recovered after a couple of days, we were told, but we never saw much of him thereafter, and Angus never said much about the day and never came again.

Another time, fishing the Cut we came across a farmer attending to one of his lambing sheep trapped on a rocky incline. The farmer tugged several times at its bloody rear and finally pulled out what we assumed was a stillborn lamb, whereupon the sheep upped and scrambled unsteadily away. We cheered and the farmer waved in acknowledgement. And I think we all cancelled sheep farming from our career plans.

We didn't have a TV in those early Thom Street days, and the radio was our main entertainment. So imagine our delight when our neighbours, the Cuthbertsons, invited our whole family to watch their new TV for the first time one Wednesday evening. We watched a programme about stately homes, presented by Richard Dimbleby or somebody with a similar upper-crust English accent, taking you through the gardens and house, pointing out the architecture, furniture and paintings room by room. It was probably slug-slow by today's fast-cutting standards, but, then, for us, staring wide-eyed at this new-fangled contraption, it was a whole new dawning. Thereafter, it was an answer to my prayers whenever a school friend invited me to watch TV after school – I was always too embarrassed to ask – and the biggest treat of all was to get to see *The Lone Ranger* with a 'Hi-ho, Silver, away!' on a Friday afternoon. We finally got a TV, but with Agnes's thrifty ways it was a long time in coming, and until then those after-school invitations were a big deal.

In the meantime, without a TV to keep us home, we went every Saturday night on a family outing to La Scala picture house, down past the Orangefield chippie by the West Station. The movies were usually black-and-white Hollywood gangster dramas and the Pathe News 'from around the world', but it was a big family event every week.

I always thought of La Scala – or 'La Bugs', as it was affectionately known – as a huge modern movie theatre, but I recently saw a picture of it and was taken aback at how small and ramshackle it actually was – and that was from the outside. I remember, one summer evening when I was ten or eleven, learning an unforgettable lesson from Charlie Sr about being overconfident, judging a book by its cover and suchlike. We were walking up the hill past the Orangefield, coming home from La Scala with the family while it was still light and I was teasing Charlie no end I could beat him in a sprint to the next lamp-post. He was an adult for heaven's sake. Adults couldn't run, or so I thought. He ignored my pestering for quite a while, until finally he said, 'OK, ye're on. Let's see.' He blew me away. I was stunned and silent the rest of the way home. I couldn't believe it. He never said a lot, but he always seemed to have a surprise up his sleeve.

Later, when as a teenager I rode the top-deck front seat of the bus with my kitbag beside me to go to train or play football, and I watched the yards along the river around quitting time, when the workers were pouring out the gates into the buses in their dungarees and dirty work clothes, some not much older than myself, I felt confused. These men were the heart of Clydeside, workers in the yards alongside my dad and brother, and yet I felt detached, and a bit ashamed that I didn't want to end up in the yards with them. If I had been open about these feelings, I would have been seen as overambitious and presumptuous, even patronising, so I was careful not to rabbit on too much. It wasn't all youthful conceit and daydreaming. I had been going great guns in schools football and then junior football. My play was attracting attention. So, on my record, I had a chance. But it wasn't something you'd have the nerve to talk about or even bring up. Shutting your mouth and getting on with it was the thing that got respect back then.

All that said, my feelings about Greenock are completely changed today. When I go back and drive down the A8 from Glasgow Airport with my wife Diane, who's from southern California, I'm puffed with pride to point out to her – even if it's raining and though she's heard it all before – the old places. The sandbanks at low tide on the river as we come down the slight incline from Bishopton into Langbank, with its long view of the river; Dumbarton Rock, sitting like a huge barnacle on the other side; the Parklea fields, lush and green in Port Glasgow, next to the river on our right as we approach the Parklea roundabout; then Gibbshill up the hill on the left, opposite the Inchgreen railhead and dry dock, where we lived after the Blitz, now looking much different, with smart semi-detached homes where the old teeming tenements used to be; Whinhill golf course, even higher to the left, up the top of the hills, cut out of the moors and gorse, where in our teens we scavenged for clubs and balls and learned to love the *other* game; the Cut along the moors, where as kids we hiked and fished and even tried to guddle trout by hand; and the swans and ducks that never seem to change in the Cowdenknowes Dam, where our family home is to this day. As an impatient teenager, it all meant nothing. But after travelling much of the world these last 40 years, often in privileged circumstances, and seeing what they say is the best that is out there, I think my home town Greenock and its heart, the Clyde, are second to none.

3

Heroes and Villains

The golf, fishing and hiking I referred to in the last chapter were, of course, what kept me busy when I was not playing football. Being a Clydeside kid, I kicked a ball as soon as I could walk, and one of the first Christmas presents I can recall was a brown leather T-panel football I got when I was five or six. It was the old-fashioned kind with a rubber bladder and cock to inflate it, which was simple enough. But then came the job of folding the cock and tying it securely with string, thumbing it down under the leather cover after it was blown and lacing the whole thing up tight without leaving a wicked bump. Charlie Sr did it for me at first, but sometimes I feel that during my childhood I spent more time fiddling with, lacing and pumping up footballs than I did kicking them.

Greenock Morton was our team. They played at Cappielow Park, close to Gibshill. It was a small ground that consisted of a timber grandstand backing onto the Glasgow to Gourock railway line with terraces on the other three sides. Their strip was white hoops and white shorts, Celtic-style, but with royal blue rather than green stripes. That's how the shirts were then, but the design has changed many times since and no doubt will continue to do so, especially if Morton ever become more successful.

The club was formed in 1874 and was so named because the founder members lived in Morton Terrace (the 'Greenock' wasn't officially added until the 1990s). Their first taste of major success came in the 1896–97 season when they reached the semi-final of the Scottish Cup, but they lost to Rangers 7–2 in front of 12,000 fans at Cappielow Park. In 1899–1900, they won promotion to the Scottish First Division for the first time when they finished runners-up to Partick Thistle. However, this was not the new dawn that the supporters might have hoped it would be, and Morton have proved inconsistent in league terms, forever yo-yoing between the top two divisions (and in more recent years the new divisions One and Two). However, their all-time pinnacle has to be their 1922 Scottish Cup final victory over Rangers, finally gaining revenge for the semi-final defeat 25 years earlier. Morton prevailed courtesy of a single goal scored by George French. Local jubilation would have been short-lived, as the following season over half of the first team resigned in a dispute over wages. The club hung on in the First Division until 1927, when they were relegated.

By the time I started attending matches, when I was six or so, the club had already touched greatness – the Scottish Cup victory was still very clear in the memories of the older supporters – but it very much retained its local feel and played many local men. Those same older supporters who could regale us with the glory of the Cup win would also tell us about a time, not so long before, when a local butcher incentivised the players by offering a leg of lamb to any goal-scorer and when the pitch was also used to graze a flock of lambs during the week.

As a Protestant boy from Greenock, the only other team I'd have wanted to support was the dream of all Scottish Proddies, Glasgow Rangers. The Gers and their hallowed ground, Ibrox Park, were only 20 miles upriver, but it might as well have been 200 to us kids, as in those days that was a long haul by rail and bus, or two bus rides via Paisley. The only times I visited Glasgow were when Agnes took Myra and me when she went up to town to buy linens, homewares and clothing at the warehouses there. She was a diligent shopper and homemaker who never let anything go to waste, and we made the Glasgow trip maybe twice a year. It was a whole-day affair, entailing an hour's train ride from Greenock West to Glasgow Central station and the same back, for in those days the steam-engine trains and their carriages with framed scenic prints above the seats stopped at every station en route. We'd leave home around 9 a.m. and get back around 6 p.m., and it was always a big event going shopping and eating lunch at the warehouse restaurant in the big smoke. But the point is that the 20 miles to Glasgow and Rangers' stadium at Ibrox were a lot more significant than that distance is today, when it's a 20-minute zip up the A8. So, for us football-mad boys, Rangers may have been our dream, but Morton were our reality.

The crowds at Cappielow were bigger then than today. It is sad to see, when I glance at a Scottish paper, that sometimes as few as two to three thousand diehards now attend home games. When I was a lad, we were still basking in the post-war attendance boom, and with no TV coverage of matches then to keep fans home, I'd guess Cappielow was pretty close to its 10,000 capacity most weeks. And when Rangers or Celtic came to town, it was packed to the rafters. Old Firm games were a people-watching riot. Fans swarmed the streets and the Sinclair Street railway bridge by the main gate. They hung on the scoreboard waving their bottles and sat astride the walls drinking and singing. Their celebrating and merrymaking was a thing to see, although it didn't take long on Clydeside to appreciate what a bottle of cheap wine can do for a soul.

We had what we thought was a good team in those days. They reached the 1948 Scottish Cup final, having taken the mighty Rangers to a replay in front of 130,000 fans at Hampden Park. Celtic had been disposed of in the semi-final. Our star player, unusually, was a goalkeeper, Jimmy Cowan, and I always remember him in his plain but distinctive yellow jersey. Jimmy became legendary, not just in Greenock but in all Scotland, for the match against the auld enemy, England, at Wembley in 1949. The 3–1 victory was largely attributed to his heroics in goal. The newspapers dubbed the game 'Cowan's Match' and deservedly so, for Jimmy denied a forward line of Stanley Matthews, Stan Mortensen, Jackie Milburn and Tom Finney time and time again. It was England's first defeat since the end of the war. Hugh McIlvanney, the legendary sportswriter, has gone on record as rating Jimmy Cowan Scotland's best-ever goalkeeper, and that's good enough for this old Morton fan.

If in our hero-worshipping young eyes Jimmy was our most illustrious asset, he did not overshadow the other players, and I can see their cigarette-card faces now and even recall their styles of play and characteristics. Tommy McGarrity was a scheming wing-half/inside-forward; Davie Cupples a quick centre-forward; Tommy Orr a tall, leggy wing-half (today we'd call him a midfielder); Billy Campbell an elegant inside-forward; Willie Whigham the journeyman full-back; Johnny Hannigan a sparkling ball-playing right-winger and centre-forward; and who can forget Jimmy White? My brother, Ian, certainly hadn't when I was researching this book. White was another wing-half and the team hard man when things turned ugly. As Ian remembered, 'He'd run the length of the field for a fight.' He reminded me of how White once chinned Willie Woodburn, the Rangers centre-half. 'He was a rough big yin, was Woodburn,' said Ian. 'He was kickin' all the Morton players and intimidating them. But that didnae stop Jimmy White.'

Saturday and a Morton home game was always a big day. I can dimly remember the first time I went to a match, walking down Gibshill Road in my mackintosh and sou'wester ('Rain, rain go to Spain', remember), turning down Weir Street to Sinclair Street and on down under the railway bridge to the main gate. Later, when we had moved across town to Thom Street, Dad and I would walk down to the West Station to catch one of the special Cappielow buses. I was just an awestruck seven or eight year old, sitting on my dad's knee if he snagged a seat or holding on to a seat rail when it was standing room only, my head buried among the working men's coats and jackets. I remember the crowds milling around outside the main gate of the ground and Dad chatting to workmates and friends. Then, when it was time, he'd say, 'Awright, Chic, are ye ready?' and he'd bend down and lift me over the turnstile. We'd walk down under the main stand and out to the small stand in front of it by the players' tunnel and sit in front of the frosted-glass windows that backed onto the home dressing-room.

I don't know if my old man was being contrary just for the sake of it or if, more likely, he didn't like seeing someone who was trying their best being hounded, but at Cappielow it seemed that when a Morton player screwed up and everybody was on his case, he would almost always pipe up with, 'Aye, but the idea was there.' As I got older and began to feel confident about understanding what was happening on the field, I would sometimes join in when other spectators barracked Charlie Sr for defending the indefensible. He would just smile as they howled all around him. Looking back now, I would guess he was winding up all his fellow season-ticket holders and gently taking the rise out of their passion and anger. It was all in good humour, as most of the men were friends and colleagues. Charlie Sr knew his football and in his younger days had played for Shawfield Juniors, but, as with all things in his past, he rarely spoke of it. For a man who hadn't signed the Official Secrets Act (presumably), he didn't give much away.

After the game, we'd queue up (often in the rain, it being Greenock in winter) for the standing-room-only buses home, where everybody swayed and bumped together as they dissected the game and the players' performances. Charlie Sr always seemed to know somebody from our part of town, and they'd get talking, often about their work and not even the game, and I'd just sit there, usually in my sou'wester, loving my day out at 'the Ton' and wondering about the rest of the day's results. At Greenock

West station, we'd buy a Saturday *Sporting Green* or *Pink* or the *Greenock Telegraph* to get the scores. Then we'd order fish and chips at the Orangefield chippie and head up Murdieston Street and round the dams, past the ducks and swans to home. Pure bliss. Those were the days.

Back home, I'd imagine I was one of my Morton heroes when I played in the park or the streets with my pals. I'd pretend I was Johnny Hannigan or Davie Cupples, who, of course, always had to be beating opponents. That was me, taking on opponents from day one, even when it was only the classic pick-up game in the streets, with jackets or pullovers for goalposts and who knows how many on each team. The sides and positions always depended on who was available at the start, who arrived during the game or had to go home in the middle of it and, of course, who was still there when darkness or irate parents ended play under the street or park lights.

The day in 1953 we went to La Scala and I saw the Pathe newsreel of the Hungarians beating England 6–3 at Wembley was a defining moment in my football life. I loved playing football, but I can trace the time when it became a passion back to that trip to the cinema. I was mesmerised by the Hungarians and especially their barrel-chested inside-forward with the educated left foot, Ferenc Puskás. England had never been beaten at Wembley, and to see them demolished in such style by the Hungarians was shocking almost beyond belief. I cannot think of it now without hearing again the distinctive voice that narrated the Pathe newsreels. The man himself never appeared on film, but for years he had a voice as well known as any in the land, including Vera Lynn's, Tommy Handley's or even Winston Churchill's. After Puskás and

England skipper Billy Wright exchanged pennants in the centre circle, Puskás juggled the ball in the air while he waited for kick-off, then kicked it high in the air and, as it dropped, stopped it dead under his left foot. I was entranced and enchanted. Such magic. Such skill. And after the game, seeing the England players in utter shock was, for us Scots, pure joy. Remember, on these bulletins all we were ever served up was Billy Wright this and Stanley Matthews that, and the unbeatable greatness of England at Wembley. In just one game, Hungary changed all that. With their withdrawn centre-forward, Nándor Hidegkuti, and their slick passing style, they simply overwhelmed the English from the off. It was a stark lesson in just how Continental football had developed and left all of us in Britain behind. And Puskás, the 'Galloping Major' of the Hungarian army, who had been spearheading the inexorable rise of this Eastern European country as a footballing world power, became a global star almost overnight.

We'd heard about him but until now had never seen him in action. I kept scrapbooks (most of the kids did) and had pasted in crudely cut-out newspaper pictures of our Scottish heroes: Lawrie Reilly, Gordon Smith, George Young, Willie Waddell, Eddie Turnbull, Willie Ormond and, of course, Greenock's Jimmy Cowan. The names go on and on. They were seared on our fertile brains. I also had cuttings of Puskás and the other Hungarians, as the papers were talking of them all the time and, in my eyes, the further abroad a player came from, the more glamorous and attractive he was. Now I was watching them and expecting to see something special. When, and this is the bit everyone remembers, Puskás scored that unforgettable goal, with his left-foot pull-back move near the right touchline to beat Billy Wright clean as a whistle and then rifle his shot past Gil Merrick in the English goal, I was stunned. It was after that day that I started juggling.

Today, they call it juggling – we called it keepie-uppie. It was a solitary pursuit, and I was devoted. I'd rush home from high school at lunchtime, bolt down my food and then get out in the back yard and juggle. I'd juggle during school playtimes and after school into the evenings. When we got a TV, I'd look out for televised circuses and variety shows featuring juggling acts and watch to see if, as well as juggling plates, hoops and rings, they also juggled balls with their feet. I diligently recorded in my head all my personal bests and set out to beat them daily. I would juggle for hours. I could tell anyone day to day what my records were for alternate feet, left foot, right foot, thigh, head and shoulder. I didn't need anybody to tell, to show off to. I only needed a ball to be happy. I truly was juggling crazy. If my circus ancestors could have seen me, they'd have been proud; anyone else would have thought I was nuts.

Now, you can't be that loony and practise that much without some improvement. I got pretty good and quick with my feet, not only at the juggling itself but also at recovering and reacting to mistakes. That combination of quickness and agility, all from keepie-uppie, stood me in good stead for the rest of my football career. In the last year of my junior school, the Highlanders Academy, I was made school-team captain, and when I went on to Greenock High School, at 11 years of age, they made me skipper, too. This was all good news for my development as a footballer, but the fact is that I picked up whatever skills I had not so much from the school games but from my keepie-uppie practice and the pick-up games we played constantly in the streets and parks around the neighbourhood.

This was a fine preparation for conditions to come, because the Greenock High School field not a quarter-mile from our home on Thom Street was abysmal, and it is a wonder that any quality footballers were produced at all. The school field was a black cinder monstrosity set into a steep hillside, which made it handy for the occasional spectator but a flesh-ripping torture chamber for the players. Our feet and socks would be black with cinder dust after a dry summer lunchtime game, but most of the time we were jumping the gullies of water running across the field from the rain washing down the hillside. There was no means to protect yourself from the skin-tearing cinder surface and, 50 years on, there are scores of Greenock men who can roll up their trousers to display black scars and buried cinder in their knees and thighs.

Still, it was playing for the High School team that helped develop me as a footballer. I played for the first- and second-year Greenock High School select teams, which, to nobody's surprise, were regularly whipped by our Glasgow counterparts. Call it learning by experience. At Greenock High School, I got the chance to play alongside boys such as Ronnie Stewart, who went on to play for Airdrie; Hugh Brown, who signed for Kilmarnock; and Billy Gourlay, who was capped for Scotland Under-15s as a goalkeeper but went on to play for Partick Thistle and Falkirk as a mazy-dribbling left-winger. How's that for versatility?

I captained the first- and second-year teams at Greenock High and, at the age of 14, I started playing for a local juvenile club, Port Glasgow Rovers. John Adam, the Rovers' manager, had heard about me from my classmate Bill Bryden's father. Bill himself was a great character and a close mate, who went on to become an acclaimed theatre director. He showed thespian qualities even then, breaking us up in class with his melodramatic James Dean impressions – 'Ma, I didn't mean to shoot him.' Unbeknown to me, Bill's dad had seen me play at school and had alerted John Adam. I went for a trial against Woodhall Boys Guild and was signed up there and then – at half-time, no less. John, it seemed, had made a quick decision and had to borrow the registration papers from his opposite number on the Boys Guild touchline – not a simple favour to ask in those days of bitter sectarian rivalries.

At Port Glasgow, there was a striker a couple of years older than me and in an older age-group team named Hugh McIlmoyle. He would later play in England and become such a legend at Carlisle United that they have now built a statue of him at their Brunton Park ground. He also played for Leicester City in their 1961 FA Cup final against the mighty Tottenham Hotspur. Other Rovers players included Ritchie Blaikie, our goalkeeper, whom we dubbed 'Dracula' because he didn't like crosses; Jack Glennie, a gutsy defender who today is a much sought after Burns Supper orator; Malky Russell; Alan Skirving (another Greenock High boy, who became chief executive officer at Lanarkshire Council); and Jim Keenan, he of Whinhill golf course fame. Jim would wind everyone up, and for a while had us all believing that John Adam was a scratch golfer, pointing to his pullovers as evidence. John had never played golf in his life. There was also a full-back whose name escapes me, who played like a big girl, but when the games ended, he donned his Teddy boy suit, slicked back his hair in his DA (duck's arse) quiff and set off to rip up some cinema seats with his open razor. The Teddy boy craze was sweeping the country, fuelled by the release of the film *Blackboard Jungle* and the emergence of Bill Haley and Elvis Presley. Most of us boys were too wrapped up in our football to get caught up in it all, but this guy lived the life to the full. He was barely 16 but had fathered a child, and his and his mates' exploits often featured in the police reports in the *Greenock Telegraph* on a Monday morning. My best pal at the Rovers, though, was Jim Geddes, a wing-half with an educated left foot, who would progress with me to the pros in the coming years.

Sports facilities aside, Greenock High School wasn't a bad place at all. Most of my memories are pleasant ones, and the school certainly has a track record of producing creative pupils who make their names in the arts in later life, so they must have been doing something right. Besides Bill Bryden, Richard Wilson, the actor from TV's *One Foot in the Grave*, novelist Alan Sharp (also my good friend and the screenwriter of *Ulzana's Raid*, *Night Moves* and *Rob Roy*), sci-fi writers Iain Banks and Ken MacLeod, and politician Sam Galbraith are all former pupils. Greenock as a whole generally produces a disproportionate but pleasing number of creative people. Our most famous son is surely the inventor James Watt, who gave his name to the unit of power. Our most notorious must be the pirate Captain William Kidd, but we don't talk about him. In between, we can boast of producing writers Peter

McDougall, George Blake and W.S. Graham; musicians John McGeoch, guitarist with Siouxsie and the Banshees, and Al Stewart, of *Year of the Cat* fame; painter William Clark; and comedian Chic Murray.

I'd guess that, given Greenock turned out such a fine assembly of writers and performers, you'd have to say that their teachers must have been pretty good. One such I can remember was 'Pop' Urie, our Greenock High School French teacher, who was so nicknamed because he had two daughters at the school. Pop epitomised for me all the best qualities in a teacher: patience, restraint and genuine concern, which I'm sure many of us didn't deserve, especially when I remember how we used to mangle the language he was trying to teach us.

There were other teachers, though, who brought unnecessary pain on themselves. One such was a geography teacher nicknamed 'Josie'. He was a strange man, who wore a suit covered in fountain-pen stains. He claimed to have taught all over the world and boasted how he had 'tamed' kids in the hardest schools, specifically in New York's Harlem district. This didn't cut much ice, of course, and it wasn't long before kids were chucking rubbers at him as he scratched away on the blackboard pretending not to notice. Some boys found out where he lived and had a ton of manure delivered to his house. Another time, they called an executive car to take him to Heathrow Airport. 'Not guilty' is all I can say.

Things went well at Port Glasgow Rovers, and playing with and against older, stronger and better footballers improved my game. I was happily looking forward to playing school and juvenile games every weekend, but the local gym teachers were bent on changing that. The schools were suffering in scheduling conflicts, as the players, naturally, chose to play the tougher juvenile games for the club teams instead of for the schools, so they made it a rule that you couldn't play Saturday morning with the school team then play again in the afternoon with a junior club team.

'Wee Pat', our high school gym teacher, defended the rule by complaining that boys playing for juvenile clubs would be too strong for their high-school teammates because of the extra training they were doing, but nobody believed that for a minute. The rule was beyond screwy to us 13 and 14 year olds. We did not believe Wee Pat's reasoning, knowing we would and could play three times on a Saturday and three times again on Sunday if it was left up to us. And our parents would never have objected. Quite the opposite, probably.

I was unwilling to pack it in with Port Glasgow Rovers and therefore found myself banned from playing in and captaining the school team. I wasn't happy, but I could live with it, knowing that club football was tougher and more exciting and what I should be playing if I seriously wanted to get spotted and make it as a pro. It was the first of many quick decisions I would make during my career based on gut instinct and without consulting anyone. The result was that I made a hash of a lot of things, I'm sure, but it also honed my ability to rationalise those decisions to myself – some might say delude myself – and get on with the job at hand. From my teenage perspective, juvenile football was where it was all happening, so I figured I'd made the right decision and took the school ban in my stride. I can't remember discussing it with my folks or even feeling any need to.

Parents didn't usually come to the games, and, strange as it may seem, I don't believe my old man ever came to any of my school or juvenile games. He certainly never accompanied me to any of them. He may well have come on the quiet, but if he did, he never mentioned it. Not having overly fussing parents had its advantages in Greenock then, too. The Catholic–Protestant rivalry was huge, and the games between the Catholic Boys Guild teams and the Rovers were barnstormers even at that level. What with all the usual 'Protestant bastard' verbals and sideline spittle jobs, there was enough to deal with without the embarrassment of having your old man on the touchline to contribute his two pennies' worth or fight your battles for you. Charlie Sr was never a big talker, and if there were things I did to try to please him or make him proud, I think one of them was that I tried to shut my mouth and get on with things – at least most of the time. Not having him at games and not discussing them at length never struck me as anything but normal.

My decision to play for the Rovers obviously irked Wee Pat, though, and it made an already cold relationship more difficult. I guess he took it personally. He was all of about 5 ft 7 in. He had dark, receding hair and a sallow Mediterranean complexion, and it was said he was Greek, which would have had no relevance except the war was only recently over, and I think it's fair to say that foreigners were treated with unfounded suspicion. Wee Pat was always dressed in navy – navy slacks with blue or black plimsolls and a white sports shirt under a navy jersey – and often wore a navy 'French' beret on his head, which only lent to his 'foreign' air. 'Inspector Clouseau without the moustache' describes him exactly. He had an unsmiling demeanour that never seemed to change and matched his personality, or at least what we ever got to know of it. You got the impression that Wee Pat never enjoyed anything to do with school, certainly not teaching or coaching the school team, even when it was winning. Part of the reason may have been that he couldn't kick a ball to save his life, although he went out of his way to hide it.

Our relationship was almost non-existent, despite the fact that I had been the school-team captain. When you were in the halls or gym class and you heard him shout, you knew somebody was in for a loud and angry 'What do you think you are doing, boy?', and if he knew the offender's surname, he'd use it, for extra embarrassment. He had been known to grab boys by the hair and shake their heads slowly and deliberately in front of everyone in time with 'YOU – STUPID – BOY'. He liked to position himself at the top of the stairs at the school entrance to catch latecomers, charging them to write 500-word essays on punctuality. He also patrolled the bus queues after school noting the names of students he deemed to be misbehaving and entering them into his 'wee black book'. More seriously, if you were caught big-time horsing around on his gym equipment, it would be six of the best. That meant he took your gym shoe, got you to bend over and whacked you on the arse with it six noisy times. He didn't hold back. He also possessed a two-tongued leather strap, which he would use on your palms if you missed his gym class. Other teachers had similar straps, but they were three-tongued, thinner and less painful. That said, it wasn't so much the pain of the punishment but his haughty tone and the public humiliation he inflicted that made him so disliked.

I discovered a year or so after I was banned from his school team that I had been pencilled in for a Scottish Schoolboys trial and that Wee Pat had deliberately kept it from me. This upset me because it would have been a huge feather in my cap and a terrific opportunity to get myself in front of pro scouts. But I soon got over it, as playing for the Rovers was fiercely competitive and gave me plenty to think about without wasting energy on stuff I could do nothing about.

However, around this time, I had won the school sprint trial and was therefore the automatic selection for the 100-yard sprint at the Renfrewshire Games in Paisley. I knew that Wee Pat would rather it had been someone else wearing the Greenock High School vest that day, and I was none too pleased about having his hopes and potential glory resting on my shoulders. Before the race, I hung around in my blue school sash and spikes whilst my opponents received pep talks, advice and encouragement from their teachers. I was as nervous as hell. I was getting ready to go against the best in the county, and the possibility of being embarrassed was freaking me out, but Wee Pat was nowhere to be seen. This was a big deal, not of Olympic final proportions, I'll grant you, but still a very big occasion for yours truly. I wandered around the infield before the race clueless, not knowing a soul in it and thinking the worst. My butterflies were out of control as we were called to the start line. I remember hearing the starter shout, 'On your marks,' which I did, but somehow, due to fear or nerves or some combination of the two, I missed the 'get set' shout. So when I heard the gun go off, I was still on my knees in the ready position watching everybody else shooting off their blocks like bats out of hell and steaming down the track. I scrambled from my knees behind the last runner, pumped my legs like I'd never pumped them before and managed to catch a couple of stragglers to finish a distant fifth. Fifth, flustered, embarrassed and ashamed. That's how I was feeling as I got dressed under the stands that night, with the others getting changed to leave or getting ready for their events, when Wee Pat came in.

'What happened to you, Cooke?' he demanded across the whole changing area, for everybody to hear.

'I missed the starter's "get set" call,' I offered sheepishly.

'How could you do that?' he sneered, before sticking his nose in the air and marching off in a huff with his clipboard under his arm. Nobody said a word, and I wished a hole would open up. If I'd had a gun, I would have shot the little berk right there and then.

Afterwards when I'd recovered a bit on the bus going home, I was incensed at Wee Pat's attitude. Did he, I wondered, think that I'd tanked the race intentionally? I couldn't believe that anybody could have thought that, and I was so upset at myself for having agreed to run then performing so badly that I vowed I'd never run another race for him or his gym class again. And I never did.

Next year, he had sprint heats in the playground to determine who would represent the school again, and that time I did tank it. My mates Davie Barr and Charlie McEwan and I got out to good starts, and I led then faded, as planned, to finish in the pack. But I've never regretted it one bit. I vowed to myself I'd never run for him again, and I kept my promise.

That wasn't the last I heard of Wee Pat. An old schoolmate, who characterised his rule as 'with an iron fist', reported that he used to see him regularly walking in

Gourock in his retirement. Apparently, he had become somewhat mellowed and nostalgic, my old school friend noting jocularly that it had come 40 years too late for us. He also mentioned that Wee Pat believed in euthanasia and carried a pill at the ready so that if he ever had an incapacitating stroke or heart attack, he would be prepared. I'm not sure what to think about that.

I heard about Charlie Cooke from a friend whose son was in his class at school. He was 13 years old, and my mate told me he was a great, really great, player. I signed Charlie for Port Glasgow Rovers Under-18s when he was 14 years old during (literally during) a trial match. I was so impressed, I borrowed a registration form from the other team and signed the boy at half-time. He had a remarkable gift for both keeping and using the ball. With Charlie in the side, we won the Morton Supporters Cup – a trophy no one gave us a chance of winning.

We trained at Parklea, and afterwards I would take the Greenock boys home on the bus so I could pay their fares. This allowed them to spend their pennies on chips, which were a significant morale-booster in those days.

I remember Charlie's problem with the PE teacher at Greenock High School. We presumed that he felt that, what with Charlie's extra training, he'd be too strong for the other boys, and that that was why he banned him from the school team, but who knows what his motives were? Charlie was always a good boy and never cheeky. He'd have the banter with the other lads but nothing more.

Competition for places was always keen, and I was a great believer in taking boys to one side and telling them if they were being dropped before pinning up the team sheet. I never had to take Charlie to one side because you could not contemplate not playing him, but I remember he was always sensitive, supportive and sympathetic to the boys who were dropped. I always remember that. After he left us and went on to greater things with Renfrew and then Aberdeen, someone asked me if I could get the autographs of the Scottish League side that were playing the Italian League side. I contacted Charlie, and he got the lot and returned them with a delightful letter offering to do anything he could. This was the loyalty and courtesy we came to know from our best-ever player.

John Adam, former manager, Port Glasgow Rovers

4

From a Junior to a Don

When I was 16 and still at Greenock High School, I had the opportunity to join a semi-professional side, Renfrew Juniors, who played at Western Park in Renfrew, 17 miles upriver, towards Glasgow. I was not at all unhappy with Port Glasgow Rovers, but, as I say, Renfrew were semi-professional (don't let the 'Juniors' bit mislead you), and the offer represented an important break and was another rung up the football ladder. Renfrew were run by Donald McNeil, a well-known personality in Scottish junior football, who had a reputation for unearthing young talents and moving them on to professional clubs. That was how Renfrew and most other junior clubs survived financially. For example, just before I went to Renfrew, a lad called Andy Lochhead, a big strong centre-forward, was moved on to Burnley, where he became one of their all-time greats. He also played for Leicester City, whom he represented in the 1969 FA Cup final. I was destined to play against him several times in the coming years.

John Adam at Port Glasgow Rovers was disappointed and tried to make an arrangement whereby I would play for both teams. I would have been agreeable, but the SFA had some rule that prevented me from doing this. John did not give up easily and pursued the matter.

'I went to Renfrew Juniors to discuss the prospect of Charlie remaining a "juvenile" [a grade of younger players in Scotland] and was ordered unceremoniously out of the clubhouse,' remembers John. 'I reported the incident to the Scottish Football Association, but they decided against us. Even though the club lost out, I well remember the banter with famous faces of Scottish football such as Tom Reid of Partick Thistle and Willie Allan who was the SFA secretary. The matter was known as "The Charlie Cooke affair".'

I was just a wet-behind-the-ears schoolboy and had no inkling whatsoever of any of this. I used to take the bus up to Renfrew two nights a week, Tuesday and Thursday, to practise and on Saturday afternoons to play. The team was made up of a mixture common at junior clubs then. There were part-time former professional players on their way down. Then there were boys and men in their late teens and early to mid-twenties who'd just missed out on full-time pro careers and were now changing clubs from time to time for a better deal, working as electricians, engineers or fitters in the shipyards, or, less often, as accountants or architects. And of course there were schoolboy wannabes such as Jim Geddes and myself from the Rovers, looking, by some miracle, to make the team and move on to become 'real' professional footballers.

Jim was well built and bigger than me, although his

game was more about touch and skill than boot and brawn. I was medium height and weight for my age, maybe a touch smaller, but fast and good with the ball. Playing and training with the pros, as I saw them, grown men with years of experience behind them at levels I could only dream about (or so I thought then), I did everything I was told, which wasn't much. 'Yes, sir, no, sir, three bags full, sir' was the refrain, and we just prayed we could do half as well as them. And we did. Jim became a starting wing-half and I the right-winger and inside-right. After a while, I even began taking the penalty kicks. It might seem bizarre that the smallest and youngest player on the team was taking the PKs, but I was juggling and practising so much and growing so confident that I thought nothing of it at the time. And, all modesty aside, I was playing well and worth my place. I think I was at one of those few moments in my life in which I was so happy and well prepared that it felt like nothing could slow me down, and there wasn't an opponent I didn't think I could beat twice and more if I had to, no matter who they were.

My time at Renfrew, maybe six months, was terrific. Win, and you got an extra two shillings and sixpence or sometimes a five-shilling bonus. Lose, and you still got 'expenses', which varied from five shillings to seven shillings and sixpence depending on the club's finances, i.e. the weekly gate. And don't forget to take your dirty training gear home and wash it. I had no idea what the older players were getting paid and didn't care. Money didn't come into it for me then. I just wanted the chance to play against the best out there and maybe get a shot at the pros. And although I say it myself, I had a terrific attitude. I didn't care about being beaten or shown up or anything like that. If somebody was better, I'd go away and try to figure out what they had that I didn't and practise to develop it. Hughie Bryceland, brother of Tommy, was a good example. I played with him at Renfrew. He was a left-footed forward, but more importantly, he had a powerful behind-the-leg scissor kick. If the ball was on his right side, he could scissor kick it powerfully, slicing his left foot behind his standing right foot and striking it with the laces of his left. The first time I saw him do it, I'd never seen the move before, and I was agog. One day in a game, Hughie shot using the kick from about 20 yards, a real screamer, with the move bringing the opposing keeper to a great save, and I vowed to learn his trick. I did – it was much easier than I thought, and I actually used it for a pass in the middle of the field at Wembley 10 years later in the 2–2 FA Cup final against Leeds at Wembley. It was a small thing, but it's a good example of how I absorbed everything around me then.

Another move I picked up at Renfrew, from our centre-forward Jim Rumble, was a roll across the body before pulling the ball back with the sole of the rolling foot and shooting with the same foot. It was the move I used for my 20-yard shot just over the bar in the 1966 FA Cup final against Dave Mackay and his Spurs side.

Learning all I could and improving was all I was interested in, but the bonuses also became important because they determined how much I had left over from the money I gave Agnes to put aside for the Carlsberg Special kitty at Davy Jones' Locker in Gourock on Saturday nights with my school-mates Jim Keenan and Alan Skirving and our pals from the shipyards Davie McGuigan and Jim McCloy. We'd get smashed at the Locker until ten o'clock closing, then head off to the Cragburn dancehall half a mile away on the esplanade, or occasionally to the Boat Club in the west end. A mixture of fresh air and a reality check meant that by the time we arrived at the dancehall we hung around in the shadows, reverting back to the shy, skinny kids that we really were.

The main thing, though, was that Renfrew Juniors were important for my game. They didn't take any prisoners in junior football, and a youngster like me, who lived to beat opponents, had to be quick and savvy. There were no special instructions from Donald or anyone else. It seemed they felt that no matter what age you were, if you'd made it this far, you must have some idea what was going on and be able to take care of yourself. I took on opponents with a passion, and the result was I was super-happy at Renfrew. I was playing out of my skin and loving it. And most importantly, I was playing at a much higher standard than I could have done if I'd stayed with Port Glasgow Rovers. That was the best thing of all, playing against older, more experienced players. Bigger, faster and stronger opponents were a guarantee you were going to get clattered a few times, and for a ball-hogger like me, a few was more like plenty. But I'd played that way all my life, taking the ball close to beat opponents no matter how tough or quick they were, and being from Greenock, I was used to getting hammered and listening to all the 'little Proddy bastard' threats and promises that you'd be sorted out after the game. One thing I'm proud of was that I blew right through all of it and kept my mouth shut, at least most of the time. I returned the physical challenges with interest when I got the chance, despite the disparity in size or weight or corner-boy twattery. It was probably a help, too, that I was still a schoolboy and didn't know any of the players we were competing with; I played against them all the same way no matter the kind of big shots they were (or imagined they were) in the junior ranks. I knew in my bones that tougher opposition was the quickest and best way to develop my game. It was exactly what I needed if I wanted to get to the pros, and I drank it all in with a passion.

Being a schoolboy, without any financial commitments or adult responsibilities, I couldn't have been happier riding the top deck of the bus from Greenock with my kitbag beside me on the almost-hour-long journey up past the shipyards to Western Park for training and games. Early on, the only question in my mind after each game was whether my name would be on the team sheet when it was pinned to the dressing-room wall the next Thursday evening. Donald never announced the team any other way, and Thursday night after training was always a nervy time, with players talking quietly or not at all until the team sheet went up and everybody learned their fate. Fortunately, after my debut I became a regular, but that tension while waiting for the team sheet, the fear of being dropped, never left me.

Those training nights and Saturday games, and my soccer daydreaming, hit my study habits hard and after I joined Renfrew my exam scores fell off a cliff. At Highlanders Academy, Dennis McKee and I had always been dux and second dux, and we were generally within a mark or two of one another. Instead of moving on with me to Greenock High, Dennis emigrated with his family to Australia. We kept in touch for a short time, and I remember his descriptions of Australian rules football, which sounded very weird. Our letters soon tailed off, though, and I've often wondered what became of Dennis.

I went into the first year at Greenock High School a year younger than everybody else, and I kept my place in the A class all the way through to the third year. But after I went to Renfrew, around fourth year, my teachers had no chance. While they were teaching the class about British history, the industries of far-off countries or the finer points of mathematics, my head was just full of images of Lawrie Reilly, Eddie Turnbull, Gordon Smith and countless other Scottish football heroes. As a result, my test scores nosedived in my fourth and fifth years. I battled on, travelling to Renfrew on Tuesdays and Thursdays to train and for matches on Saturdays, while staying out or going to the movies, especially Hollywood Westerns, to get out the house when we had relatives visiting, and cramming for exams the night before. By some miracle, I got my Highers in English, maths and art, and Lowers in history and French. I was happy to have got something for Agnes's sake, but the results meant nothing to me, as I had thoughts only of playing football, nothing else.

These fitbaw ambitions weren't all just fantasy, because I was playing in one of the best teams in junior football at the time. Our full-backs were a man called Billy Collins, who was an impossibly ancient 39 years old, and another guy called Jimmy Millen, who signed for Stirling Albion. Then we had the youngest half-back line around – Jim Harvey (18), Alan McGraw (18) and Jim Geddes (17) – as well as our flying left-winger Hughie Bryceland, the man we all wanted to emulate. We put Irvine Meadow, the holders, out of the Scottish Junior Cup, so I was beginning to enjoy some success and could almost taste and smell the good times ahead.

Things went well at Renfrew, and by the time I'd played six games, Bobby Calder, the chief scout at Aberdeen, had, unbeknown to me, come to see me play several times and liked what he saw. Just before a home game against Saltcoats Victoria, he corralled Jim Geddes and me together outside the clubhouse. He told us he'd been watching and admiring us both for weeks. Flattery got him everywhere. He wanted to talk with us and our parents about us signing provisional forms for Aberdeen.

Now, there had been lots of reports in local newspapers in Renfrew and Greenock that many clubs from both sides of the border had an interest in signing Jim and me. Manchester United were said to head a long queue of big clubs readying to offer me terms. At that age, I still believed what I read in the papers, and my head was in the clouds. Maybe I should have known better, for there were even reports that I had already secretly visited an English First Division team down south to discuss a contract. I don't recall that, I thought, and figured, in my schoolboy mind, that it must just have been an honest journalistic error. The galling truth was that not one club had made any contact with me or my parents, at least not as far as I knew. Many years later, I read a clipping from the *Greenock Telegraph* in which Charlie Sr was reported to have warned Manchester United off when I was still in high school as he wanted me to finish my education. Maybe Donald knew more than he was saying, for moving players on was his business, and I assumed he orchestrated signings and player departures to suit Renfrew's needs. Whatever the case, I was completely in the dark. It was great for my ego that there were so many flattering reports, but they became like a thorn in my side as they appeared more and more frequently, even in the *Telegraph*, which never, in the normal run of things, printed anything about Renfrew sport.

So when Bobby Calder approached us, all dapper in his camel-hair coat and soft hat, I was all ears. He already had a reputation, although Jimmy and I didn't know it, for identifying young talent, keeping it away from Celtic and Rangers and sending it up to Aberdeen, and he was to continue doing this long after I had passed through his hands. Tommy Craig, Jimmy Smith, Bobby Clark and Willie Miller would all be unearthed by Bobby. He reminded me of my father, with the same sort of wiry build and lean, bony, narrow face, and maybe that's why I felt so comfortable with him. The truth is he was great at making you feel important, not to mention the great PR job he did with your parents. His plan was that Jim and I would move after Renfrew's season finished in the early summer and join the Dons full time for the start of their 1960–61 season sometime in late June or early July. We were excited to get the Dons offer, the first concrete one we'd had, and we both readily agreed that Bobby would come down early the following week to visit and get the OK from my parents in Greenock and Jim's in Gourock.

From my point of view, there was nothing to think about. Here I was in high school, and not only were Aberdeen offering me money for doing next to nothing, it seemed, except for signing a form, but I was also finally getting the thing I wanted so much – a chance at a pro club. Nobody else had even come close, despite all the twaddle about cross-border visits and reports of 'great interest' and 'pending signing'. Call it youthful impatience, but I wanted things to start happening and couldn't wait to sign. The Aberdeen offer fitted so nicely. It meant a chance to move on in the game and getting paid for it, too; even the timing was perfect, as it was nearing the end both of Renfrew's season and my sixth and last year at Greenock High. With nothing else on the horizon, at least as far as I knew, I couldn't see my parents objecting.

I trotted out onto the pitch afterwards and contributed to a Scottish Junior Cup victory over Saltcoats, even though I was now fantasising about setting Pittodrie, home of Aberdeen Football Club, alight and putting three goals past Celtic at Parkhead. If I had known what else my day had in store, I would probably not have been able to pull on my boots and play. I was getting changed in the locker room after the game with the rest of the team when Donald McNeil came walking through followed by a well-dressed man in a soft hat. This was an afternoon for soft hats, it seems. They passed everyone else and came and stood in front of me, looking down at me as I looked up at them. 'Charlie, this is Mr Jim Smith, the chief scout for Rangers,' said Donald.

I suppose a modern-day equivalent might be 'Charlie, this is Mr Smith, wealth adviser for the National Lottery.' I was lost for words. He proffered his hand, and I shook it.

'You had a good game today, Charlie.'

'Thank you,' I said, embarrassed, not used to accepting such compliments in company.

'I've been hearing good things about you, Charlie. How

would you like to visit Ibrox Park next week? We could show you around, and perhaps you could have a chat with Mr Symon.'

Mr Symon. Scot Symon, the Rangers manager. This was big: for a Scottish working-class Protestant boy, as big as it gets. Ibrox. Glasgow Rangers. The Gers. In my wildest dreams, this is where I ended up. And here in front of me was Mr Smith, offering me the fast track to Scottish immortality and heaven. My mind was racing. I tried to gather my thoughts. There was no contest between Rangers and Aberdeen. But I had given my word to Bobby Calder only two hours earlier, and, still a schoolboy and not wise to the ways of the world, I was naively honest about everything. Nothing had been signed, but I'd given my word.

Flustered and lost for words, I didn't ask for time to talk to my agent, who didn't exist, of course. I didn't ask how I might escape from the proposed contract with the Dons, or what Rangers might pay, or whether a verbal promise was a contract in law. No. I just looked at him and blurted out, 'Sorry, sir, but I've already met with Mr Calder and promised to go to Aberdeen. He's coming down to visit with my parents next week.'

I don't know who looked more shocked: Donald, who clearly had no idea that Bobby Calder had been lurking around earlier and was maybe worried for the survival of his relationship with Rangers; Mr Jim Smith, who was surely unaccustomed to scruffy teenagers turning down the prospect of playing for one of the biggest clubs in Europe; the other lads witnessing this little drama unfold; or me, saying the words that I'd never thought I would or could say. Mr Smith was charming. He wished me well, shook my hand again and left. Strangely, he made no attempt to change my mind or point out that I was making a life-changing decision and that I should give it further thought. Donald didn't say anything either. Heaven knows what he was thinking. I never found out whether the whole business upset the dynamic between the three men and their clubs. Bobby Calder won the day and I know he had no regrets, for I read an interview with him years later, when he retired from Aberdeen after a long and successful tenure as chief scout, in which he said he rated me as his best-ever find. It is strange how reading a little comment like that in an old clipping can bring pleasant chills that even winning a cup final cannot.

And that's how it all came down. In less time than it takes to walk the tunnel at Stamford Bridge, the Scottish Protestant boy's dream of a lifetime had come and gone. You might think I should have been crushed that it happened so quickly and apparently thoughtlessly, but by the time I boarded the bus back to Greenock, I was already rationalising it all to myself and feeling better about the day's events. The Gers were a dream, no question, but they were also a big club awash with the finest talent, and a youngster could easily get lost in the crowd. Aberdeen was a smaller pond and probably a better bet for a youngster who wanted to make it. But above all else, I had been offered an opportunity to become a full-time pro at a First Division club, something that I had begun to think was never going to happen.

When I told my folks everything I could remember of the day's conversations, they took it all in with surprising calm, and Agnes fussed more about when she could expect Bobby Calder to arrive the following Tuesday evening, so she could have the house shipshape, than about the details of the proposed contract. Charlie Sr didn't say much, but I could tell he was very pleased, and that made me happier than almost anything else. And me? I was excited beyond words that night as I got dressed and met up with my pals at Davy Jones' Locker, contributed my share to the kitty, got smashed with them in celebration and had a grand time afterwards at Cragburn. My dream was coming true. What was there to complain about?

Bobby Calder came down on the Tuesday and met with my parents, and we signed the provisional agreement. In fact, he was at the house before me that evening, as I was away playing football with my pals when he arrived. Under the terms of the agreement they started paying me right away, and the twelve shillings and sixpence a week I received on top of my wages from Renfrew was like manna from heaven to me. I was chuffed to be able to give all my Aberdeen money, and occasionally even more from my Renfrew monies, to my folks and still keep enough to get drunk on Saturday nights and go to the Cragburn with my mates.

'A funny thing happened to me' is a gag line, but it really did to Jim Geddes and me. Sometime before the end of the season, Bobby Calder invited Jim and me up to see Aberdeen's away league game against Rangers at Ibrox. After the game, which the Dons lost, we were ushered into the Blue Room for refreshments. It was incredible. Everything was blue, the wallpaper, the crockery, the tablecloth, the carpet. Waitresses were offering cucumber sandwiches, and directors, complete with bowler hats and paper collars and cuffs, were launching themselves into large whiskies – the whole bit.

Jim and I skulked around for a while, hoping that some players might arrive and camouflage us a bit (although being the scruffy schoolboys we were, that was wishful thinking). Eventually, after loitering aimlessly and snacking on the cucumber sandwiches for ten minutes or so, we summoned up the nerve and approached the bar ready to order a couple of beers we'd been eyeing. Just as Jim was about to order, who of all people should appear beside us but Scot Symon, the top man himself.

'It'll be orange juice for you boys, then,' he said, his voice sounding like we imagined God's would. And Jim ordered two orange juices.

I played out of my skin for the rest of the season with Renfrew, anticipating the pro soccer season ahead. I was super-confident and felt there was no opponent or team that I couldn't handle. Just towards the end of the junior season came a game I'll always remember. I was 17, still at high school and living at home by the dam with my parents when Bobby Calder called to say that Tommy Pearson, the new Dons manager, wanted to see me play before the final call-up. It was a game for Aberdeen reserves against Clyde reserves at Shawfield in Glasgow in late May '60. It was on a Wednesday afternoon, and Dad and I made sure to get a bus that would get us there in good time. This was the first time in all the years I could remember that my old man had taken time off work and accompanied me to a game. I had never known him to even attend any of my games, never mind travel with me to one, and, as I mentioned earlier, this had been just fine with me. Sounds weird, I know, but that's how it was for me and, I think, for many of the guys I played with and against. Terrence Gurney, a fellow

Greenockian and a former apprentice at Chelsea, tells of the embarrassment of one of his youth teammates when, after playing in a Greenock juvenile game, he found out that his mother had been at the match and had knocked somebody's lights out because they had been giving her son some stick. Occasionally, when I was very young, I'd ask Charlie Sr, like kids do their old man, to do up my football-boot laces, and he'd tie them firmly, with the laces around the sole and the knot on the outside; or I might get him to pump a leather ball with a rubber bladder and lace it up, but there was never anything in the way of formal coaching or even simple advice from him. On the other hand, if he expressed disgust at a Morton forward for poor control or shooting, or especially for an inability to go past his man, I got the message loud and clear. The fact that he took time off work to come to that game at Shawfield made it all the more important to me.

When I got to the Shawfield dressing-room, the whisper among the team was that George Herd, Clyde's Scotland international inside-forward, was playing. I could not believe I was about to be sharing a pitch with a real-life star international footballer. He had helped Clyde to a Scottish Cup victory over Hibernian in 1958 and was coming back from injury. Being the awestruck schoolboy that I was, I thought it was fantastic just to be on the same pitch as him. I remember it was a beautiful sunny day, and we drew 1–1. George was a small fellow with tricky skills, and I was saucer-eyed at his every touch and move, probably investing him with abilities that weren't really there. The truth is I'm not sure whether he was taking it easy and just playing himself back into fitness or giving it all he had. He did well and looked a cut above some of his teammates, but he sure didn't dominate.

More importantly for me, though, I had a cracker of a game, beating opponents with ease, giving spot-on passes and generally looking more mature than my years. I hadn't known what to expect and played very simply at first, but as the game wore on, I realised the pace wasn't beyond me at all, and I grew in confidence and ambition and had a spanking good game. If there truly are defining moments in careers, then this was one for me. That match and the praise I received afterwards from Tommy Pearson and Bobby Calder, and especially from Charlie Sr, was a great confidence-builder. The Dons confirmed after the game that I'd be called up the next month, and I left Shawfield prouder and happier than I can say. I was pleased almost more for Charlie Sr and Agnes than for myself, and it was a joyous ride home together to Greenock. I'll remember my happiness for my old man that day for the rest of my life, and I can even feel the prick of a tear in my eye as I recall it now.

It's ironic that Charlie runs a coaching school because, though he'd probably shoot me down for saying this, nobody could have coached Charlie Cooke. He brought the skills he learnt on the streets and in the playground to the top table. I thought one of his greatest assets was his ability to stay clear of injury. Guys like him and Kenny Dalglish rarely missed a game. Charlie was always a great player in my book, and I never saw him play a bad game. He could perform with any players, anytime, anywhere. The original Martini footballer. He was a master of the ball, in a literal sense. His absolute control was mind-blowing, and combined with style, strength, aggression and just the right amount of arrogance, it made him one of the finest players ever to come out of Scotland. He'd be a £20-million player today, for sure.

Jim Geddes, teammate at Port Glasgow Rovers,
Renfrew Juniors and Aberdeen

5

The Match

Wednesday, 18 May 1960 at Hampden Park, Glasgow, not long after the Shawfield game, was another night I'll remember for the rest of my life. I was yet to embark on my dream of becoming a full-time pro at Aberdeen and was still just a schoolboy, living at home on Thom Street by the dam and the swans.

I remember that night not so much for exact details or incidents, although they included a 127,000 crowd, three cracking goals from Real Madrid maestro and captain Alfredo Di Stéfano and four fantastic finishes from the 'Galloping Major', my Hungarian hero of Wembley '53, Ferenc Puskás. And all this on a night when both teams played brilliant attacking soccer and Real Madrid swept to an imperious 7–3 win over an excellent Eintracht Frankfurt side in the greatest European Cup final ever. But that match was more even than the sum of its parts and the effect it had on our whole nation; that night we connected with the very essence of soccer – skills, speed and grace under fire

– and left with an understanding of why and how it stirs us and millions of others around the world so.

In historical terms, it was a night of all sorts of European Cup records. Real won their record fifth European Cup in a row. The biggest-ever European Cup final attendance, 127,621 mostly Scottish fans, yielded the best-ever Euro Cup receipts, of £55,000. Seventy million viewers around the world, more than ever before, watched it on television, and the 7–3 result made it the highest-scoring final in the history of the competition.

But the records and the history books can't do the occasion justice either. They'll never be able to describe what happened there on the field and terraces that night. I don't have words adequate to it, because what took place at Hampden that evening was, I believe, more than just a good game or even a great one. It was an epiphany, an appreciation of Europeans and football by proud, underachieving Scots not used to admitting anything to foreigners other than bragging, 'Wearrragreatest!!!' The match that night showed the sublime heights the game could reach in real life and not just in our Scottish dreams, and our gratitude to both teams took over Hampden like a virus. We were drenched in the magic of football that night. How many members of that enormous crowd remain alive, I have no idea, but each and every one of them would tell you the same.

The set-up couldn't have been better. Scotland and Hampden had been chosen to host the final for the first time in the Cup's history, causing great excitement in Britain, as it was thought that, with the home-field advantage, Wolverhampton Wanderers, England's best at that time, or Scotland's own Glasgow Rangers could win the whole thing. Wolves were the first to go out when Barcelona whipped them 9–2 over their two-leg quarter-final. Rangers advanced to the semi-finals to meet Eintracht by beating Sparta Rotterdam 3–2 in a quarter-final replay at Highbury.

Eintracht's part-timers had arrived on the European Cup scene under everybody's radar, and Scotland was abuzz about the Gers' chances of getting to the final and winning it at Hampden. But Eintracht thrashed the Gers 6–1 in Frankfurt, in front of 80,000 German fans, and 6–3 at Ibrox, for an unbelievable 12–4 aggregate. So impressive was Frankfurt's speed and so comprehensive their domination at Ibrox that Rangers' fans applauded them off the field at the end of the game, which was all the more remarkable considering that not so long ago the two countries had been bitter wartime enemies.

Meanwhile, in the other, all-Spanish semi-final, Real met Barcelona, managed by the famous Helenio Herrera, who would one day be my coach when I played for a World XI eight years later at the Bernabéu.

Barça and Real had been battling one another in the Spanish league all the way to the final games of the season, with only goal difference separating them at the death. Barça eventually came out on top in the league, but Real had made the European championship their own and were aiming for their record fifth win. Under their new manager, Miguel Muñoz, they earned a 3–1 win at the Bernabéu, where Barça had two goals disallowed, then sped to an early 3–0 lead at the Nou Camp on two goals from Puskás and one from Francisco Gento, with Barça only managing a late consolation goal from Sándor Koscis and a 3–1 final scoreline.

Real's 6–2 aggregate thrashing of their biggest opponents had set the Hampden final up as one for the ages, and it didn't disappoint.

I was more excited about this game than any I could remember going to see. I was finishing out the junior season with Renfrew, and had the new season at Aberdeen to look forward to if all went to plan. But I was still only a 17-year-old schoolboy and felt like the excitable kid I had been 7 years before watching the Pathe News at La Scala and seeing the Galloping Major for the first time. Who could forget Puskás pulling the ball back with the sole of his left foot and leaving Billy Wright for dead? This was a chance to see Real and Puskás live, with the rest of his superstar teammates like Di Stéfano, Gento and a little guy I would play against four years later for the Scottish League against the Italian League in Rome, Luis Del Sol, and nothing could make me miss it.

Strangely, no matter how many mates I asked, nobody else was up for going. I couldn't believe it. Here was the chance of a lifetime, as far as I was concerned, and everybody had ice-cream vans to drive or movies to see. Or girlfriends. Go figure.

However, nothing could have stopped me that night. I took the train up to Glasgow alone and got settled high on the terraces with the other 127,620 expectant fans. What, we wondered, were we going to see?

We didn't have to wait long. Frankfurt took up the running immediately. A Meier cross shot in the first minute almost beat Domínguez in the Madrid goal, but he managed to touch the ball onto the bar and to safety. Kress and Pfaff also tested Domínguez early before, at the 18-minute mark, Kress volleyed a low cross into the Madrid net to give Eintracht a deserved lead. It was at this point that Di Stéfano and Puskás whipped the hitherto lethargic Madrid side into shape, and we were treated to perhaps the finest team display ever as Real Madrid proceeded to take the fine Frankfurt team apart at the seams. Di Stéfano got three magnificent goals while Puskás got four, showing his whole repertoire, including narrow-angle power shooting, technically perfect volleying and penalty-spot coolness.

Eintracht were no slouches, but it was clear even to them that we were witnessing something special. The 7–3 outcome may have been a bizarre one-game scoreline, but it was also indicative of the sublime attacking soccer we saw from both teams that night.

If the game itself was full of brilliance like we'd never seen before, the ending was moving beyond belief. When the final whistle sounded for what had truly been a game for the ages, most of the record crowd of fans, predominantly Scottish, stood their ground and never moved as they applauded and cheered and wept for 45 minutes after the final whistle. Hampden was overflowing with love and gratitude and rivers of tears that night, directed towards both teams in thanks for an occasion we'd remember for the rest of our lives. When the Real team circled the field with the trophy for the last time, the roar from all of us still standing transfixed by it all was deafening.

Never has any foreign team played so brilliantly and inspiringly or been so rapturously applauded and loved by people on British soil as Real that night. If we get a chance to touch the mysteries of life and football only a few times in our life, that was surely one time for me, and, I believe, for every other soul who was present.

I walked to the train home to Greenock in a happy daze. I was sad that it was past and gone but happy, oh so happy, to have been there and seen it all live. I'll never forget that feeling. And as I rode the train home, I knew more than ever that if it was ever within my power, I wanted sometime, someplace to play the beautiful game that beautifully.

6

Bonnie Prince Charlie

Even today, I can remember my excitement that summer of 1960 after the Real versus Eintracht final and the Clyde game as I prepared to leave for Aberdeen, where I would spend the next four years. Aberdeen was known as 'the Granite City' due to the number of homes and fine historical buildings that are constructed from the hard silver-grey stone, which is plentiful in the north-east, and when I walked down Union Street in the city centre, I wasn't disappointed. It was and still is a beautiful town.

In fact, it's not too far north of St Monance in Fife on the north-east coast, yet despite our family holidays in St Monance, I'd never been to Aberdeen. I discovered it was a major fishing port and also known as 'the Rose City' because of the Aberdonians' success in cultivating the plant itself in all its diverse glories. My time there predated the oil-industry jobs and infrastructure that now abound there.

But all that was sidebar stuff to me compared with the

fact that the Dons, despite their brushes with relegation in 1957–58 and 1958–59, were among the bigger clubs in Scotland, with home attendances of ten to twenty thousand if they were playing well. At that time, they were one of a small group of clubs, including Hibernian, Hearts and Dundee, which could realistically claim to have a chance of challenging the Old Firm's supremacy.

With my single suitcase filled with all my earthly schoolboy belongings (which weren't many – all I really needed were my boots), I was primed and ready for this whole new life ahead of me. It was a four-and-a-half-hour train ride across the country to the north-east, beginning with a one-hour trip on the steam train from Greenock West to Glasgow Central, then a short taxi ride to St Enoch station followed by a three-and-a-half-hour journey to Aberdeen in the long-distance Pullman carriages with their passageways and sliding doors and the watercolour prints of seascapes and rural castles that decorated British Rail coaches then.

I remember that ride like it was yesterday. As the train rat-tat-tat-tatted over the rails out of Glasgow, the Scottish countryside rushing past was a summer idyll, with grazing sheep and cows, and kestrels hovering over green fields and hedges. Farmers with their shirtsleeves rolled high were driving their tractors and walking the fields with their sheepdogs in the sunshine, and, surprisingly, as the scourge of myxomatosis was at its height, there were rabbits and hares galore. As I got off the train and walked down the platform at Aberdeen, I couldn't have been more excited about or ready for my big adventure.

I was going to Aberdeen on a full-time professional contract. My wages would be eight pounds a week in the reserves and twelve pounds a week in the first team with a three-pound win bonus and a one-pound-and-ten-shillings draw bonus – that is, if I ever made it to the first team, which by my reckoning was a long shot. The money had me swallowing hard, but the idea of making first-team wages, and especially the win bonus, seemed like stuff from another planet, and I didn't expect it to happen for a long time, if ever.

But I was in schoolboy heaven. Only seventeen, I didn't have a care in the world except paying my two-pound-a-week digs at Mrs Anne Robertson's three-storey granite house on Great Western Road, where I was to live with several other young players from out of town, and occasionally sending something home to Agnes and Charlie Sr. I was excited beyond words to be getting a chance at the thing I wanted most in the world to do, and about being as far away from Greenock as it was possible to get in the Scottish First Division. I had made the decision to join the Dons completely on my own, and here I was, again on my own, on my way to start a whole new adventure in a whole new world. It never entered my daydreaming mind that it could all end abruptly and I could be back home in Greenock scrounging for work faster than it takes to sprain an ankle or tear a ligament. Call me stupid, but I had never considered any of the things that could go wrong.

One good thing that did come out of my daydreaming, though, was a tremendous attitude. I was focused and excited like it was a cup final every day. I was fit out of my schoolboy skin and ready for just about anything. I assumed all the players would be excellent and mostly much better than me, and I was afraid that I might not be good enough, no question about that. But I had always gone into games thinking that opponents were better than me, and it was an attitude that had served me well and really wasn't new or hard to live with. My background in the religious bigotries and battles of Greenock juvenile football meant I was pretty used to the rough and tumble of older competition, being on the end of stupid tackles and threats, and giving back the welly, if I could, in spades. I wasn't big, but I was strong and quick with a bit of a temper, and I wasn't at all intimidated by older, bigger and stronger players. In fact, in a strange way, I used to think they were all the same size when I had the ball at my feet. It was the great equaliser, for me.

But I knew my place going in as a schoolboy at Aberdeen. I would shut my mouth and work my butt off and be a royal pain in the arse to play against no matter who the opponent was. Just about anybody could do that, I figured. If I got the chance to do things with the ball, I'd try to do them; that was what I wanted to be known for. And if I didn't make it, well, I'd take care of that when it happened. I had no plans if the Dons didn't want me. I didn't have a single contact in the professional game apart from Bobby Calder, and the only people I could have turned to were Agnes and Charlie Sr.

What I found was different from what I expected. Funnily, 'Pittodrie' is Gaelic for shit heap. Seriously. It is also the name of Aberdeen's football ground, and before Aberdeen Football Club was formed in 1903, the site was used by the local police force as a dunghill for their horses. Although they were decent performers for the first 40 years of their existence, the Dons had to wait until 1946 before winning their first honour when they beat Rangers at Hampden Park in front of 130,000 to take the Scottish League Cup. In the following year, under the stewardship of Dave Halliday, they beat Hibernian to win the Scottish League Cup and lost to Rangers in the Scottish Cup final. Dave Halliday, who in his day had been a great centre-forward for Sunderland, managed to take the club to two more Scottish Cup finals, in 1953 and 1954, before delivering the ultimate – the league championship – in 1955. Halliday left to take over at Leicester City, and Davie Shaw stepped up from trainer to manager, keeping the good times going by taking his team to victory in the Scottish League Cup in 1956. This was truly Aberdeen's first golden age, but that cup final win over St Mirren was followed by a steady decline in the club's fortunes. The next few years saw a fall in league positions and early exits from the cups, until in 1959 there were signs of a revival when the Scottish Cup final was reached again. This time, though, the team faltered against St Mirren. Relegation loomed. Davie Shaw reverted back to the trainer position, and Tommy Pearson, an old Pittodrie favourite as a winger who had also played for Newcastle United and Scotland, was installed as manager, and this is where I came in. I'd like to say that this is where the club's fortunes changed too, but that was not to be. Tommy Pearson had also been a local sportswriter and a harsh critic of the team and its manager in his columns over the previous two relegation-threatened seasons, so I cannot imagine the feelings swirling around within the club when Davie was unseated for Tommy. All of this was unknown by me so I wasn't looking out for tension, but as far as I can remember, Davie got on with his job with no hint of resentment.

Aberdeen's second purple patch would come long after my departure, under manager Eddie Turnbull and with players like Martin Buchan and Joe Harper. They beat Celtic in the Scottish Cup final in 1970, but not until the arrival of Alex Ferguson as manager did the team enjoy their greatest-ever age. With players like Gordon Strachan, Steve Archibald, Jim Leighton, Alex McLeish and Willie Miller, Ferguson broke the Celtic–Rangers axis and, incredibly, won the league in 1980, 1984 and 1985, the Scottish Cup in 1982, 1983, 1984 and 1986, and the European Cup-Winners' Cup in 1983. No wonder Manchester United snapped him up. All that, of course, was a long way into the future at the beginning of the 1960–61 campaign.

In 1960, Tommy Pearson was in the vanguard, I think, of the new breed of white-collared GM-type coach/managers who fancied the business-suit boardroom role and listening to themselves talk at pre-game meetings more than actually getting their hands or tracksuits dirty on the training field or at the chalkboard. I wasn't surprised at all to read that shortly after parting ways with the Dons during season 1965–66 after five less than brilliant seasons, Tommy played golf in the British Open. That was exactly how I could imagine him. To me, he always seemed much better suited to raising his glass in the members' lounge and toasting the gathered guests than to rousing weary players to battle at the start of overtime in a muddy Scottish Cup replay.

1960 was also a time of change in the Dons' playing personnel. Just as the season was coming around, several great Aberdeen servants and fans' favourites from the 1955 league championship days – men like GK Fred Martin, centre-half Jim Clunie, wing-half Archie Glen, inside-forward Bobby Wishart and left-winger Jackie Hather – were all retiring or moving on, and it was probably as good a time as any, despite the previous season's relegation struggle, for youngsters like myself, Desmond Herron from Duntocher Hibs, Doug Fraser (ex-Blantyre Celtic, already with a season at Pittodrie under his belt) and local boy Doug Coutts to be arriving at the club.

The weather for pre-season near the Aberdeen beaches was beautiful and I couldn't get enough of training. I was loving it, and after the first few days getting used to the new surroundings and bus schedules, the new faces and characters and the funny sing-song north-east accents, gradually deciphering some of the more unusual words and meanings – 'Far ye ganin?' for 'Where are you going?', for example – I was having a blast taking anyone and everyone on in practice, no matter who they were.

In sprints, I was surprised to find that I could be first over the first 20 yards against almost anybody, and the only guy who would consistently catch me over 100 was Ally Shewan, although if I got a good start, I would pip him. Skill-wise, I didn't see anybody do things that surprised me, although Jimmy Hogg, our captain and left-back, had an educated left foot and looked to play the ball on the ground and keep possession much more than we were used to seeing in full-backs in those days. He was no Carl Lewis, but he read the game beautifully and was a terrific calming influence on the whole team. 'Hedger', as we called him, was a good example of an excellent player who was never recognised by the national squads simply because he played in the boonies and not with the Old Firm in Glasgow. Everyone who watched him regularly and those of us who played with him had no doubt that he had the talent and mentality to have a successful international career. But, like many others outside of Glasgow, he was overlooked.

Billy Little, the Dons' slight but sharp front man, impressed me from the first day with his unassuming, workmanlike attitude. He was a few years older than me, with a First Division season already on his résumé. He'd been a schoolteacher when he got the chance as a pro, and he took it carefully and methodically. He wasn't the feinting, faking kind of one-versus-one player I was but a thoughtful, calculating type with sharp feet, a savvy eye and a clinical finish. He wasn't a big guy, 5 ft 9 in. or so, but he was the classic inside-forward/front man who could 'keep the line moving', with terrific vision and a great nose for goal. He lived in the same digs with several of us at Great Western Road, but there the similarities ended. Billy was a straight-living non-drinker, about to get married, and he looked after himself in exemplary fashion, not at all like the rest of us, who were drinking and gambling and generally up to all the stuff young footballers with too much time and money get up to. That said, I liked Billy's quiet, down-to-earth approach. It was the way I'd have wanted to be if I hadn't been as impulsive and compulsive as I was. Interestingly, despite his great attitude and plentiful skills, Billy's playing career never really took off, and, surprisingly to me, knowing his relatively reserved demeanour, he went on to manage Queen of the South and Falkirk.

I think it's one of the mysteries of the game how talent doesn't always win through. Often the reason a career falters is obvious. Poor work habits, lack of skill, speed or heart, or maybe injury. But sometimes there's no apparent explanation, and the players you think the most able don't always rise to the top.

Things, for example, did not run smoothly for my chum Jim Geddes, who was signed from Renfrew with me by Bobby Calder. Jim was a classy wing-half who could easily have done well, but he didn't hit it off with Tommy Pearson and tells me that 'Tup', as he was known to us, from his initials, never once spoke to him. He was paid the minimum wage and got the odd letter from Tup headed 'Dear Geddes'. Very odd indeed. Part of the reason may have been that Jim picked up an ankle injury early on that took a time to clear up, and he was never able to establish himself fully after that. Eventually, he moved on to Third Lanark, after which we played against each other once, and I (Jim informs me) scored the winner in a 2–1 victory.

When Thirds were relegated, Jim took himself off to play in South Africa and was just beginning to flower when he had his leg broken in a tackle and found himself in plaster again for nine months. To make matters worse, the guy who did it, 6,000 miles from home, came from Greenock and used to play with Jim for Greenock Juniors. By 1969, he was out of football and pursuing a successful career in engineering. I learned most of this only recently, when I contacted Jim back in Gourock in an effort to liven up my memory cells while I was writing this book. He also told me something I had no idea about at the time and, considering how much it upset me to hear about it, God only knows how it must have felt for Jim when it happened. Seemingly, Bobby Calder had gone on record, gone on the radio even, saying that he only signed Jim to ensure he got me, thinking that if he offered terms to my pal as well, I would be more likely to sign. It was hard for Jim to hear, and it was insensitive and crass of Bobby Calder to say it, even if it was true. I'm embarrassed I was so wrapped up in myself that I had no idea what was going on around me.

Thankfully, Jim is made of the right stuff and is philosophical about his footballing career. He still runs daily and works out twice a week, and he retains his great sense of humour – he recently told me he still watches the game, 'But if they don't ban passing the ball back, I may stop.'

The rest of the lodgers at Mrs Robertson's house on Great Western Road were a motley crew, as they say. Doug Fraser, a swarthy, handsome, muscular young wing-half from Glasgow, was a couple of years older than me and already had had a season in the Dons' first team. Doug was strong and quick, more of a ball-winner than a creator but a good physical presence. He was a natty dresser, particular about his clothes and appearance, and was not unsure of himself. He later moved south to West Bromwich Albion for a decent £25,000 fee and won an FA Cup-winner's medal when Albion defeated Everton 1–0 at Wembley in 1968. He captained West Brom and gained caps for Scotland before moving to Nottingham Forest and then on to Walsall, where he became manager. After leaving football, he joined the prison service.

Gordon Sim, too, was a year or two older. He was a left-back, and we used to kid him that his right foot was for standing on. He had impeccable manners and an upmarket accent, from one of the better schools in Edinburgh was my guess, although he had come to Aberdeen from Shettleston

Juniors. Gordon had serious ambitions, I'd say, to being something other than a footballer. He dressed in smart tweed jackets and read the *Financial Times*, and I think did his best to dumb down to fit in with us of rabble status. I had six years of secondary education behind me but never hinted as much in Gordon's presence. Gordon was a good guy and one day in pre-season was kind enough to take us new boys, my room-mate Desmond Herron and me, for a game of golf at the Bridge of Don club. Just as we were teeing off, Gordon asked if we wanted a drink, and Desmond and I had a Coke while Gordon had a beer. Lo and behold, when we arrived home to Great Western Road, Tup was waiting for us already informed that we'd been seen 'drinking' and questioning what we were up to.

Willie Callaghan was a short, barrel-chested winger who had an irrepressible gusto about him. Willie had arrived with plenty of noise, much of it self-generated. He had the Glaswegian patter and knew his way around the game, but he never really had the extra pace needed to crack it as winger in the first team, and a couple of years later he moved on. Willie Allan was an east-coaster who had smooth ball skills that I always admired, and he became my inside-forward partner for a while in the first team before he too left Aberdeen. I always liked Willie. He had no pretence about him and smoked like a chimney. In fact, that's how I remember him best, with his curly blond hair, that beautiful shuffling dribble of his and a cigarette in his hand.

It's said that footballers pass like ships in the night in pursuit of their careers, and that's certainly been the case in my experience. I didn't form any great bond with any of my lodging mates, or indeed any of my Aberdeen teammates, despite being there for four years. Wille was a good example. We played, trained and lived together but never really got to know one another except for on the field. So much so that years later, on a visit back home to Greenock, I was surprised to see him in a team photograph of Greenock Morton. I never knew he'd gone there.

Bobby Cummings was another ship-in-the-night lodger. He was a slim, bustling front man, an ex-miner from Ashington, near Newcastle, wiry and strong and excellent in the air. He too was older than the rest of us, and he was the old head of the lodgings. He was a charmer, with a broad Geordie accent and an infectious passion for the horses. At least, it was infectious for me. Many a Friday pay day, I was broke by the evening after an afternoon session in the bookies with Bobby. I'd lose everything and have to borrow my rent money from one of the boys, or, when I got to know Mrs Robertson better, I would ask her for a week to pay. Thinking back now, I can't believe we were so crazy. Bobby stayed around for a couple of years before moving back to his home-town team, Newcastle United. I was glad for Bobby that he got the move he so hankered for. And I was glad for myself that I could start paying my digs on time.

Willie Lamb, another east-coast lad, from Macmerry, was a forward who had his housemates Billy and Bobby, along with Norman Davidson and Ken Brownlie, competing with him for the first-team centre-forward spot. Willie was a quiet guy who kept to himself, which made it tough for him to catch Tommy Pearson's eye, and he too moved on not too long after the 1960–61 season.

Desmond Herron, a right-winger with decent pace and a cannon shot in both feet, roomed with me for a while. Desmond was another Glaswegian, with all the patter and an unstoppable string of jokes to keep us all laughing. He started out the first season with me at the vanguard of Tommy Pearson's much-vaunted youth policy but got a chance to join Celtic legend Bertie Peacock, who was managing out in Canada, and moved in 1962. Today, Des works on the oil rigs off the north-east coast. He spends two weeks on and two off and says that by the time this book is published, it will be two on and three off. Des does stand-up comedy as a sideline. Joe Kerr is his stage name. Geddit. Joe-kerr. Yeah, sure you do. He tells me that after he left Aberdeen, he played for 13 clubs. When John F. Kennedy was shot, he says, he was playing for Barnsley, in case anybody needs to know.

He also tells the joke about the Pope flying over to Birmingham for the investiture of a bishop. Unfortunately, the weather was bad and the papal jet was diverted to Gatwick. So he gets in the big papal Bentley at Gatwick and tells the driver to put the foot down, they're going to be late. So the driver is driving right on the speed limit, and the Pope's getting lairy about the time.

'Can't you go any faster, my son?' asks the Pope. 'We're going to be late.'

'I can't go any faster, Your Eminence,' says the driver, pointing to the speedometer, 'I'm doing the 70 speed limit.'

After a minute or so, the Pope asks the driver to pull over. The Pope then gets in the driver's seat and puts his foot down. They're hammering along at 135 mph when a wailing police car signals for him to stop. When the young cop sees who he's pulled over, he calls up headquarters.

'Searge, you should see who I've pulled over here. He's very, very important.'

'You mean Prince Charles?' asks the sergeant.

'No,' says the young patrolman, 'more important than that.'

'Prince Philip?'

'No, more important than that,' says the patrolman.

'Who's more important than that?' asks the sergeant in frustration.

'Well,' says the patrolman, 'the Pope's driving him.'

OK. I thought it was funny when I first heard it. Blame Desmond.

The Friday a week before the start of the 1960–61 season was the night of the annual intra-squad pre-season game. I was still a kid from Greenock having a blast playing football every day and having more money in my pocket than I'd ever known, and didn't know what an intra-squad game was or what to expect. So I took whatever jersey I was given and just continued where I had left off in practice, looking for people to beat and enjoying myself. That included Ian Burns, the occasional first-team captain and hard man, who didn't mince words or tackles and whom I'd be grateful to have in my team in seasons to come.

It's hard to describe without sounding bigheaded or carried away, but I was in the zone, totally focused, without a care in the world. I was following through on my promise to myself to work my butt off and be a royal pain to play against. My confidence was growing daily, and it didn't matter to me who I was playing against,

Ian Burns or the latest trialist. I had a cracker of a game, beating opponents almost at will, and immediately got fan attention on the night and press headlines the next day. The following week, the *Aberdeen Press and Journal* headlines announced that I was in the first team, along with 18-year-old Desmond Herron, for the opening game of the season against Ayr United at Pittodrie the next Saturday. I couldn't have wished for it to happen any quicker.

In the build-up to the opening game, Tup announced to the press that he was going with youth. From the club's financial viewpoint, after two years of flirting with relegation and a £13,000 operating loss the previous season, the youth policy was a certainty in the boardroom before Tommy ever claimed to have dreamed it up.

But it worked. The fates were with us. We beat Ayr 4–3 that day, and the team got rave reviews. Some came my way – the press called me 'Twinkletoes' and suchlike – but most applauded 'courageous Mr Pearson' for being so daring in his youth policy. My excitement at the success of my debut was short-lived, because Tup promptly dropped me for the next game, against Raith Rovers. He said he didn't want to burn me out. Fat chance, I thought, not realising it was Tup spinning and that he had another young player a couple of years older than me, Jimmy Robertson, up from Edinburgh whom he wanted to look at with a view to signing. Jimmy was maybe 5 ft 7 in. and a slick ball player, and Tup obviously liked the cut of his jib in training. Unfortunately for Jimmy, the Dons went down 4–1 in that next game, and I was recalled in Jimmy's place. I went on to play the most league games that season of anyone in the whole squad, my 32 league appearances equalled only by our free-scoring left-winger, George Mulhall. George, after scoring 40-odd goals in 150 games for the Dons, went to Sunderland, where he forged a formidable attacking partnership with a man who found the back of the net for fun – Brian Clough. Later, George became a manager with Bolton Wanderers and, more successfully and recently, with Halifax Town, where he restored their Football League status.

I was also third-top scorer for that first season, with ten goals. I never thought anything of it at the time but in retrospect, considering the way I came to ignore scoring more and more during the rest of my career, I'm pretty proud now of that first season when I was a 17-year-old player. I only wish that I had carried on in that vein, scoring freely, but over the seasons I began to believe that playmaker/midfield-engine press nonsense and fooled myself into believing that my role was to create goals for others. I read the tag 'midfield schemer' so many times I subconsciously curbed my own goal-scoring instincts, believing that that was not what I was for. I went from notching up double-figure tallies in a season to being happy with just a handful. I saw scoring goals as a bonus, not an aim in itself, and I regret that. Indeed, what I say to the kids who ask me for advice nowadays is that if you want to be a good midfielder, you have to carry a scoring threat. That way you'll always have a team to play for.

In that first season, I helped the team improve its league standing, and we finished 6th with 36 points, 8 more than the previous season and, of course, well clear of the relegation that everyone had tipped. Not only did I establish myself as a Dons regular in my debut season but

I also became a fans' favourite because of my dribbling skills and willingness, some might say compulsion, to take opponents on. 'Bonnie Prince Charlie' they called me. 'The Bonnie Prince'. I never thought anything of it at the time, but now, looking back, I'm flattered and proud no end of the name.

Hugh McIlvanney, then a young reporter on *The Scotsman*, watched me in a 1–1 draw at Clyde. I was proud of his analysis and opinion at the time and kept the report, in which he said:

> Cooke, who is 17, has the fresh-faced, clean-cut look of a schoolboy but it does not hide the mature touches of a class inside-forward. His smooth ball-play and fine passing combined perfectly with the efforts of Davidson. He's a clean-limbed boy, strong of shoulder, with a good idea of the duties of an inside-forward.

It wasn't all good, though, with one paper running a headline after a game against St Johnstone that read 'Selfish Cooke Forgot About His Colleagues'.

This would be a recurring theme in my career, but in general the press were terrific to me. They called me 'the Boy Wizard', 'Prince of the Dribble', all that kind of thing. It might have been enough to turn a young boy's head, but my home-town newspaper, the *Greenock Telegraph*, ensured that didn't happen. An article printed in December 1960 began: 'Greenock Boy Is Dons Favourite. Greenock boy Hugh Cooke is one of the big stars in the revival of Aberdeen this year. Each week Hugh is earning praise from sports writers.'

A year on, despite the fact that I was a household name

in Scottish football, the *Telegraph* were sticking to their guns: 'Local Boy Gets Training Course. Since going to Aberdeen, Hugh Cooke, a one-time local juvenile player, has made rapid strides.'

When this book goes on sale, I'm inclined to have an alternative cover made up with my name given as Hugh Cooke – it might sell better in Greenock. A little later, I was bemused to read in the *Daily Mail* that: 'Arsenal are interested in Ian Cooke, the Aberdeen forward, who they believe could be the player to get the best out of George Eastham.'

The press obsession with my dribbling and 'greediness' sometimes went overboard; one journalist was even moved to write a poem about it:

> Ah said that Charlie was a 'dilly'.
> He's aye been that, but willy-nilly
> Tae 'dilly' he oft added 'dally',
> And Dons fans found that hard to swally!

> But Charlie noo is learnin' fast,
> His dallyin's a' in the past.
> Like any craftsman – it mak's sense –
> He's learned frae hard experience.

Interestingly, it was my 'selfish' ball-playing skills at Aberdeen that brought the attention of a whole procession of English clubs interested in plonking down £20,000-plus to sign me when I was only a couple of months into that first Dons season and straight out of school. It was an astonishing sum to see in the headlines and great for my ego, but after the phantom signings sagas at Renfrew, I was at least a tiny bit better prepared to handle it.

It definitely boosted my confidence, though, and helped me deal with the 'greedy' criticisms. I always spun it to the press that I understood everyone's frustrations and wanted to curb my dribbling inclinations, but in truth I didn't think people knew what they were talking about if they thought it could be turned on and off like a tap. If anything, I didn't want to dribble less but dribble *better*. I played the game as I found it, just like we all do, passing or dribbling according to what I thought I should do. I felt my one-on-one skills and the opportunities they opened up for me and my teammates were some of the most important things I brought to any team I played for. When all was said and done, I thought beating opponents was the most difficult and also the most valuable skill in the game. It was what the best players did, and what I wanted to do. If I was given the chance to do it all over, apart from scoring more goals and cleaning up my drinking habits, I wouldn't change a thing.

At the end of that first, highly successful season, I did what might seem a strange thing to most people and got a job as a bricklayer's labourer in the close season. I didn't have to. I was getting paid my basic close-season wages by the Dons and I could have been off, like everybody else, for a couple of weeks in the Costa Brava and spent the rest of the summer on the golf course. But I had a weird guilt thing about not having had a 'real' job since I'd left school. I had come straight into football, and for whatever reason, despite working my tail off in training, as I always would throughout my career, I felt bad about having somehow got off lightly by not having to do an apprenticeship. It was crazy, in a way. Many of my classmates had gone on to university, were still there studying and would go on to fine careers and even into the arts, as Bill Bryden did. But for some teenage reason, I still felt guilty that I hadn't gone into the yards at 15 like so many of my Greenock pals and contemporaries. Maybe it was because I'd never wanted to go there and deep down felt ashamed about that. But all I'd ever wanted to do was play football, and here I was doing it, getting a free pass, or so it seemed, and it felt like I'd cheated somehow.

So, through one of the Dons directors, I got fixed up to work on a building site as a brickie's labourer as soon as the season was over, and I worked there for the remainder of the holiday. I figured it would strengthen me and generally toughen me up physically and also take care of the guilt thing. I worked like crazy – far too much in the first few days, in fact, as I came home stiff as a board and wasn't right for more than a week. I clearly remember mixing mortar and then, like a real novice, overloading my wheelbarrow with it and trying manfully to negotiate up the plank that led to where the bricklayers were working in the buildings and what an impossible struggle it was. Weaving and stumbling like I was, I must have looked like a drunk. I quickly learned you just half fill the barrow, or even less if you're inclined, so you can do the job quicker, more efficiently and for a longer period than you ever can trying to prove you are Tarzan.

The same thing happened when I was loading my hod with bricks for the layers. At first, I loaded it up until it was impossibly heavy and stumbled and swayed up the planks, thinking that was the way it was done by 'real labourers' and the problem was just that I wasn't used to it and maybe had to get stronger. The old labourers, though, in between their constant cigarettes, quickly taught me how wrong I was and that lighter is better.

I remember, too, unloading the bricks from the trucks and how the straw they were packed in would come clouding off with the brickdust and get in our eyes – there was no easy way around that one. I copied the old workers, though, cutting holes in square rubber sheets to use instead of gloves, and after several days I figured out how to handle the bricks properly, without ending up with raw blisters and painful, smooth, tender fingertips and palms every night.

It was an instructive summer, I'll say that, and I'm sure I was stronger for it. But if you don't use it, you lose it, and I don't think it had any lasting effect on either my build or my game. And my guilt was only partially appeased. Go figure.

7

The Zero-Cost Team

November 1960, and the newspapers were speculating about various English clubs coming to watch me, with a Newcastle United rumour being particularly persistent.

Tommy Pearson, meanwhile, put out the spin that the club wasn't interested in letting players go, especially the younger players, that he was building a youth policy for the future, for the club, the fans and the city, and that I was there to stay. It all sounded pretty impressive.

Things went well for me in those early years at Pittodrie, and there was no shortage of highlights. We famously defeated Rangers at home by a thumping 6–1. I laid on two for teammates and scored myself with a near-post header. We saw off Rangers and Celtic at their home grounds, too. Other domestic games I will never forget include a 10–1 drubbing of Raith Rovers, when I had a good game but only managed 10 per cent of the goal tally. In 1961, I was named among the 29 players summoned to a World Cup get-together in preparation for the following year's tournament. I didn't make it to Chile in the end, but, nevertheless, it was good to know that the Scottish selectors had me in their sights.

In November 1962, I received an international call-up, to play for a Scottish League representative side against the Italian League in Rome. It was not a full cap, but it was a terrific honour. I'd just turned 20 and was tickled pink to be on such a glamorous trip and in such exalted company, visiting the Vatican and being photographed at St Peter's with Old Firm stars like Jim Baxter, Jimmy Millar and Willie Henderson of Rangers and Paddy Crerand, Jim Kennedy and John Divers of Celtic, as well as guys like Ian Ure and Alex Hamilton of Dundee. 'Hammy', as we all knew Alex, made up for his lack of Old Firm status – the thing that usually got press and selection committee attention – with his sheer energy and personality.

We played in the half-full Olympic Stadium, and I was awed even during the game by the marble statues that surrounded the ground, never mind by the star-studded team we faced that day. Soccer stadiums then weren't thought of, as some are today, as works of art or even community assets, but the Olympic Stadium was something else to my young eyes. What with visiting St Peter's and the rest of the historical sites we'd been to on a tour of the city the day before the game, I was blown away by Rome and the whole trip. I was still only familiar with Greenock and Aberdeen, and had made visits to some of Britain's larger cities, so Rome, dripping with culture and history, knocked me out.

The Italian attack that day was anything but Italian, with an array of foreign stars that reflected the make-up of the top Italian teams. It thrills me to name them even today. Up front, they started Kurt Hamrin (Fiorentina), Luis Del Sol (Juventus), John Charles (Roma), Helmut Haller (Bologna) and Gianfranco Petris (Fiorentina), with superstar players like Omar Sivori (Juventus) on the bench. Del Sol had recently moved from Real Madrid, Haller was starring for Germany, and who could mistake big John Charles? The Welsh giant was then enjoying Beatle-type adulation when the Beatles themselves were still only session musicians in a Hamburg backstreet.

Lining up for us, we had Willie Henderson (Rangers) on the right wing and Davie McParland (Partick Thistle) on the left, Jimmy Millar (Rangers) at centre-forward, Willie Hamilton (Hibs) and me at inside-forward, Jim Baxter (Rangers) and Pat Crerand (Celtic) as wing-halfs; Ian Ure (Dundee) was centre-half and captain, Alex Hamilton (Dundee) and Jim Kennedy (Celtic) were in defence and Sandy McLaughlan (Kilmarnock) was in goal. John Divers was our substitute.

The Italians took a 3–1 lead, with goals from Del Sol, Haller and Petris against a John Divers goal, as they outplayed us in the first half on a heavy field. But we came back strongly in the second half and played some good stuff to tie it on goals from Jimmy Millar and yours truly, when, in the 72nd minute, I put a near-post header past Fabio Cudicini of Roma in the Italian goal.

'Cooke pounced on a lobbed centre and headed in' is how one Scottish press report described it, putting it, I thought, way too simply and limply. I worked my tail off on the muddy field the whole game that day and puked up afterwards, I was so tired. The goal itself wasn't cloaked in glory, but I think it was a tad better than the 'pounced and headed in' billing it got. I had sprinted hard through the mud to the near post when I was dog-tired, past equally tired Italian defenders, and had risen ('like a hawk', we always used to kid each other at Chelsea) to put a perfectly placed near-post header past Cudicini (Recognise the name? Yes, that's him, the father of current Chelsea goalkeeper, Carlo), who was glued to his line. Not a 30-yard Bobby Charlton-type screamer, I grant you, but quite a nifty little goal at a key time – everybody was tiring, including myself, and that highlighted the Italian defence's wobbles and Cudicini's indecision. As you can tell, I was very proud of it.

Unfortunately, John Charles chested down a corner from Petris two minutes from the end, and Hamrin, one of the smallest players on the field, smacked the ball past our Sandy McLaughlan for the winner.

What could and should have been a well-deserved draw against the star-packed Italian team went into the record books as a loss. Our bad luck seemed to be underlined when the Italians turned up at the after-game reception, held in the beautiful marble banqueting room of a hotel, looking like millionaire film stars in beautifully fitted blue blazers, grey slacks and matching shirts and ties courtesy of the Italian League. The only thing missing to complete the Hollywood backdrop was Sophia Loren. We returned home to Scotland deeply frustrated with the result and totally routed in the fashion show to the usual press bleatings and self-flagellations that accompany Scottish defeats, even undeserved ones.

Fortunately, the result did not hinder my slow scramble up the international ladder, and in December 1962 I was called up to play for the Scottish Under-23s against Wales at our own Pittodrie. We won 2–0, and I helped make the opening goal.

The letter from the SFA summonsing me for international duty reads like a historical document and gives a little flavour of the times. Bear in mind that we were supposedly the cream of Scotland's younger international footballers. The following commands, and the financial compensations, make interesting reading:

1. Those travelling from Glasgow and Edinburgh should assemble respectively at the Buchanan Street and Waverley stations.
2. Players must bring their own boots, properly studded, shin guards and any other special equipment they may require. Jerseys, shorts and stockings will be provided.
3. Players will receive a fee of £20.
4. Players are forbidden to comment on the match in television, radio or press.
5. After the match players will dine in The Imperial Hotel with the Welsh players.

So there.

Another memorable game during my Dons period was a friendly against the touring Brazilian 'Tournament Champions', as they were always described, Bahia. It was a friendly in name only, under the floodlights at Pittodrie. It was simply a money-maker for both clubs, with nothing at stake, but, that said, we wanted to win and played that way, as did the Brazilians, I think it's fair to say.

It was the first time I'd played against a Brazilian team

and it was an eye-opener. We tied 1–1, but they played the ball around like it was on an invisible string linking them all, and at times they made us look like fools. If you'd read the reports the next day – and especially the praise for me, saying I'd shown the Brazilians a ball-playing thing or two – you would have thought we had done OK. Remember, we were still suffering from that superiority complex that typified British football then as now. Bahia, who may or may not have been champions of anything, who knows, certainly played as if they were and gave us a chasing that night; the only thing that didn't reflect that was the 1–1 scoreline. There were plenty of clattering tackles from our guys, who were just itching to get a piece of the Brazilians – and remember, we had Ian Burns, our fiery wing-half, and George Kinnell at centre-back, who could dish it out with the best. But the Bahia players handled all the rough stuff beautifully, with none of the chest-bumping and referee-baiting that's such a negative feature of the British game. It was a great reminder of how beautifully football can be played, just as Puskás and the Hungarians had shown us at Wembley in 1953 and Eintracht and Real Madrid had done at Hampden in 1960, and of how there was plenty out there to learn from and adapt for ourselves if we had a mind to.

Tup, meanwhile, was still spinning away about his youth policy, although now, a couple of years on, the youth weren't quite as young as they'd been. Sometimes managers get carried away and the 'building for the future' twaddle is just that – twaddle. As if to prove it, over the next two years Tup and the Aberdeen board, headed by Charlie Forbes and Dick Donald, proceeded to shred the team and improve the club's bank balance.

In September 1962, George Mulhall, our quick, goal-scoring left-winger, was shipped off to Sunderland for around £25,000. A year later, Doug Fraser, our right wing-half, was transferred to West Brom for a similar fee, and two months later, our captain, the rock in the middle of our defence and occasional centre-forward when we were desperate for goals, George Kinnell, went to Stoke City for £32,000. These were big fees then. In that same period, Bobby Cummings, Chris Harker, Jim Clunie, Norman Davidson and Ken Brownlie also left for lesser sums, which, when added together with the three star transfers, totalled close to £160,000 – a huge sum in those days. New players came, like solid centre-half John McCormick from Third Lanark and forward Andy Kerr from Sunderland, along with winger Don Kerrigan from St Mirren, but none for big fees, and thereafter we scrambled to stay in mid-table and out of relegation trouble.

Luckily, my own career was flourishing. In the space of 18 months, from being a schoolboy wannabe playing at Renfrew, I'd become a first-team regular at Aberdeen, been selected for Scotland's Under-23s and the Scottish League team and was being touted even by Glasgow pressmen as a full national-team candidate.

I continued to play well over the coming seasons, scoring too, and at the end of the 1963–64 season, I was voted Aberdeen's Player of the Year, an honour of which I was, and remain, immensely proud.

So, things were going well for me, and I think I had every right to be optimistic for the new season. But the start of the 1964–65 season saw the results of the last two years' transfer exits come home to roost. Astonishingly, the club were now trumpeting the fact that they were fielding a zero-cost team. The first team included six players who'd arrived for free from local leagues: John Ogston (Banks o' Dee), Dave Bennett (Sunnybank), Doug Coutts (Banks o' Dee), Dave Smith (ALC Thistle), Ernie Winchester (Torry Academy) and Lewis Thom (Banks o' Dee). They, combined with the rest of us, who had cost only the £20 registration fees – Willie Allan (Bo'ness United), Bobby Cummings (Ashington), Jimmy Hogg (Preston Athletic) and myself (Renfrew Juniors) – made up the sum total of the zero-costers.

The zero-cost team maybe made a nice PR story and a bunch of money for the balance-sheet, but it did nothing for results on the field at the start of that 1964–65 season. We took only 13 points from 15 games, and there was no sign from Tup or the board that there would be any changes to their zero-cost initiative, no sign of the cheque book being produced.

With my Player of the Year award and my selection for the national-team squad a definite possibility, I felt my career was at a tipping point and that, with just a little bit of luck, a regular full Scotland place might materialise. But the way things were shaping up at Pittodrie, the team was going to struggle in the relegation zone for the rest of the season, and it would be near impossible for me to beat out better connected Old Firm challengers or highly thought-of Anglos for international selection.

It looked to me like the zero-cost nonsense could cost me my Scotland chance and possibly any move in the near future to a bigger club in England. So, just as I had made my decision without consultation with anyone else eight years before to forgo schools football with Wee Pat and sign for John Adam's Port Glasgow Rovers, and as I had made my quick agreement with Jim Geddes and Bobby Calder to join the Dons from Renfrew, I consulted with nobody, only my own intuition, decided that I wanted a transfer, and if I was going to stay, I wanted a raise, and I went to see Tommy Pearson to ask for a move. It was as simple as that, although the club's later version of events didn't quite relate it that way. I remember Tup giving me the big one about the club salary structure and how they couldn't change it for one player. I told him that if that was the case, I wanted away, and as a result I was transfer-listed.

One transfer story that had some legs, which is of some interest now in the light of what came after, was that Leeds United and Aberdeen were deep in conversation over doing a straight swap for me and Billy Bremner. Billy, it was said, was unhappy playing in England and wanted to return to Scotland. Although Don Revie was by now the manager at Elland Road, the mighty machine had not quite clicked into gear yet and Leeds were still a Second Division side. The Leeds story never went anywhere, but I didn't have to wait long to find out where I was going. Dundee boss Bob Shankly, brother of Liverpool manager Bill, came in with a Scottish-record bid of £40,000 – £8,000 more than the £32,000 record transfer fee Aberdeen had received the year before from Stoke manager Tony Waddington for George Kinnell and way beyond the previous record between Scottish clubs of £27,000, paid by Rangers to St Mirren for George McLean.

History had not yet consigned Bob Shankly to exist only in the huge professional shadow cast by Bill. Sure, Bill had just won the championship as manager with Liverpool but the years of the dynasty and domination for the Merseyside club had only just begun. At this point, Bob had arguably achieved more, having taken Dundee to a Scottish League championship in 1961–62 and, incredibly, the semi-finals of the European Cup the following season. I was summoned to the Dons boardroom, where I met and agreed terms with Bob Shankly almost as quickly as I had with Bobby Calder, and before the local sportswriters could pound any keys to complain, I was a Dundee player.

Wolves, Coventry and a whole host of English clubs were left at the post by Shankly's quick response, or at least so it was reported. Dundee had finalised a drawn-out and acrimonious transfer of Alan Gilzean to Spurs just a few days before, for £72,500, and Shankly and the Dundee board had chosen (wisely, as it would prove, bearing in mind what they would get for me not too much later) to reinvest a bit over half the Gilzean fee on me.

The Aberdeen press reaction was predictable, especially since I had gone to one of the Dons' key rivals just down the coast. The *Press and Journal* claimed the board and I had failed the fans and the city and gave us laldy. The back page was handed over to the supporters, and many blamed me for signing a new contract with the Dons several months previously only to renege on it and ask away. Some criticised the club for caving in and not holding me to my current contract, and a couple gave me the benefit of the doubt, saying I had every right to do what was best for my career.

As for me, I had no feelings of shame or guilt whatsoever. The Dons had signed me for nothing on provisional forms as a junior four years previously. They had got an excellent

4 years of service, 34 goals and bunches of free publicity at the Under-23, Scottish League and full international levels while paying me as little as they could get away with, only increasing my wages when I pressed for it. Now they were cashing in. It was the biggest bonanza they'd ever had, on top of all the other windfalls they'd squirrelled away over the last few seasons. I didn't feel I was cheating the board, the fans or the city one bit and wasn't about to apologise to anyone. In fact, after seeing the way it was all reported I felt just the opposite and even quite belligerent.

'The offer made by Dundee was so good that Cooke had to be brought into the discussions and the player decided he wanted to go to Dens Park,' was how Tommy Pearson stated it officially for the club, and I had no problem with that neutral characterisation of it. But that wasn't the end of it.

The Dons lost 3–0 at home to Clyde that weekend in front of 4,000 fans. James Menzies reported in the *Daily Record* that the team had been slow-handclapped and Tommy Pearson booed as he went to the sidelines to make a late substitution.

Chairman Charlie Forbes denied that the Dons were 'deliberately selling their personality players'. He elaborated:

> It is the policy of this Board of Directors to consider offers for dissatisfied players. It is no good keeping anyone on your staff who repeatedly sends in transfer requests. We will never be able to build a team that way.

This remark, quoted in various newspapers, incensed me, as the implication was that I had been some kind of regular visitor to Tommy Pearson's office, which was total tosh. I had visited once and made my feelings known to the manager up front and crystal clear, and that had been it. If there had been more press speculation in the meantime, which was perhaps what Charlie Forbes was referring to, it hadn't been at my instigation, as I had zero relationships with any of the press in Aberdeen. Otherwise, I had trained and played my socks off for the team, as my Player of the Year award attested, and never at any time got into any kind of discussions about transfers or planted any stories about my dissatisfaction. It just wasn't my way. I kept these things close to my chest, and the suggestion that I was a regular complainer or a difficult or high-maintenance individual was so off the map it had me seeing red.

On the Monday morning following the Clyde game, local scribe Norman McDonald wrote a column subtitled 'Disgruntled Aberdeen Football Public Have Lost Confidence in Pittodrie Set-up'. Then, under a picture of a deserted Pittodrie: 'Saturday's Feckless Fumblings Will Lead to Empty Terraces'. And, in bold type across the whole page: 'Cooke Fee Must Be Splashed On New Dons'.

Fat chance, I thought, and that's how it played out. The Dons stumbled through to the end of the 1964–65 season, during which Tommy Pearson resigned to sell jewellery in Edinburgh and work on his golf game, and Eddie Turnbull took over.

The week after I signed with Dundee, I was tempted to write a response to the *Aberdeen Press and Journal* in my own defence but, happily, thought better of it. Like all storms in teacups, it was soon forgotten, and I'm happy to say that every time I've been back to Pittodrie since then, the fans have been great and treated me like they always did – like their Bonnie Prince.

While it may have seemed that the three and a half seasons I spent at Pittodrie ended on a sour note, I felt quite the opposite about my whole time there. I had met and married my first wife, Edith, and it was a happy, busy football-playing time in the Granite City that I enjoyed a lot, even when learning, expensively, to play cards with George Kinnell, Hedger and Desmond Herron. Many a Saturday morning and evening on the train to and from away matches, we'd have games, with hands still being counted and kitties being grabbed as the rest of the squad was already getting into the team bus.

George Kinnell, 'Kinkel', as we called him, was our captain, and what a character. Politically correct he was not. 'Kinks' called a spade a spade, and you could always find him wherever the card game was. He was a fellow Fifer, from Cowdenbeath, a cousin of Jim Baxter, and I think he must have had that same happy-go-lucky family gene that characterised Jim. George was a rambunctious character whom you'd hear laughing and shouting to someone in his lilting east-coast accent before you saw him. He would often meet up with his family members after games, and they were the most gregarious, happiest and noisiest family groups around, no matter where we were. George's mother, Daisy, was a great character, who knew more about the game and what was going on than we did. She had an infectious laugh and a zest for life, and it was easy to see where George got his energy. George could drink and carouse with the best of them and always had a fag in his hands, too, like Willie Allan, only George insisted on his Senior Service full-strength, never tipped.

John Anderson, one of the Dons directors, used to give George two or three packs of Perfectos after every home game. That said, George is proud to say that on 3 January 1999, on finishing a Christmas present of Senior Service full-strength from Malta, he ended 54 years of smoking like a chimney just like that and hasn't smoked since.

On the field, he was a terrific athlete, a tough tackler, good in the air and a great team leader. He was overlooked for Scotland national-team honours, along with the likes of his teammate Jimmy Hogg and another full-back I played with at Dundee a couple of years later, Bobby Cox. I'm not alone in thinking all three should have been capped and would have been if they'd played in Glasgow. George played once for the Scottish League, along with our teammate George Mulhall, against the Irish League, in Belfast in 1962, but never added to that tally, something that he puts down, in his typically unvarnished way, to the fact that he never wore the green-and-white or blue-and-white of the Old Firm. He was a rock for us at centre-half but was such a good all-round athlete he could play just about anywhere. He sometimes played up front when we needed a lift and scored a hat-trick in our 4–1 win over Le Havre in 1962 after we'd drawn 1–1 at Pittodrie. George was almost knocked unconscious by a direct free kick in the home leg at Pittodrie. He was seeing double and was taken to hospital after the game with a suspected concussion. 'When they X-rayed my head, they said they couldn't find anything,' he recounts. 'I told them I wasn't surprised,' he laughs.

Thinking about George and that Le Havre away game when he scored the hat-trick reminds me of the session we had in a Le Havre dockside bar that night after the game. We were celebrating our nice win, and the drink was flowing copiously, as always, when one of the veteran players (no names, no pack drill) puked his teeth down the Continental urinal, which was in effect a cement hole in the ground. He then drunkenly pulled rank, demanding that one of us younger players retrieve them for him. We scarpered like he was a poison skunk, and he emerged about ten minutes later, one sleeve rolled high and the teeth restored to his gums. Don't ask.

Above all, George was always himself, with few pretences, and was brutally honest no matter who he was speaking with, whether it was directors, the manager, teammates or fans. When I remind him of how I used to lose in the card games he organised, he laughs that infectious chuckle of his. 'It costs ye tae learn,' he says, in his east-coast accent. He's also quick to remind me, after more than 40 years, how I pipped him for the Player of the Year award at Pittodrie in 1964. Embarrassingly, I didn't even remember who was second. After he moved to Stoke and I went on my own travels, I never saw anything of George, other than playing against him a couple of times in England. He now lives in retirement in Aberdeen, after spending several years playing and coaching in Australia after spells at Stoke, Sunderland and Oldham. I feel privileged to have played with him. He was and still is a special, fun guy, and he was a great player.

So I had lots to be thankful for, and I have only affection for Aberdeen. It is where I launched my professional career and where the people took a boy from miles and miles away and looked after him, made him welcome and then took him to their hearts. A big part of my growing up and my flowering as a footballer was done in Aberdeen, and I am eternally grateful to my teammates for helping me become a better player and providing me with an eye-opening social life and especially to the fans for anointing me their Bonnie Prince.

8

Having my Dundee Cake and Eating It

Dundee's most famous son is 7 ft 6 in. tall, wears a cowboy hat and has stubble like sharpened spikes protruding from his chin. Munching on cow pie, Desperate Dan is followed closely by a cat called Korky and a bear called Biffo. Yes, these days the town of Dundee on the east coast of Scotland is most famous for being the home of DC Thomson, the regional newspaper group and publisher of the children's comics *The Dandy* and *The Beano*. It is also known for the manufacture of jam, its celebrated cake and two football clubs, namely Dundee and Dundee United.

The town, not unlike Greenock, grew from a fairly small but busy shipping port in the eighteenth century to a bustling industrial conurbation in the nineteenth, when the jute industry thrived. Immigrants, mainly from Ireland, poured in to satisfy the growing need for labour, and other industries, including shipbuilding, sprung up. Scott of the Antarctic's ship *Discovery* was built in Dundee and is tied up there today as a tourist draw. In more recent years, the Timex watch company was a big employer, but, as with the jute industry, it fell victim to the importing of products manufactured at a fraction of the cost in the Far East.

By the early twentieth century, the population had swelled to over 130,000 and was able to support a number of football teams, two of whom – Dundee and Dundee United – saw the others off and continue playing Scottish professional football to this day. Unlike with Celtic and Rangers in Glasgow or Hibernian and Heart of Midlothian in Edinburgh, there is a belief (borne out, to some extent, statistically) that if one of the Dundee clubs does well, the other falters.

Dundee Football Club was formed in 1893, and two years later their arrival on the Scottish soccer map was duly noted when they lost 11–0 to Celtic. Form obviously improved, because in 1903, 1907 and 1909 they finished runners-up in the league, and in 1910 they won the Scottish Cup. Fans at the Dens Park ground would have to wait another 40 years to see 'the Dark Blues', as Dundee were nicknamed, come good again. In 1949, they almost won the championship, letting it slip away on the last day of the season when they lost to Falkirk. But two years later, Dundee lifted the Scottish League Cup, beating Rangers 3–2 in the final at Hampden Park. Tommy Gallacher and Billy Steel up front, Doug Cowie in defence and a youthful Bill Brown in between the sticks were the team heroes. They won it again the next year, 1952, defeating Kilmarnock 2–0, Bobby Flavell netting both goals, although the team had fallen to Motherwell in the Scottish Cup final a few months before.

It was at the beginning of the next decade that Dundee produced arguably their greatest-ever team, under the shrewd management of Bob Shankly. It was certainly a team I knew all about, had played against and admired. Willie Thornton, the manager whom Shankly succeeded, laid the foundations by signing players such as Alex Hamilton, an exciting overlapping full-back who played many times for Scotland; Ian Ure, a solid blond-haired centre-half who also served his country but really made his name down south with Arsenal and Manchester United; and, crucially, a boy called Alan Gilzean. In 1961–62, with Bob Shankly having moulded the squad into a deadly mix of experience and youth, Dundee surprised everyone by winning the championship and lining up for a European Cup adventure the next season. Pat Liney in goal, Bobbys Seith and Wishart and Ian Ure on the half-back line and Andy Penman, Gordon Smith and Alan Gilzean in attack were true Tayside heroes.

In 1962–63, Dundee did Scotland proud by reaching the semi-final of the European Cup, but they could not overcome the experience and skills of AC Milan. Although I did not fully appreciate it when I pitched up at Dens Park in 1964 (having sore memories of them thrashing Aberdeen, me included, 6–0 at Dens Park), the club had been in decline since that failure to make the European Cup final.

It was widely reported that I had been brought in to replace Gilzean. If you don't have a keen interest in Scottish football, it is easy to overlook just how big a deal he was for Dundee. The target man in the legendary championship side, he remains the club's highest ever goal-scorer, with 113 goals, and holds the record for most goals in a season with an incredible 32 in the 1963–64 campaign. Although he had a distinguished and glittering career at Tottenham Hotspur, I always thought he was a touch unlucky to share a forward line with one of the few goal-poachers in the game at the time who could out-poach him – Jimmy Greaves.

'Gilly' had been playing for Scotland by this stage, and when he roomed with John White, who had moved from Falkirk to Tottenham Hotspur, they compared notes. Young Alan was flabbergasted at the difference between his wages and those of John in England. He knew there was a differential but was shocked by the size of it. Like Ian Ure and Bill Brown (who was now keeping goal for Spurs) before him, he decided that his destiny and his opportunity to improve his bank balance lay south of the border. Bob Shankly did not want to let his star go, but Gilly was so determined that he even went on the dole until the club relented. Spurs manager Bill Nicholson, who had such success in taking Scots down south – witness Bill Brown, John White and especially Dave Mackay – stepped in, and Alan Gilzean finally got his wish.

Unfortunately for me, the spin was that I was the replacement for popular Gilly, who had gone to Spurs six days before, and I figured that no matter how well I played, Gilly's departure would still be a big part of the stories in the press, especially if I performed poorly. That said, I thought it was all pretty stupid, comparing us. We were nothing like each other in style or skills. Gilly was a terrific front man, especially with his back to goal. He thrived on getting on the end of crosses and half chances, and he was probably as good in the air, in the open field and in front of goal as any player in Britain then. I was completely different, in that all I wanted was the ball at my feet, opponents to beat and chances to create for teammates and occasionally myself. I had more than respectable statistics from midfield then, but any attempts to make goal-scoring or stylistic comparisons between me and Gilly were just plain daft.

As it turned out, I didn't have to worry, and my debut for Dundee on 20 December 1964 couldn't have gone better. While the Dons were losing 0–3 at home to Clyde and Tommy Pearson was getting booed, I was scoring a goal and helping Dundee to a comfortable 4–0 win over Airdrie at Dens Park for my new manager Bob Shankly and 9,000 happy Dundee fans. I don't mention the Dons game or Tup's troubles to gloat over his discomfort but to highlight that I hardly gave the Dons' plight another thought, I was so engrossed in my new team and the job at hand. This was something that was to happen throughout my career after each move, and I'm not sure whether to brag about it as a sign that I was focused on the present and not distracted by the past or if it represented ingratitude and lack of compassion for those who helped me get to where I was. Maybe it was a bit of both. But the fact is I hardly gave the Dons another thought from that day forward, never wished them ill in any shape or form and was always delighted and without the least trace of envy when they were successful. In fact, to this day, I'm still made up when any of the teams I played for do well.

The headlines were more than approving the day after my Dundee debut: '£40,000 Charlie Makes a Hit', 'Cooke Turns on the Style for New Fans', 'Cheers for Charlie'. Under the headline 'Cooke Peps up Dundee Front Line' Alan Saunders wrote in the *Daily Record*:

It took 175 days to bring the Alan Gilzean transfer saga
to an end . . . yet in 90 minutes Charlie Cooke had erased
the whole wearisome episode from the minds of the Dens
Park fans. In Dundee's 4–0 win over Airdrie on Saturday
Cooke entertained the crowd with an immaculate display
of inside-forward play.

I continued as I'd started off and played a strong second
half of the season, notching up 7 goals in 18 league games,
which was more than respectable and had me feeling good
about my contribution.

Gilly's departure and my arrival had gotten the
headlines, but, in what I came to think later was a
strange turn of events, Andy Penman, Dundee's other
most popular and potent forward along with Gilly, put
in a transfer request to the board just as I was signing. It
was news too but almost got buried in all the fuss about
Gilly's departure and my arrival. I hardly gave the whole
thing a thought that first couple of weeks. I was driving
90 minutes up and down from Aberdeen each day to
Dens Park to train and play, arriving pretty much on time
and leaving sharp after games or training sessions, with
no real chance to read the latest press stories or think
much about them or even, at first, to get to know the
other players. Perhaps it was that lack of involvement
or interest in Andy Penman's affairs that soured things
between us, but in my 17 months at Dens, Andy and I
hardly exchanged more than a civil 'good morning'
to each other. This was all going on, mind you, while
I had perfectly good relationships with everyone else. I
was never one to form tight bonds with teammates. It
wasn't my style. But, by the same token, I was almost

always on good terms with just about everyone, and my relationship with Andy was one that, while not openly hostile, never quite blossomed even into what I would call friendly banter.

Andy was swift and skilful, and the word that I always think described him best was elegant. He always seemed to have time to do things, no matter how tight the marking, and always had that extra half-yard when he needed it. He had a terrific shot in both feet and a great nose for goal. He was a superb talent. But I think he felt left behind when Gilly went south, and it only added insult to injury when I came in with all the hoopla about my being the most expensive player in Scotland, when he no doubt considered himself the star of the team. After I left, Andy got his move to Rangers and was capped for Scotland, too. Although we never became friends, I was sad to hear that he died at 50 years of age in 1994.

Coming to Dens felt similar to my arrival at Pittodrie four years earlier: a new club, new manager, new teammates and lots to prove about the kind of player I was and what I could do for the team. The record fee hardly entered my mind, believe it or not, as there was already speculation that other players would soon be moving for more. The most important thing to me was to prove my worth as a teammate. So I worked my butt off and made it a point, as I'd done at Pittodrie, to be at the front in all the physical training, something that was a part of my regime at every club I played for. It was all done in the spirit of good-natured competition, of course, but underneath it all it was my Greenock way of showing who I was and, hopefully, letting my feet do the talking.

The drinking that had started in my schooldays with the

133

Carlsberg Special kitty at Davy Jones' Locker in Gourock continued apace at Aberdeen and then at Dundee, where we had long sessions at Bobby Cox's pub after games (if we won, to celebrate; if we lost, to commiserate). Golf games and shooting trips were always a good excuse to hang one on, too. We were not in any way unusual. Drinking is what young, fit, working-class Scottish men did, and as we were in peak condition, a night's boozing could be shaken off with ease the following day. It was the same at all my clubs: we'd put almost as much effort into finding out where the night out would be after the game as we did into winning it.

On the field, I stayed focused and played well and aggressively for the second half of the 1964–65 season. The best that could be said for the team was that it finished in the top half of the table, but, all in all, considering the move and the transitional phase that Dundee were in, just like Aberdeen had been at Pittodrie, I was happy with my own game and the team.

I felt great going into the 1965–66 season and continued to work like crazy in training. I was strong and quick and playing with a passion, and I didn't care who we were up against or what their reputations were, especially Old Firm opponents. In fact, I took special pride in giving it everything I had against the Old Firm, at home or away, feeling that if you were going to prove something, it might as well be against the best. I played wing-half and forward that season with equal success and was rewarded with the Player of the Year trophy in my first full season at Dundee. I felt great about that trophy, more so than the award at Aberdeen two seasons before. I felt not only that I had contributed well to the team but also that I had played some of the best football of my career so far. In fact, I played one of my best-ever domestic games north of the border in that season. It was against Falkirk, and we won only 2–0, but I can remember feeling like I was 'in the zone'. Everything I tried worked. We should have won by ten, and Archie Baird in the *Sunday Express*, an ex-player and a sportswriter I respected, recognised it:

> Charlie Cooke, after giving one of the greatest displays of his career – one of the finest exhibitions of pure football skill I have ever seen – sadly trooped off the Dens Park pitch sharing in the Dundee players' humiliation of listening to slow handclaps and boos from their own fans. This was the occasion for a standing ovation for this almost one-man show of brilliant ball-control, deadly passing and general inspiration. Cooke was behind every worthwhile move. The whole field was his stage, and he strode it with an elegance that was at once effective and enlightening.

I was particularly proud, too, in that first full season at Dens, because I was a relative newcomer yet I'd won the POY trophy over more familiar faces and prolific scorers like Andy Penman and Kenny Cameron, fans' favourites Bobby Cox and Alex Hamilton, and up-and-coming youngster Stevie Murray. The competition was hot. So to say I was proud of the award hardly does it justice. Let's just say it was the proudest moment of my career to date.

Yes, we had some fine players at Dundee at that time. Bobby Cox, our captain and left full-back, Stevie Murray, our young midfielder/forward, and Alec Stuart, a fine wing-half, were guys it truly was a joy to play with. And who could forget Alex 'Hammy' Hamilton, our international right-back? 'Coxer', as Bobby was known, was a short, wiry, quick defender whom every Dundee fan (not to mention his own teammates) was convinced should have been an automatic choice at full-back for Scotland. Unfortunately, through much of Bobby's career, long-time Rangers defender Eric Caldow was the automatic selection for the Scotland position. Eric was an excellent, hard-tackling full-back and had an outstanding career, but I agree with those who say that if Bobby had got his dues, which he probably would have done had he been an Old Firm player himself, he'd have had a long and distinguished international career too. He was an inspirational captain and a hard-nosed competitor, no matter who he was playing. He was a great tackler with a terrific recovery speed, and he read the game beautifully. Of all the great underestimated players I played alongside during my career, Bobby was the one who deserved recognition the most. He was that good.

Stevie Murray was inspirational in a different way. He was young, skilful, fit and highly competitive whatever position he was asked to play. Sometimes it was wing-half, sometimes forward, and he well deserved his success at Dens, his eventual transfer to Celtic and the Scotland caps that followed. Wherever he played, Stevie seemed to know what was needed. He could adjust instantly, grafting with the best of them in midfield and just as easily making and scoring key goals up front. Stevie was one of those players you could play anywhere and know you'd get your money's worth – the kind of teammate every player appreciates. Alec Stuart was a powerful figure with an educated left foot that reminded me so much of Jimmy Geddes. Alec was a strong and skilful presence on the field and the kind of player managers instinctively look to for leadership and to build their team around.

Alex Hamilton, with his spiky blond hair and mile-a-minute chatter, brought his seemingly boundless energy to any situation. He played a mean piano and wasn't at all slow to inform you how good he was – at the piano and on the field. To this day, I'm proud to say he didn't beat me in any fair (and I stress 'fair') 20-yard sprint, no matter how often he disputed the results and got our teammates to side with him. Alex played 24 times for Scotland, the highest number of caps awarded to any Dens player. He was one of those personalities you meet in the game that you know you won't forget easily.

Another, much less flamboyant player, in fact a quiet and modest man, was part-timer Alan Cousin. Alan played throughout Dundee's 1963–64 league championship and European Cup years and followed Bob Shankly to Hibernian at the end of the 1964–65 season. Alan was a tall, scoring forward during Dundee's halcyon years, but, throughout it all, he was also a classics teacher at Alloa Academy, and it's anybody's guess what he thought of the Dens locker-room banter. Not exactly classical Greek dialogue, we can be pretty sure.

Bob Shankly, the manager who spent the record fee on me, wasn't a chatterer like Hammy. I probably spent more time with Shanks when I signed for Dundee in Aberdeen, maybe all of five minutes, than I did all the while I was with Dundee thereafter. To be fair, there weren't a lot of opportunities, as he left two months later to take over Hibernian after Jock Stein left Easter Road to manage Celtic. Years later, I read somewhere that Shanks left Dens because of his frustration about being unable to bring to

Dundee the kind of success he was used to. That's a new one, I thought.

Sammy Kean, the first-team coach, was appointed interim manager when Shankly left, and I think his two-month tenure, from February to April 1965, is a terrific example of how a good performance doesn't count for much when the board is determined to get their own man. During his reign, Sammy was responsible for a string of good results, including a 7–1 win over Hearts at Tynecastle, a 4–1 win over Kilmarnock, a 3–3 draw with Dunfermline and a 2–1 win over Hibernian, at a time when all four of these clubs were vying for the 1964–65 league title. In fact, that victory of ours over Hearts eventually led to them losing the title to Kilmarnock by 0.04 of a goal! On all measurable criteria, Sammy should have been a shoo-in for the vacant job. But on April Fool's Day 1965, Sammy left to take over as manager of Falkirk as Bobby Ancell arrived to take over at Dens.

The board who made such decisions – including, presumably, choosing to buy me, or at least giving their assent – was the Gellatly family, owners of a well-known father-and-son accountancy firm in Dundee. They didn't mix much with the players socially, and there was talk within the club that the board needed to sell a forty- to fifty-thousand-pound player each season to keep the club financially sound. A look at Dundee's transfer history would seem to prove the point, as they sold consistently almost each year, starting with Ian Ure to Arsenal in 1963, then Alan Gilzean to Spurs in 1964, me to Chelsea in 1966, Andy Penman to Rangers in 1967 and Stevie Murray to Aberdeen for a £50,000 intra-Scottish-club record fee in 1970. Again, it's just hearsay, but it was said that many of these deals took place without the manager's agreement and in some cases even without his knowledge.

Thus it was that Bobby Ancell, a star full-back and hero at Dundee in the '40s and '50s, was appointed to the manager's seat. Bobby was cut from the same cloth as Bob Shankly and Tommy Pearson, as far as I could see, being a white-collar boss who clearly enjoyed the boardroom and left much of the training-field duties to his staff. Like Tup, he loved his golf, and we players used to have fun joking about his philosophical bent and invariable team-talk references to the fairway game. His claim to coaching fame was the attractive Motherwell team of the early '60s that contained Pat Quinn, Willie Hunter, Ian St John and Bobby Roberts. They had pleased the eye with skilled players and a sweet moving style for a short time, but the top players were sold, and the team never won any honours. Bobby's record and his previous Dens popularity obviously impressed the Dundee board enough to make them sign him, but he was unable to reverse the dearth of success that had characterised Bob Shankly's last two seasons.

One thing I have to give Bobby credit for, though, was getting me a new and improved contract early in the new season. Managers in those days invariably pleaded the board's case and tended to take up an adversarial position vis-à-vis players looking for more money. That was their job then, and I suppose to some extent it still is. But I had finished the previous season strongly and felt in great fettle for the new campaign. I was prepared to argue my case and ready for the usual club riposte about the importance of their pay structure and the dangers of breaching it, coupled with the old standby of pleading poverty. The latter would have been hard to swallow bearing in mind the influx of funds from the transfers of Messrs Ure and Gilzean. Bobby surprised me, though, and listened to my case. Instead of the back and fore I expected, it was a brief, non-confrontational meeting, and a couple of weeks later I signed a new two-year deal. Whatever anyone else outside the club may have felt, especially in light of my move to Chelsea nine months later, I thought it was a smart deal on the club's part. I got slightly improved monies and the club got an extra year. Dundee took the opportunity, remembering the Alan Gilzean fiasco, to claim that what they had done with me was unique, quite different from their normal way of doing business, and proof if proof was needed that the club would do all in its power to keep its best players. The fans obviously saw it that way too, as their unhappy reactions to my transfer to Chelsea would testify. But I didn't think the board did anything special at all. I figured they were making an easy financial accommodation while avoiding a public transfer request and getting another year on the contract term, with some free public relations into the bargain – their side of the deal was worth far more than the small amount extra they would pay me.

Call me cynical, but over the previous four seasons I'd seen the season-ending free transfer lists at Aberdeen, Dundee and every other club. We were all aware of the fine line walked by footballers; an injury or loss of form or favour can end a career in the blow of a referee's whistle but it's still a shock to see it happen before your eyes to players you've been training with week in, week out. After watching Tommy Pearson and the Aberdeen board (and every other board for that matter) make decisions to suit themselves,

Jim Geddes being a good example. I felt Dundee would do the same when the time came. I'd escaped serious injury so far, but I'd seen how it could change a career overnight. I was no longer the fresh-faced 16 year old on the British Rail car with my suitcase on the rack, ready to believe everything I was told. Even as I signed the new deal with Dundee, I felt that the Scottish First Division still wasn't the best, and if I had my druthers, I'd play in England eventually. One reason I had no compunction in signing the new contract was my feeling, deep down, that, irrespective of all their team-building talk, just like the Aberdeen board, if there was an attractive offer down the road, the Dundee board would have no hesitation about taking it.

That deal came quicker than any of us expected – nine months later, at the end of the season. Early on the morning of Tuesday, 26 April 1966, having received the Player of the Year award at the supporters' annual dinner-dance downtown the night before, I caught the train to Edinburgh to meet with Tommy Docherty at the Royal Caledonian Hotel and sign for Chelsea. It might sound like a whirlwind ending to my time at Dens, but in fact it was less sudden than it appeared.

It had started six months earlier, with my first cap for Jock Stein's full Scotland team, against Wales at Hampden on Wednesday, 24 November 1965. The Wales game was part of the Home International Championship. But, far more importantly for Scotland and its fans, it was also a dress-rehearsal for the second leg of Scotland's World Cup qualifier against Italy in Naples three weeks later, which Scotland had at least to draw to qualify for the 1966 World Cup in England.

Jock Stein's famous attention to detail was quickly

141

on show, when it was announced we would play the Hampden game against Wales not in the usual navy-blue shirts but in the all-white colours Scotland would wear against Italy. The Scottish team against Wales was minus Billy McNeill of Celtic, the Spurs goalie Bill Brown, Liverpool's wing-half Willie Stevenson and forwards John Hughes and Denis Law of Celtic and Manchester United respectively, all through injury.

On paper, I was picked in midfield alongside Jim Baxter of Sunderland and Celtic's Bobby Murdoch, but in reality, I played a deep role akin to a sweeper alongside Jim's teammate Ronnie McKinnon. Alan Gilzean played alongside the Rangers trio of Jim Forrest, Willie Johnston and Willie Henderson up front, with the two Willies playing wide.

Wales were captained by Mike England (Blackburn Rovers) at centre-half, ably assisted by Terry Hennessey (Nottingham Forest) at wing-half and Peter Rodrigues (Cardiff City) at full-back. In midfield, they had Ivor Allchurch (Swansea Town) and Roy Vernon (Stoke), with Gil Reece (Sheffield United) and Wyn Davies (Bolton Wanderers) up front.

Jock Stein enjoyed God-like status among Scottish fans and players at that time. His Celtic team were conquering all before them, and the press, fans and selection committee alike hung on his every word. I was a big admirer too, so when he said he wanted me to play a deep role, basically behind Baxter and Murdoch, almost like an attacking sweeper, I took him at his word. And the rest is history, as they say. We won 4–1, and I had a cracker of a game, never putting a foot wrong. In truth, I thought it was a breeze doing the Beckenbauer role at the back, picking up runners and through balls, and setting up teammates going forward. It was altogether less strenuous and pressured than what I'd experienced in the middle of the field. In a sense, it confirmed what I'd always thought about the position: that it was a bit of a doddle if you could play at all and that it was maybe a good place for a talented midfielder who's getting on and has lost a yard but not necessarily for a youngster early in his career who still feels he has stuff to prove, as I was then.

But the press were ecstatic and went to town with high hopes for the Italy game in Naples. 'Real Cookie' was the headline splashed across the whole back page of the Scottish *Daily Express*, with the subheading 'Charlie Is Hampden's Darling'. 'Cooke, Murdoch Star' was the full-page *Press and Journal* headline the next day. 'Cooke Shows Potential as a Great Player' was the headline in *The Scotsman*, where John Rafferty wrote:

> Charlie Cooke was the joker in Jock Stein's planning. He used him as Real Madrid used Di Stéfano in their great days, picking up the play near his own centre-half and racing through with it. It may sound sacrilegious to say so but he was Di Stéfano all over again. A great player and the find of the match.

Under the headline 'Cooke Must Play in Naples', Alex Cameron also declared: 'Charlie Cooke was the find of the match.' On the same page, under the headline 'Now Bring on Italy', Alec Young said: 'Defenders have scored four of the five goals in our last two internationals. This must give team manager Jock Stein something to think about. But Cooke's marvellous display certainly eases the tension.'

Finally, as if to give a clue about things to come not too far in the future, Tommy Docherty was quoted in *The Scotsman*: 'Scotland played wonderful football. They were going all the time and seemed to be playing like a club side. I thought Murdoch and Cooke were outstanding.'

During the next three weeks leading up to the game in Naples, the country was abuzz about the World Cup qualifier. The Wales result had caused a degree of euphoria among the fans and soccer scribes. What before had seemed like a tall order – to go to Naples and hold the Italians to a draw – maybe wasn't so much to ask after all, was the thinking. Everybody and his brother had an opinion about who would play and what Jock Stein's tactics might be.

The tension and the atmosphere as the game approached were fantastic, but at the same time, Jock Stein's options were narrowing fast as the injuries just kept mounting. The situation became so bad that John Mackenzie of the Scottish *Daily Express* expressed his belief that this was perhaps the most jinxed Scotland team ever. Jim Baxter, the team captain against Wales, had damaged ligaments in his ankle in that game and had to miss the Naples match. So too did Denis Law, who still hadn't recovered from an injury that had kept him out at Hampden. Ditto Bill Brown in goal, Willie Stevenson, who was starring at wing-half for the all-conquering Liverpool, and Billy McNeill in the heart of the defence. Such was the uncertainty surrounding the team going to Italy that Jock Stein delayed announcing the line-up, and even on the morning of the game, there was more bad news – the shocker that Willie Henderson, a key man for us up front, was unfit. This caused uproar in the press, and some unfairly pointed the finger at Willie, claiming he must have known before boarding the flight to Naples whether he'd be able to play or not.

The fact is that Jock knew all the tricks and how to play the foreign press, and I'd guess that he knew Willie would be doubtful but took him anyway just to keep the Italian press and team guessing. Meanwhile, recognising that the atmosphere in the San Paolo Stadium in Naples would be red-hot, Jock bet on defence and selected Ron Yeats, Liverpool's man mountain, at centre-forward. He was number 9 on the team sheet but in fact became a second stopper alongside Ronnie McKinnon, Davie Provan and Eddie McCreadie in the back four.

I was in midfield with John Greig and Bobby Murdoch, while Billy Bremner picked up Rivera deep in defence, virtually acting as a fifth defender, with Jim Forrest and John Hughes left to forage as best they could up front.

We played well enough to keep the Italian fans quiet for about 30 minutes or so, but the place erupted when they took a 1–0 lead after 38 minutes on a scrappy Ezio Pascutti goal from a cross that could have been cleared. The second half was a battle, in which we gave as good as we got but created few chances. The Italians got a goal from Giacinto Facchetti, a beautiful although maybe somewhat lucky lob over Adam Blacklaw into the top corner of the net at 73 minutes, and then a grounder from Bruno Mora in the penultimate minute to seal our fate.

After the game, our depression was total as we pondered our nicks and what could have been and the feelings back home, where a headline story in the *Greenock Telegraph* on the day of the game read 'Absenteeism Soars as Scotland Play Italy'.

Thousands of Clydeside shipyard workers were absent from work after lunch this afternoon and the presumption was that they stayed at home to watch the big football match on TV. 'We calculate that 40 per cent of our workers have not turned up,' said a spokesman at Scott's Shipbuilding and Engineering Company.

'Arrivederci' was the banner across the whole back page of the Scottish *Daily Express*, bemoaning our exit and the four-year wait until the next World Cup.

Despite calls for him to take up the Scotland job permanently, Jock Stein went back to Celtic, dealing a blow to the many players and journalists who felt he would have been the perfect man for the job.

For me, it had been a dramatic introduction to the full Scotland team. A new coach, a new role as a sweeper and a terrific free-flowing win against Wales, followed by a familiar midfield role and a grinding defensive slog, crowned by the biggest disappointment Scottish football had experienced in years.

But after midweek European and international games, domestic league matches come at you fast, leaving you little time to brood over disappointments or celebrate successes, and at 3 p.m. the next Saturday, I returned to Dens ready to pick up where I'd left off. Disappointingly, Celtic beat us 2–0 in the second round of the Scottish Cup. I got some satisfaction, however, when we beat my old home-town favourites Greenock Morton 5–1 at Dens in March. Fate made up for that when, early in April as the season was coming to a close, we lost by a heartbreaking 0–1 scoreline to Rangers at Ibrox. I was very proud of the way I played in that match and felt that we should have won. This Old Firm loss was important because a win would have been something to hold on to in a season that had otherwise been a washout in terms of trophies and cup runs.

That said, I had finished the season strongly and was delighted with my form. In the 17 months or so I'd been at Dens, I'd made 59 appearances, scored 11 goals (only 4, though, in this last season) and made plenty of untabulated assists. I had also played in the Scottish Under-23 team against England and for the Scottish League versus the English and Irish Leagues, and, of course, I'd made my full international debut. It had been an immensely satisfying time, and I couldn't have been prouder to receive the Dundee Player of the Year trophy.

I was truly touched and honoured when I stood up and received the award at the dinner on 25 April 1966. I can't remember what I said in my brief acceptance speech. It would have been sincere, because my time with Dundee was and remains one of the best periods of my life, but my inner emotions were a gut-wrenching turmoil of guilt, embarrassment and excitement, because as I held the award aloft, I was the only person there who knew that the next day I was travelling down to Edinburgh to meet Tommy Docherty and, barring an unforeseen disaster, sign for Chelsea Football Club.

9

Blue Boys

When I was a boy, Chelsea Football Club rarely crossed my radar. I knew the name, as I did that of every English and Scottish league club, but their exploits rarely made the Pathe News at La Scala, and they had few top star players. I was aware that they played in London and that Scottish football legend Hughie Gallacher had played for them for a while. He was one of the 'Wembley Wizards', as the Scotland team that defeated England 5–1 at Wembley in 1928 became known. Hughie was a phenomenal goal-scorer for Airdrie and Newcastle United before he plied his trade at Stamford Bridge. His life was the stuff of legend. Controversy dogged his career, and rumours of excessive drinking, bar-room brawls and financial catastrophes swirled around him. Tragically, when his playing days were over, and having lost his wife to illness, he threw himself under a train. A happier story was that of Tommy Walker, famous for building the great Heart of Midlothian side of the 1950s and as a playing hero at Tynecastle, who also played at Chelsea for a period. This I knew, but little else.

I later learned that a successful businessman named Gus Mears decided in the first decade of the 1900s to build Stamford Bridge in order to provide London with a stadium in which big football matches could be staged. Gus had watched the growth of football over the previous 20 years with a sharp commercial eye, and he drafted in Archibald Leitch, an engineer from Scotland, to design the ground. By the end of his career, Leitch would be responsible for Highbury, White Hart Lane, Old Trafford, Goodison Park, Ibrox and Hampden, among others. So, unlike most of the other clubs that pioneered the game of football in Britain, Chelsea were born not from a team seeking a ground, but instead came into the world as a ground seeking a team. Fulham were offered the opportunity to play at Stamford Bridge but declined.

Chelsea eventually got out of the stalls in 1905, playing their first Football League match in September of that year, but would not win any major honour for half a century. Saddled with the nickname 'the Pensioners' due to the close proximity of the famous home for old soldiers, it was often hard for them to be taken seriously, and they regularly climbed up and fell down the top two divisions without ever troubling the supremacy of Huddersfield Town in the 1920s or Arsenal in the 1930s.

As manager, it was a player from that almost impregnable Arsenal team who delivered the first piece of silverware to a Chelsea board of directors. Ted Drake was a good old-fashioned centre-forward who started out at Southampton but had been snapped up by Herbert Chapman for Arsenal and teamed with the likes of Alex James, Cliff

Bastin, George Male, Joe Hulme and Eddie Hapgood to form perhaps the most effective club side of the twentieth century. He is in the record books for scoring seven goals in a match against Aston Villa, and if the Second World War had not curtailed his career, he would surely have racked up one of the highest goal tallies of all time. Not a man to waste his allotted time on the planet, in the close season he played top-level cricket for Hampshire County Cricket Club.

Ted Drake arrived at Chelsea as manager in 1952, having taken Reading out of the old Third Division South. Chelsea were flirting with relegation from the First Division, but within two seasons, Ted had lifted them into the top half, and in 1954–55 Chelsea confounded everyone, including themselves, by winning the championship for the first time in their history, surpassing the all-conquering Wolverhampton Wanderers by four points. Roy Bentley, the England centre-forward, was the hero and the captain. Ted Drake could pride himself on having banished the 'Pensioners' image once and for all and dispelled the hoodoo of no major honours since the club's formation. Things didn't go too well for Ted and Chelsea after the 1955 championship season, though, with the team dropping into the relegation zone in the very next season and struggling to recapture their top form in subsequent campaigns. In 1961, the board drafted in Tommy Docherty from Arsenal as coach, with a view to adding impetus to Ted Drake's management style. There was no immediate improvement and Chelsea were relegated to the Second Division at the end of 1961–62. Ted had already been relieved of his duties early in the season and young Docherty had been given the reins.

Tommy Docherty was born and raised in a single-end tenement in the Gallowgate area of the Gorbals in Glasgow. The family lived in such poverty that Tommy, his mother, father and sister all shared one bed, and there was no bathroom. National Service first took Tommy out of the Gorbals and then gave him the chance to develop his football ability, enabling him to stay away permanently. He was signed by Celtic but never secured a regular first-team place, and when Preston North End came in for him, the ambitious young man did not hesitate to take the plunge. Tommy's stay at Deepdale coincided with a resurgence in the club's fortunes. They won promotion back into the First Division, and in 1954 they reached the FA Cup final at Wembley but lost to West Bromwich Albion. Their star player at the time was Tom Finney, whose fame had certainly spread north of the border when I was a kid, but Docherty soon established a reputation as a fiery and competent defender. His country capped him 25 times, and he was a member of the team that represented Scotland in the 1958 World Cup finals in Sweden, where the world first witnessed the precocious talents of the 17-year-old Pelé. In that same year, Tommy transferred to Arsenal and enjoyed three seasons with them before leaning towards coaching.

Although Tommy had been unable to avoid relegation in that first season at Chelsea, the impact he had was like a whirlwind around the corridors of Stamford Bridge. He had struck up a good relationship with chairman Joe Mears, and that gave him the confidence to be bold in his approach. Not that Tommy Docherty could operate any other way. Players used to the more sedate and polite style of Ted Drake were now faced with a bundle of tartan energy, shouting, swearing, laughing and blasting everything and everyone in his path. The very next season, he brought his young side straight back into the First Division, and Tommy told everyone who would listen and those who wouldn't that his Chelsea side were going to make waves. The press christened them 'Docherty's Diamonds'. Most of the team had come up via the youth system. There were the Harris brothers, Ron and Allan, Terry Venables, Barry Bridges, Peter Bonetti, Bobby Tambling, Ken Shellito, who had been recognised by England, and a full-back named Eddie McCreadie, whom Tommy had signed from East Stirling on his first foray back to Scotland looking for undiscovered talent and with whom I had already played as an international.

In that first season back in the top flight, Chelsea finished in fifth place, only seven points behind the champions, Liverpool. In 1964–65 they improved to third, finishing only five points off winners Manchester United, and they took the League Cup, beating Leicester City in a two-legged final. They only just failed to make Wembley for the FA Cup final, losing to Liverpool 2–0 in the semis. The mix of players was changing: Ken Shellito was being forced out by injury; George Graham, a Scot, had been signed from Aston Villa; Peter Houseman, John Boyle, John Hollins and Marvin Hinton were all young lads banging on the first-team door; and, perhaps most significantly, a tall, gangly centre-forward who had been laying bricks in Windsor had made his debut. He was called Osgood.

1965–66 promised much. Terry Venables, a confident young man who had strong views and wasn't afraid of airing them, was captaining the side. Bobby Tambling, a forward with a rapier of a left foot, was finding the net like there was no tomorrow, and Peter Osgood, like a young deer finding his feet, had started to show an eye-popping talent. A creditable fifth position, a better away performance than any other First Division side and another FA Cup semi-final appearance, as well as a semi-final against Barcelona in the Fairs Cup, were enough to prove that the momentum had not been lost.

However, an incident at Blackpool – which, strangely enough, came to be known as 'the Blackpool incident' – changed everything. It happened when Chelsea played a league game against Burnley in April of 1965, and it was the beginning of the end for Chelsea and Tommy as an item, and the end of the end for the dream of Docherty's Diamonds.

Chelsea had got into the habit, when playing in the north of England, of having a brief break by the sea in Blackpool, and this is what they did before an important league match at Turf Moor. This was the season when they finished third, and at this point, with two matches left before the end of the campaign, there was still a small chance that they could win the First Division. The manager gave permission for his lads to go for a drink, but there was a curfew hour, by which most of them had not made it back. Tommy was furious, seeing this behaviour as a direct affront to his authority, and in the morning, as the players trickled down sheepishly for breakfast, he stood there handing out rail tickets instead of cereal bowls. Eight players were sent home, and a weakened team proceeded to lose 6–2, dashing any hopes of Chelsea becoming champions. The following season, relations between Tommy and some of the players deteriorated, with the manager and Terry Venables in particular often sparring in a war of words. Transfer requests had been tabled by others.

Of course, I knew nothing about the politics at Stamford Bridge. As far as I was concerned, here was a club who were playing exciting football, with an ebullient, go-getting young manager, and who were on the brink of even bigger things. When I met Tommy in Edinburgh, he nigh on floored me with his charm, his banter, his directness and his self-belief. I couldn't get pen to paper quick enough. His team were being presented as natural successors to the 'Busby Babes' (Sir Matt Busby's young Manchester United side, many of whom had perished in the Munich air disaster), and I admired their hard-working, fast-paced style. I can honestly say that at that moment in time if I could have chosen to play for any team in England, it would have been Chelsea. Tommy was at the peak of his powers of persuasion. What 'The Doc', as the press called him, failed to tell me was that he was buying me as a replacement for Terry Venables; it was even more absent-minded of him not to mention that the man in question had not yet left the club or been told himself. When I met up with Tommy 40 years later, he told me that he had already agreed a fee of £80,000 with Bill Nicholson of Spurs for Terry but had asked that it remain confidential until the Fairs Cup was out of the way.

Back in Dundee, an almighty row had erupted over my transfer. No matter what the club, the press or anyone else (except maybe the fans, who, I think, always have a legitimate beef in these situations) had to say about the move to Chelsea or how it had come about, I reckoned it was win-win all round. Dundee got their

British-record-equalling fee of £72,000 plus a friendly against Chelsea at Dens the following season and a hefty profit on their original investment into the bargain, after only a season and a bit. Chelsea and Tommy Doc got a player who'd win three Chelsea Player of the Year awards, a record equalled only by Gianfranco Zola. And I got my wish, to further my career in a league where I'd be challenged more than ever, playing against some of the best teams in the world – which, in the end, was what really mattered to me.

Back in Dundee, though, there were no celebrations. Bobby Ancell took the opportunity to cover his arse big-time. He told *The Scotsman*:

I stand a chance of being hung, drawn and quartered for this, but we felt we had no option. Since being with the Scotland party at the Hampden international Cooke has been a disgruntled player. And disgruntled players are no use to any club. Despite his two-year contract he has been a daily visitor to my office stressing his determination to leave Dundee. I made up my mind that it would be better getting money and spending it on a player or players who did want to play for us.

Let's be kind to Bobby, give him the benefit of the doubt and say only that his 'daily' description is a tad overdone; but the notion that it was he who had made the decision and that he was going to spend the money on new players was just tosh.

To go back to the original contract, I had squeezed out a marginally better deal, maybe five or ten pounds a week more, and the club got another year on the term.

How that was some wonderful act of generosity on the part of the club is still a mystery to me. On reading his comments that I was disgruntled and that such players are 'no use to any club', I might have asked him and the board how much better off they'd have been without my butt-busting Player of the Year performances and with someone instead who 'wanted to play for the club'. As for him spending the money they got for me on new players, that was just empty talk for the fans. The Gellatlys would make that decision as they did all the others, and in the end the money did not go in that direction.

The truth, I think, was quite different. Alex Hamilton and Andy Penman had already asked to be transferred before I had, and they, like me, had been told by the club that they had to honour their two-year contracts. The reason they held Hammy and Andy to their contracts but relented in my case is pretty simple, I think: a large transfer fee was waved in front of the board, while there weren't any, or not big enough ones, for Alex or Andy, at least not at that point in time. So the Dundee board snaffled up the record fee, and, with their PR machine running at full throttle, Bob's your uncle, I was suddenly a disloyal player who had been making life intolerable for the board and the manager – the only solution was to take the money and a game at Dens the following season and ship him out. And, of course, let the press and fans know just how intolerable it had been for the club to have to put up with it all for so long.

I knew it was CYA time for the board and Bobby Ancell and I was silly to let it get to me, but it bugged me because I knew how hard I had worked and what a nonsense the 'daily visitor' stuff was. It didn't end there. Alex Cameron in the *Daily Mail* yelled: 'The Worthless Contract!' He went on to say that player contracts were:

> a worthless scrap of paper on which are printed imposing words that mean nothing. It is legal verbiage which big money will storm through like elephants in a cabbage patch. There is one question which is irresistible: was Cooke tapped directly or indirectly? I am not saying he was, I'm only asking.

I liked Alex, but this was just hypocritical crap and smear. This tapping stuff was way off the mark. I wasn't tapped up directly or indirectly. Believe it or not, as with every other move I made in the game, I was gambling that I'd get the transfer I wanted. Not necessarily to Chelsea but hopefully down south. I was, I believe, one of those unusual players, some might unkindly say socially repressed, who didn't have a network of contacts in the game at any level, especially not down south or in the Glasgow press mafia which Alex was a member of and which floated all their pals' stories and greased all the Old Firm wheels. I kept to myself and was never a telephone nut or a press hound, and everything I knew about what was happening in the game was roughly no more or less than most fans knew from reading their sports pages – sometimes less, because I didn't always read them. So every time I asked away, it was a much bigger gamble in my mind than any of the directors, journalists or fans ever believed.

I had no idea that Chelsea were making a bid for me, and I had never had any conversations with Tommy Doc or anyone I knew who would have contact with him.

The first I knew about the Chelsea deal was when I got a call from Bobby Ancell telling me to be ready to travel to Edinburgh the next day. During subsequent talks with Tommy Doc in 2006, he confirmed that, no matter what anyone thought to the contrary, after initial contact was made between managers, many transfers were in fact conducted almost exclusively by the club secretaries and included the manager only when the final signing was made and the press release issued.

Be that as it may, Hugh Taylor in the *Daily Record* added his two pennies' worth with the headline, above a photo of Tommy Doc and me, 'This Makes a Mockery of Scots Football'. He went on to say that, while he wished me luck and I was a great player, my transfer sickened him. He then quoted Players' Union secretary John Hughes, whom I had never heard of in my life, unless it was John 'Yogi' Hughes who played for Celtic, and I don't believe it was. These official types are always around, it seems, and being quoted when you don't need them. 'The public have been kidded,' complained the mysterious Mr Hughes, 'and I think that fewer and fewer people will be going through the turnstiles at Dens Park next season.' I don't know who this Hughes guy was – he was certainly anonymous to me and, I'd bet, to every other player in the Dens dressing-room. He had never to my knowledge officially visited the players at Aberdeen or Dundee, and suddenly he's weighing in in the national press against one of his purported members. Who the heck was he to know anything about my move, and, in his total ignorance, was he implying I had done the kidding?

The only positive note that seemed to be struck was a

quote in the *Daily Express* from the chairman of the Dundee Supporters Club, Matthew McGrath. He said:

> Charlie Cooke would have got the Player of the Year title even if the Chelsea deal had been announced a month ago. He is a great player, which means of course that other clubs would be interested in him. Obviously he will be getting much more money and that is what he is in the business for. I am sure every Dundee fan will join me in wishing Charlie all the best with Chelsea.

Another lifelong fan saw it differently, however. Graham Thompson thought that: 'Cooke should never have accepted the title of Player of the Year with this signing in the wind. He should have stood down and allowed the title to go to another player.' I didn't feel that way at all. My transfer request had been public knowledge for months, and the fans had made their choice. The Chelsea bid was unfortunate timing, but I figured I was being honoured for my performances, and on that score I wasn't feeling embarrassed or guilty at all. The tacky part of it was not being able to be totally honest about everything on the awards night.

Alex Cameron's and Hugh Taylor's columns were just flat-out hypocrisy by old pros who knew better. Players had been getting transferred and clubs coining it in while covering their backsides for yonks, just the way Bobby Ancell and the Dundee board were doing and Tommy Pearson and the Aberdeen board had done before them. I can only assume it was a slow news day for Scotland's best, or they were miffed they hadn't got an exclusive on the deal.

As I rode the train into Edinburgh that May morning, whinging columnists couldn't have been further from my mind. I was thinking instead of what Stamford Bridge would look like and how it would feel playing alongside Bobby Tambling, John Hollins, Peter Bonetti and the rest of Tommy Doc's young squad. Chelsea were exciting, and I was excited to be going there. I couldn't wait to sign and get on with it. In Edinburgh, I met Tommy, Dr Boyne, the Chelsea club doctor, and assistant club secretary Alan Bennett. After I had signed, Alan hustled away to get my transfer papers formally lodged with the SFA and then raced off full pelt down to London to the English Football Association headquarters, where my registration would be finalised. The idea was that Alan would rush all this through so I would be available to play in the Fairs Cup semi-final tie with Barcelona that Wednesday evening. Documentation complete, Alan rang Tommy and reported proudly, 'Everything is taken care of. Charlie is fully registered and can play tonight.'

'No, he bloody can't,' Tommy boomed back, 'he's got a bleeding bad ankle.'

I had, having injured myself the previous week. I had shown it to Dr Boyne and believed it would clear up in a couple of days, but while Alan was running around London like a blue-arsed fly, my ankle continued to swell, and I missed the first leg of the tie.

While Alan was racing about with my papers, I was flying down from Edinburgh with Tommy Doc and Dr Boyne to Heathrow to join the Chelsea squad on its way to Barcelona for the Fairs Cup semi-final tie. Unbeknown to me, I was also heading into the fermenting turmoil among the players. The Blackpool incident was still reverberating within the club, it seemed. I had read about it, but that had been some time before, and I thought that this kind of stuff went on at many clubs and that it would be long forgotten by the time I arrived. More fool me.

According to Barry Bridges in the book *Upfront with Chelsea* by Chris Westcott, Tommy Doc had recently had further run-ins with him and Terry Venables following Chelsea's 2–0 defeat to Sheffield Wednesday in the 1966 FA Cup semi-final. It was the second year in succession that Chelsea, under The Doc, had fallen short at the last but one hurdle, and the disappointment was huge. According to Barry, Tommy accused Terry and him of not trying in the Wednesday game, which, in fairness to them all, was no doubt an overreaction to a result that was bitterly disappointing, especially as Jim McCalliog, recently released by The Doc, had scored for Sheffield.

But the upshot of it was that Barry was left out of the team for the next league home game, against West Brom at the Bridge. Barry's omission was the only change since the Sheffield Wednesday game, and when he saw the team sheet, Barry, in his own words, 'went spare'. He searched for Tommy all over the ground but couldn't find him before or after the game.

Tommy, of course, was in Edinburgh signing me. It's not hard, then, to imagine Barry's emotions when Tommy and I rolled up at Heathrow. Tommy introduced me to everyone, and then, as Barry recalls:

[Docherty] eventually walked into the bar and I asked to speak to him. He said he didn't have time and I just flipped. We had a terrible row and I said, 'If I'm not playing, I'm not going,' which was maybe a bit harsh. He said I was not playing so I got my bags off the plane and walked out. The press saw the whole thing and the next day the papers were full of it, but I don't regret it.

When Barry left and word got around, I'd be lying if I said it didn't feel a bit awkward, being the player arriving as another was stomping out the door, even if I knew nothing about their conversation or the events that led up to it. It's moments like these that put a thick skin on your hide, I suppose. And was it just coincidence, I could maybe have been excused for wondering, that players like Barry suddenly demanded to leave, as Andy Penman had done at Dundee, when I arrived? As they say, it's a funny old game.

Describing the Heathrow Airport scene further, Barry continues: '[Docherty] wasn't at the airport for the flight to Barcelona the next morning, as he was signing Charlie Cooke, which was the beginning of the end for Terry [Venables].' In the foreword to *Upfront with Chelsea*, Terry says something similar:

> But after we were beaten in two FA Cup semi-finals Tommy Docherty lost his patience and wanted to break up the team. When he came into the dressing-room before my last game against Barcelona and introduced Charlie Cooke, I knew my days were numbered.

Both were correct, of course. But, wrapped up as I was in the excitement of my move, and being naive as a boot boy about the manager–player relationships at the Bridge at the time, I didn't know it and sure couldn't see it. As I mentioned, Tommy didn't tell me at the time about

Terry's Spurs transfer or that I was intended to be his replacement, no matter how many players or reporters, including Terry, thought they already knew. The players and press already knew about 'Buller' (Ron Harris) taking over the captaincy from Terry following the Blackpool episode and what that signaled about Terry's future at the club. Call me stupid, but I was still thinking Terry and I could be teammates.

As Barry got his bags and stormed out, the rest of the players had to be wondering who'd be next. Although Terry's move was still a secret, my arrival no doubt had everybody thinking something could be in the works. Bridges and Bert Murray would move to Birmingham in a matter of days, and of course Terry would be gone very soon after. But that day at Heathrow, that was all still in the future. The well-dressed Chelsea party may have had a business-as-usual look to it as we boarded the plane that day (including 'Venners' and John Hollins doing their 'dropped coins in a queue' party piece, which raised a bit of strained laughter), but the atmosphere as we embarked for Barcelona was definitely edgy, to say the least.

For the trip, Tommy Doc put me in a room with Peter Osgood and John Boyle, and the result, as I can see in hindsight, was so predictable. The room had twin beds and a roll-away to accommodate the three of us. 'Ossie' and John, being the upstanding teammates they were, figured we should cut for who was to be in the roll-away. So Ossie gets out a pack of cards, shuffles them extravagantly, lays the pack on the table and says, 'OK, seeing you're the new guy, we'll give you first cut.' So I get up, and just as I'm cutting the cards, Ossie and 'Boylers' leap into the empty twin beds, laughing hysterically and pulling the sheets over them and pointing me to the roll-away. And that was my introduction to my new teammates.

In fact, I couldn't have asked for a better reception, from everyone, including Terry, and my memories of those early days among the new faces of the Chelsea team are mostly happy ones. One negative story that surfaced, though, was that there was animosity between me and Ossie and that it had ended in some kind of fisticuffs in the locker room. Total rubbish. I have no idea where that came from, although Joe Fascione told me, 40 years later in 2006, that we did have a rather loud shouting match when we were out on the tiles one night in the West End around the time I first arrived. I'll plead guilty, but for the life of me I have no recollection of it. We'll blame it on the beers. As for me and Os fighting in the dressing-room or anywhere else, the only thing we'd have been fighting over was who was buying the next round. And knowing how quick I was with my kitty money, it had to be Os or Boylers on the bell! In fact, Os, Tommy Doc and I laughed about the story at the time and thought of maybe staging a mock wrestle at the Mitcham training ground for the press, just for a joke; but, knowing how these things can go wrong, we thought better of it.

Another negative idea that I don't think we should have to live with is that when the old team was broken up something inferior took its place. In the same foreword I referred to before, Terry Venables says that the early 1960s team felt they could have been one of the best sides in the land, while the new team 'continued to do well, but in a different style, with more individual players'.

It's hard to know for sure what Terry's really saying there. If he means that the early '60s Chelsea were terrific and might well have gone on to great things, he'll get no argument from me. They were a superb team with a great record. But if he's suggesting the team that followed wasn't one of the better and more exciting teams in British football in the late '60s and early '70s, I think he's talking tosh, and I believe there are thousands of true Blues fans who'd say the same. It's worth pointing out that not all the Docherty Diamonds were sold or let go and many were still at the Bridge through the golden years. They were part of a side that made reaching finals, winning cups and achieving top-five league positions certainties for a few years, and that also provided as much if not more entertainment and exciting soccer as almost any team in the country, including those Terry played for.

As for describing the team as individualistic, I doubt Terry will read any apologies from Osgood, McCreadie, Hollins, Alan Hudson, David Webb or any of the other players who might have symbolised that individualism, and he certainly won't hear any from me. That's who we were, and I'm thankful for it and for the fact that we weren't swallowed up in the coaching twaddle of the day back then.

Think back, if you can bear it, to England's performances since those 1966 World Cup days. Sir Alf Ramsey's teams were far from exciting at the best of times, but the 'wingless wonder' stuff that followed for many years after was positively lame. The playmaker role became almost a parody of itself. Joe Bloggs would run twenty yards back to take a five-yard pass from his full-back, pass it five yards square to a defender teammate, get it back and pass it five yards to another player. And the ball still wasn't over the halfway line. There was plenty of coaching baloney about playing short to draw opponents then releasing long balls for forwards who would run behind defences (words I think I've heard from Terry himself, if my memory serves me), which, of course, never happened in a month of Sundays, not against foreign opposition who invariably played with sweepers. There was the occasional strong England performance to keep Charles Hughes and the Loughborough College coaching fraternity happy and building their power bases. But as the years rolled by, Bobby Charlton slicing through and scoring from 20 yards became a dusty memory, and the idea that players like Ossie and 'Huddy' or other exciting talents like them would take Bobby's place and make their marks in the national squads remained only a dream in their minds and those of the fans.

I'm thankful Chelsea were the kind of team they were. We may have underachieved – perhaps that's a book in itself – and heaven knows we've got plenty to answer for, but I wouldn't have changed our style one iota even if I could have.

Charlie Cooke was a show-off. When he first came to Chelsea, he was a revelation, and as a young boy, I was blown away by the tricks he could do with the ball. There were not many around in those days in the English First Division who could master the drag back and nutmeg people with such impudence. George Best, perhaps. But Charlie was at the Bridge in front of my very eyes, and, in a team full of stars, he became my firm favourite. The thing about Charlie was, I reckon, his first priority was to entertain punters and to win at all costs his second. That is why he divided fans, managers and other players so sharply. It depends where you sit on this football lark. I like being entertained. I met Charlie once at a charity match in Los Angeles, and it was a huge thrill. He was very humble and understated and seemed surprised that I wanted to shake his hand. I'm not sure he realises what an impact he had on so many people.

Paul Cook, musician and former Sex Pistol

10

Spurred

After the conservative Tommy Pearson at Aberdeen and Bob Shankly at Dundee, Tommy Docherty was like a breath of fresh air for me. It would not be fanciful to say that he spoke to me more in the first few days of playing for him than the other managers did in my entire time with them. He was truly larger than life: tough, blunt, boisterous and a laugh a minute, with rapier-fast repartee for any occasion. It was a talent that often brought the house down but could occasionally have less happy results, when players and officials didn't appreciate finding themselves on the sharp end of his jokes or being eclipsed by Tommy's fast-talking personality. High-octane characters like Tommy attract their share of critics, but I am pleased to say that the years have not worn down his natural ebullience or his razor-sharp wit. He was in typical bantering form when I met up with him recently for the first time in a quarter of a century.

'How are you keeping?' I asked.

'Great,' he chirped, in his now diluted Glasgow brogue. 'If I had known I was going to live this long I'd have taken care of myself a bit better.'

'Don't be silly, you look great.'

'I've told you a million times, Charlie, don't exaggerate,' he fired back, laughing contagiously at his own funny.

Later, when his audience had doubled (Tommy Baldwin had joined us), he recounted his experiences at one of his other managerial appointments: 'So, at my interview, I said to the chairman, "I will take this club straight out of the Second Division," and he gave me the job there and then. I kept my promise, for the very next season we went straight into the Third.'

One of his strengths was his ability to rouse his players to battle. He was a terrific leader for someone like me, with my Greenock background, and for those who enjoyed his earthiness and humour. He brought tremendous energy to any situation, and wherever he was, a group would explode with laughter when he joined it. His energy was infectious, and spirits and confidence hit the roof when he was around. Sadly, he was not to be at Stamford Bridge for too long after my arrival. He enjoyed a perfect relationship with Mr Chelsea, Joe Mears, our chairman, whom Tommy has described as being like a father to him. When The Doc wanted a player, all he had to do was ask, and Joe would be straight as to whether the funds were available or not. Joe never questioned his manager's judgement in these matters and did not interfere with team issues; likewise, Tommy had no aspirations to become involved in club business and confined himself to the playing side of things. When Joe died in 1966, Tommy was unable to establish a similar relationship with his successor, Mr Pratt. Indeed there was a series of run-ins, and their fractious coexistence was as much a reason for Tommy's eventual departure as any of the repercussions of the Blackpool incident.

At the beginning of my first season proper at Chelsea, 1966–67, we travelled to Dens Park to play Dundee in the pre-season friendly which had been part of the Chelsea–Dundee agreement and which meant that the real value of the transfer deal was the highest up to that point between a Scottish and an English club. Alex Stepney played in goal for us, as Tommy had bought him from Millwall as a replacement for Peter 'the Cat' Bonetti, who was among the unsettled group at that point. Fortunately for Chelsea and Peter, the differences were worked through, and Peter was soon back where he belonged as Chelsea's best-ever goalkeeping servant. Alex, meanwhile, went on to a European Cup victory with Manchester United, so things didn't turn out badly for him either. We prevailed that day at Dens, winning 2–1 with goals from George Graham and Ossie.

We next played VfB Stuttgart in Germany in another pre-season game, and by now I was finding my feet. A bunch of us – Buller, Ossie, Marvin 'Lou' Hinton, Eddie Mac, Boylers and me – had a night on the town that evening, and at 2 a.m., the worse for wear, we piled into a taxi back to the training camp. On the journey back, Lou began to feel queasy, and we had to roll down the window so that he could tip his head out and have a good old puke as we sped along. Relieved, he settled back to recover, but a mile or two later he panicked when he realised something was missing from his mouth. He had a couple of false front teeth, and the retching had sent them flying. Not wanting to spend the rest of the trip looking like Albert Steptoe, he ordered the taxi driver to turn around, and after a surprisingly short search, given that it was the dead of night in the middle of nowhere in the German countryside with only the illumination of the car headlights, we found them. Lou took plenty of stick for it for a long time after, believe me.

My first league game for Chelsea was in the opening match of the 1966–67 season, against West Ham United at Upton Park. It was a beautiful sunny day, and as we arrived on the coach 90 minutes before the kick-off, the contrast between the English and the Scottish game could not have been starker. The coach had to crawl the last half an hour through the football traffic, and the streets were already thronged with boisterous, colourful fans. Touts, tinkers and tradesmen flaunted their wares. Mounted police and some with dogs kept the more excitable fans apart. The sense of occasion was fantastic. Only 10 days before joining Chelsea, I had played for Dundee in a First Division league game against Hamilton Academicals at Douglas Park watched by 700 hardy souls scattered around the terraces. Outside the main entrance, half an hour before kick-off, the place was deserted, so much so that the players could not give away their complimentary tickets.

The Hammers were cock of the walk, and rightly so, as three of their players, Bobby Moore, Geoff Hurst and Martin Peters, had been included in the team that had just won the World Cup at Wembley. They had also recently triumphed in the FA Cup, in '64, and the European Cup-Winners' Cup, in '65, and with the added impetus of World Cup euphoria, it wasn't only folk from east London who felt that West Ham had a good chance of winning the league championship that season. As this was the first time many Chelsea fans were to see me in the flesh, it was a big day for me. We had a great game and won 2–1, and in the 71st minute, I did myself a big favour by scoring the winner in my debut. I remember well picking up the ball in our half, beating two defenders, feigning passes that sent other West Ham players scurrying away to mark someone else and then hitting a low left-footer that Jim Standen in goal must have thought was going wide, for by the time he dived, the ball was in the back of the net. At the other end, Peter Bonetti played a scorcher that afternoon to keep Geoff Hurst and his pals at bay, and we came away from Upton Park with two valuable league points to kick off our season.

The headlines and comment in the Sunday papers the next day were pleasing: 'Cooke Snatches Chelsea Victory', cried the *Sunday Express*; 'Bonetti and Cooke Excel', said the *Sunday Times*; and 'Cooke Adds Depth to Chelsea' was *The Observer*'s verdict. The *Sunday Citizen* had me grinning even wider. Under the lead-in 'West Ham Are Cooked by Charlie', Howard Whitten wrote: 'Cooke looked from the outset a thrilling ball player in the Denis Law mould. His control was precise, his change of direction quicksilver and his passing inspired by split-second vision which tears defences apart.' I duly posted my cheque to Howard on the Monday morning.

The following Wednesday night, I finally made my home debut, against Nottingham Forest, and experienced the roar of the Shed for the first time. They gave me a rousing reception and made me feel at home immediately. Forest were a vastly improved side, led by guys like Terry Hennessey and Henry Newton in defence and

Colin Addison and my old Scotland teammate Joe Baker up front. From finishing 18th the previous season, they would end this one runners-up to Manchester United. We didn't play as well as we had against West Ham, but Forest weren't any world-beaters that day either, and we managed a creditable 2–1 victory. It was perhaps a measure of how exciting the game was that it was noted by the press that the combined surnames of the goal-scorers on both sides – Peter Osgood for us, twice, and Ian Storey-Moore for them – contained six 'O's. Yes, I know, I know.

The future was bright, though. Tommy Baldwin had joined us from Arsenal in a swap deal that saw George Graham going the other way, and it was soon apparent that he was the perfect foil for Ossie, who was coming into his own and getting better and more confident with every game. Tommy was as sharp as a tack and a tireless worker who took a lot of close-marking pressure off Ossie, and his contribution to the flowering of Peter Osgood has often been overlooked. After Forest, we drew a couple and then thrashed Southampton 3–0 at the Dell. We dumped Charlton Athletic out of the League Cup 5–2, and then there was that superb virtuoso performance at Villa Park in which Bobby Tambling scored an incredible five times in a 6–2 drubbing of Villa and didn't even finish the full game, coming off with a hamstring injury a few minutes before the end. Arsenal were next up and went down 3–1 to us at the Bridge, Bobby suffering withdrawal symptoms when he netted only twice. After that, we travelled up to Maine Road, where we slaughtered Joe Mercer's Manchester City by four goals to one. James Mossop's appraisal was fun to read, but, I think, just a tad over the top: 'Contempt was the Chelsea attitude. They held Manchester City aloft on a palm of iron, and with one mighty puff blasted all Maine Road's tactical claptrap into oblivion.'

We remained unbeaten and going gangbusters in the league when we travelled up to Blackpool for a League Cup third-round tie on the cold misty night of 5 October 1966. Morale could not have been higher. We were gelling together nicely and felt we were a match for anyone. We knew that we would be there or thereabouts come the end of the season. In the 21st minute, Ossie went into what looked like a pedestrian tackle on Blackpool's promising young defender Emlyn Hughes, but Peter came out of it writhing in agony, with what turned out to be a badly broken right leg. I can recall seeing Tommy Docherty's face creased with worry as Ossie was stretchered off and Allan Harris came on to replace him. Here was another Blackpool incident that Tommy Docherty, Chelsea and, most of all, our brilliant young number 9 could do without. It was a terrible blow for all of us; what had been a carefree and successful young group was suddenly confronted with the harsh reality of the professional game. Bones and spirits can be broken on the turn of a foot. Careers can be ended in the blink of an eye or the pull of a tendon. There but for the grace of God and all that. Such was Ossie's playmaking skill and his goal-scoring value to us, especially in the air, that it knocked us all for six.

The season had promised so much, but we soon started to falter. We lost the next league game, at the Bridge to Burnley, and then Blackpool dumped us out the League Cup in the second leg of the ill-fated tie. Tommy moved fast to limit the damage and promptly signed Tony Hateley from Aston Villa to fill the void left up front, where we were used to Ossie's dangerous and incisive presence. Tony was superb in the air – perhaps the best in the league at the time – but he didn't have Ossie's ball-playing or playmaking ability on the ground. That said, he played a key role in the FA Cup run that compensated somewhat for our dipping league form, and it is not often said, but I think without Tony Hateley we might never have made it to Wembley that season.

Before we became embroiled in the Cup run, there were some memorable league matches. A 3–0 victory over Spurs at home with Tommy Baldwin netting two was pleasing, especially for Tommy Doc, I imagine, as Terry Venables was now firmly ensconced as midfield general at Tottenham. Then there was a 5–5 draw with West Ham at Christmas, which was a sizzler for the fans and heart-stopping for us players but had us cursing ourselves for some slack defending. For West Ham, it wasn't quite as surprising because although they were a high-scoring side, with Geoff Hurst and Martin Peters leading the charge, they also gave up a lot of goals and were known to be a bit soft defensively. We, on the other hand, were also high-scoring but prided ourselves on being hard to beat and stingy defensively, and those five goals apiece were as much a shock for us as a delight for the fans.

I had one of my better games in a match against Southampton just into the new year of 1967. We hadn't won in eight games, and we were increasingly nervy, but we ripped the Saints apart, pleasing and relieving our home fans in equal measure. The final score was 4–1, and I laid on two of ours for 'Sponge', as Tommy Baldwin was now known among his teammates, and Johnny Boyle. 'Cooke Supplies Tonic for The Doc', said Ken Montgomery in the *Sunday Mirror*, whilst the *Daily Sketch* hailed 'Cooke the Conqueror'. Desmond Hackett of the *Daily Express* was lyrical:

> This gliding, feinting master of the sleight-of-foot conjured well-loved memories of Stanley Matthews and Tom Finney. Even the followers of Southampton purred their pleasure over the impudence and delightful skills of Cooke. So far as I am concerned there could not be too many Cookes to spoil the present dulled system of regimented football.

Although I had only been at Chelsea for half a season, the press debate over whether I was gifted or greedy broke out again. I'd seen it at Aberdeen and at Dundee but did not think it would be of particular importance on the English First Division stage, where George Best, for example, strutted his stuff. I had plenty to say on the matter but found myself muttering platitudes in public, trying not to fan the flames. Alan Hoby, a highly respected writer on the *Sunday Express*, devoted nearly a full broadsheet page to the 'problem'. On the one hand, he described my game as follows:

> When he takes off, when he surges through the middle or sizzles down the wing, this poker-faced Scot brings an incandescence to the game – a glitter and glow of excitement which makes the blood run hot. Twisting and turning, the ball stuck to his foot as if by sticky tape, Charlie Cooke is a throwback to the days of the great dribblers.

However, Alan continues:

> He can enrage as well as enchant as he runs into trouble
> or holds the ball too long. At such times dribbling seems
> to become a disease with him. The ball becomes his own
> exclusive property. He will not, or cannot, pass. On and on
> he runs, exasperating, infuriating, right up a football cul-
> de-sac of his own making.

Strange as it may sound, I didn't take much of all this
seriously, except maybe the cul-de-sac stuff, which made
me seem pretty dumb. Otherwise, I was being played
wide and was doing what I believed my manager, my
teammates and the fans wanted: taking players on and
getting into positions to cross and create chances. I could
understand the press's frustrations, but I wasn't about to
change, at least not yet. If I had been dropped because
of my selfishness, that would have got my attention. But
press criticism went straight over my head.

The path to Wembley began with third- and fourth-
round ties against opposition from lower divisions. We
beat Huddersfield Town 2–1 at Leeds Road, and Brighton
and Hove Albion tied us 1–1 at the Goldstone Ground
before we overcame them 4–0 in front of a 54,000 full
house at Stamford Bridge. In the fifth and sixth rounds,
we put paid to the city of Sheffield's FA Cup aspirations,
first beating United 2–0 at the Bridge before 40,000 fans
and then defeating Wednesday 1–0 at home in front of
another 54,000 full house, setting us up for a third FA Cup
semi-final in succession – this time against Don Revie's
ever-improving Leeds United. It turned out to be a heart-
stopping barnstormer of a semi-final, played at Villa Park

before 63,000 fans, which we won narrowly 1–0. Tony Hateley repaid his hefty fee several times over when he headed in from my cross. Even more dramatically, however, Leeds had a last-minute free-kick equaliser that Peter Lorimer had crashed past Peter Bonetti disallowed when referee Ken Burns judged the kick to have been taken before the whistle. The Leeds players and fans went nuts, but television coverage later proved that it was a good, and brave, decision by Mr Burns.

The FA Cup has a way of throwing up ties that are laced with romanticism and brimming with plots and sub-plots. Our opponents for the final at Wembley on 20 May 1967 were to be Tottenham Hotspur, and no final had been as keenly anticipated for some time. It was the first all-London final, for a start. The managers' personalities were contrasted: would Tommy Docherty's flamboyance triumph over Bill Nicholson's dourness and reserved demeanour? Who would have the last laugh – Terry Venables or Tommy Docherty? Would Tottenham's redoubtable tough Scot Dave Mackay seal his comeback from a second broken leg by captaining his side to victory? Would it be Cooke or the man he'd followed at Dundee, Alan Gilzean, who would be among the goals? Would the £100,000 spent on Tony Hateley prove to be the shrewdest money of the season? Pat Jennings or Peter Bonetti in goal – who would save the day? Could Jimmy Greaves be the man to deny his first club their first-ever FA Cup? It was mouthwatering fare that immediately caught the imagination of the football-loving public. The touts certainly benefited, flogging tickets at 20 times their face value.

As can often be the case, though, that which promised

much delivered little, and the 1967 FA Cup final did just that. Whilst Tottenham Hotspur players and fans were delighted with their 2–1 victory, it was not a historic or particularly entertaining game. We played awful. Lacking in rhythm and sharpness, we lost to goals from Frank Saul and Jimmy Robertson, and although Bobby Tambling pulled one back near the end, it was academic by that stage. Mike England, Spurs' Welsh centre-half, was superb on the day. He prevented Tony Hateley from striking and marshalled the Spurs defence around him to close us all down. Some nice things were said about how I had played personally, but as a team we were devastated. It was not because we had lost to Tottenham – they were a class act and deserved their victory. There was no shame in that. We were just pig sick at how all our ambitions to put on a great Wembley performance for Tommy, to rescue a disappointing league season (we ended in ninth position), had come to naught, and we had performed as sluggishly as we did. I cringe even today when I think about it and still feel guilty that *our* failure as a team that day was another contributing factor in Tommy's departure from Chelsea not so many months later.

The good news at the start of the 1967–68 season was that Peter Osgood had recovered from his broken leg and was fit to play. Tony Hateley was briskly moved on, and we settled down to try to recapture our groove from the start of the last season. Tommy's blunt and sometimes unsettling honesty was on show after a 1–1 derby at Fulham. He pulled Ossie off after an hour, much to Ossie's disappointment. He was playing only his third league game after recovering from his broken leg and was just getting back into the swing of things. Tommy told the press bluntly, 'He's fit, but he wasn't running. I'll carry him all season if I have to, but he has to work. I can't do any more, it's up to him to work it out.' I don't think he could have put it better, for Ossie or the press.

At the same time, John Hollins had asked for a transfer in a dispute over the terms of his new contract. The board, under new chairman Pratt, was stalling and trying to put a freeze on all expenditure pending ground reconstruction financing. Tommy had no problems telling the press how he saw that one, either:

> So far as I'm concerned what John is asking is not unreasonable. And if it was up to me I'd give him the Bank of England. He was brilliant against Fulham yesterday, even with this hanging over him. I don't blame Hollins for trying to get as much as possible from the game.

However, that old groove was proving hard to find, and in August and September we suffered some of our worst results under The Doc's reign. One week, we surrendered 5–1 to Newcastle United at St James's Park, and then the next we were crushed 6–2 by Southampton at home. In both matches, we were outplayed by aerial predators: Wyn Davies for the Geordies, who scored twice, and Martin Chivers and Ron Davies for the Saints, who scored two and four respectively. Liverpool and Forest both put three past us, while we only managed one between the two games. But the ultimate humiliation came in October 1967, immediately after Tommy Doc's sacking, in Dave Sexton's first game in charge, when we crumbled to Leeds United 7–0 at Elland Road. Flower power had swept the Western world, and Scott McKenzie was at the top of the charts singing 'If you're going to San Francisco', and, frankly, after that terrible day in Leeds, we'd rather have gone anywhere than back to Stamford Bridge.

Tommy had been sacked or had resigned (they are very often the same thing) after the 1–1 tie with Coventry City the previous Saturday at the Bridge, but it had been in the wind for weeks. There was the 'failure' of the previous season, the abominable start to this one, a public row over bonuses, and non-stop press speculation about Tommy's future that only a deaf and blind man could have missed. But when it happened, we were still stunned and numb. In the background, there had been an inquiry over a derogatory remark Tommy had made to a referee in Bermuda, and in the end the Football Association decided to suspend him. For Mr Pratt, the chairman, not exactly on best-mucker terms with Tommy in the first place, it was the final straw. We were playing in the forecourt at the Bridge when Tommy had a couple of words with Buller by the ivy-covered office inside the main gates and then got in his Jaguar before any of us could speak with him. We stood open-mouthed as he drove past us, giving us a short papal wave, and was gone.

I, for one, was sad to see Tommy go, for I felt I had much to be grateful to him for. He had admired my football from afar and, not being afraid to take a chance, gave me the opportunity to come to Chelsea. It was where I wanted to play and the whole experience didn't disappoint. The ground was spacious and ramshackle, and with the dog track around it and the Shed End pushed back away from the field, it didn't have the intimate atmosphere of some league grounds. But the fans made up for that with their intensity, noise and humour, and the big-hearted embrace they gave us all. The Doc had also brought me to London, Fulham and Chelsea – places I'd grown to love. It was Tommy who'd made it all possible, and I am always reminded of his part in shaping my life when I open up a scrapbook and read this quotation from him, given many years after we had gone our separate ways:

My favourite Chelsea memories, I suppose, concern Charlie Cooke. I brought him down from Scotland for £72,000 to replace Terry Venables. He would have been a £20-million player today. He was quick, brave and had outstanding skill, a Brazilian touch. He was a fellow Scot and I trusted him. He never let me down.

They are the kind of words that make me want to play again.

I first remember catching sight of Charlie's face on the front of a Chelsea programme, at Blackburn on 4 May 1966, announcing the Prince's arrival at the Bridge. Immediately, he looked the part! Cunning, with a twinkle in his eye, somewhat resembling an American sleuth. We were told he was to replace Terry Venables, and his first appearances were indeed in the number 10 shirt vacated by TV.

As a ten year old on holiday on the south coast, I remember being allowed to stay up late to watch the first Match of the Day *of the 1966–67 season, West Ham v. Chelsea. The programme opened with the reception for Moore, Hurst and Peters to mark England's World Cup success that summer, but the highlight was a wonderful goal from our new man – a 25-yard strike after a mazy run from the halfway line. 'We all live in a yellow submarine' was the Shed Choir's song of the day (Charlie and the boys wore the change strip of yellow and blue), drowning out 'Bubbles'.*

Despite the obvious disappointment of losing to Spurs in that season's Cup final, we knew, at least, that another legend was upon us. Charlie Cooke had arrived, and many of the banners at Wembley had proclamations recommending Charlie not only for the Scotland team but for Prime Minister. The following season, I recall the BBC's Kenneth Wolstenholme describing Charlie's tormenting of England at Hampden. 'The crowd just want the ball to go to Cooke as quickly as possible,' he said. This made me very proud, as I could never understand how Bonetti, Osgood, Hollins and Tambling were regularly overlooked for England. I almost wanted to be Scottish!

Strangely, Charlie was not a prolific goal-scorer. He was a scorer of great goals, though. Sometimes, after one of his mesmerising dribbles, he would appear almost embarrassed and literally 'pass up' a scoring opportunity, to provide a teammate with the chance of glory. Ossie's diving header against Leeds could only have been provided by the Prince. Charlie departed the Bridge for Crystal Palace in 1972 but was only gone for a short while, returning midway through the next season.

Upon his return, Charlie's game changed somewhat. One hack observed that Cooke had realised that a scoring shot was only a hard pass to the back of the net! Indeed, between 1974 and 1977, Charlie weighed in with more goals than in his previous reign. More importantly, though, Charlie was a wise old head who, no doubt, was able to impart some of his genius to the likes of 'Butch' Wilkins, Garry Stanley and Kenny Swain when another Chelsea era emerged.

Spurred

His performances at Old Trafford and in Athens will be long remembered by Blues fans worldwide. I still have vivid memories of him tossing his number 4 shirt into the crowd after we had clinched promotion back to the top flight at Molineux in 1977. My only regret was that I was not in the right position to claim the prized memento. Soon, it would be 1983 and Pat Nevin – Charlie's reincarnation!

Neil Smith, Chelsea supporter

11

The Mighty Atoms

Dave Sexton couldn't have been more different from Tommy if he had tried. Their personalities were chalk and cheese. Where Tommy was loud, funny and as mad as a hatter, Dave was reserved and unassuming, although he certainly had a humorous side to him when the mood took him. But if Tommy was the wisecracking gunslinger, Dave was the backroom accountant, no question. He was born in 1930 in Islington, London and enjoyed a career as an inside-forward with Luton Town, Crystal Palace, West Ham, Leyton Orient, and Brighton and Hove Albion. At Albion, he was part of the side that gained promotion from the Third Division South to the Second Division. In 163 league matches, he scored 69 goals. He joined the coaching staff at Chelsea and for a while worked with and for Tommy Docherty, getting to know the club and many of the players. He had coached at Arsenal and briefly been manager of Leyton Orient before Mr Pratt offered him the Chelsea job. Appointing an unproven manager was a bold step by the board, but I can remember the veterans at the club being delighted by his appointment, and their instincts would prove to be spot on.

His tenure started on 7 October 1967 with the lashing at Leeds after Tommy Doc's departure earlier in the week. That was followed by three draws and a loss, which could have put the skids under lesser men. But right in the middle of this developing disaster, he got our attention in a team meeting, talking about the properties of the atom. Considering the pressure he was under at the time, I thought that was pretty cool. He made the usual points about opponents' strengths and weaknesses and our plans for and against corner kicks and free kicks and so on, all the normal stuff; but he went further this time and talked about the importance of our mental and emotional commitment and the effects of our actions on our teammates. He spoke of the atom's constantly moving but never colliding particles, held together by an incredibly strong magnetic field. He wanted us retreating and compressing smoothly in defence, then counter-attacking with speed and power and unstoppable energy and team spirit, as strong as the atom's field. He was preaching more than talking, and although these kind of team sessions can sometimes seem condescending and patronising rather than energising, it must have worked because we went out and worked our butts off and beat Sheffield Wednesday 3–0 at Stamford Bridge. Of course, successful managers need pragmatism as well as preaching, and I think Dave had a pretty good balance.

When he first arrived, he didn't know me from a lump on a log, nor I him. He could only judge me from what he saw or heard, and as my pal Tommy Baldwin and I were part of the social drinking crowd, presumably it wasn't good. What I saw in him was a quiet, self-controlled guy looking to get things right without the post-game shouting and blow-ups that can usually be expected in losing situations. I liked that. It made me think he'd be good if things got really ugly, which they already were.

Whether I was right about his impression of me or not, it was obvious in those early days that he was giving me a wide berth. I'm a shy type, and I think Dave was too, so it wasn't all that surprising that we weren't bosom buddies. But it soon became clear why he wasn't making an effort to forge a relationship with me when, within a couple of weeks, he came to me, told me that Sheffield United had made an enquiry and asked me if I'd like to speak with their manager, Johnny Harris.

I was stunned. My first reaction was, 'Holy Christ, this guy doesn't even know me, but he wants rid of me.' I wasn't a complete dummy, and I knew that, contracts being what they were then, he couldn't force me to move. I could have tried to make a case for myself or argued with him, or at least asked him point-blank what his problem with me was. He was playing me every week but wanted to trade me. It would have been worth knowing. You always second-guess yourself and think later of all the things you should have said. But what the two managers, the clubs or anybody else wanted never entered my head. I didn't want to leave the Bridge. That was it. Period. When I gathered myself, after all of two seconds, I told him thanks but no thanks, and, no, I don't want to speak to anybody. Thank you. You have a nice day too.

After a few days, when the dust had settled, I was still steamed up. I felt I hadn't been given a fair shake, not even close – especially in comparison with other players Sexton knew from before, some not even starters, whom he was willing to keep and trust. That's what it boiled down to for me: trust. He had taken over a team that was in trouble, at least temporarily, with only eight points that season from a possible twenty-two, and was quick to talk up the qualities that would be needed and the kind of trust players would need to have in each other, and he in them. But I wasn't one of them. That's how it looked to me, and far from sensing a chance to jump a sinking ship, quite the opposite, I was angry that I wasn't one of the ones he felt he could trust.

Dave, of course, could say that I was all wet, that he was already picking me for every game and that any proposed deal didn't necessarily indicate his feelings. I wasn't so wound up that I couldn't see that side of things, but it was small comfort and would have sounded like damage control if he had put it to me in so many words. But blow me down if he didn't say as much a couple of weeks later. The American Express offices in Piccadilly used to show the previous week's American football matches, and for a while Dave took us up to watch them. I think he liked the ferocity and competitiveness of the games and felt they would inspire us. The two of us were travelling back to Fulham Broadway on the Tube from the weekly NFL review when I took the opportunity to ask how the Sheffield deal had come about. I thought Dave might do a swerve or come up with some excuse, but not at all. Quite spontaneously, he responded that it hadn't mattered to him whether I'd chosen to talk with Sheffield or not, that I was playing well, and he was happy I'd stayed.

I was floored at the way he was able to brush the whole

thing off so easily. I had realised he might want to avoid an awkward conversation and my antennae were ready for the slightest hint of a swerve, but I believed he was sincere. In time, I would come to realise that that's how Dave always was: sincere. About everything he did. We might disagree about his judgement and even his decisions, but I think he always acted as his heart told him he should.

But even after this 'explanation', I was still crushed by the offer. So I got my head down and worked like billy-o, just like I'd always done only more so than ever. It was easy because I was so angry, and it paid off big-time. I was on the team sheet for every game thereafter in that 1967–68 season, playing 47 games in all, second only to Ossie's 48. After a horrendous start to the season, we finished a very respectable sixth in the league, with 48 points, and we were a much happier club, and I a much happier camper, by the end of it.

There were some great matches in the run-in to the end of that season. We thumped Liverpool 3–1 at home. 'Chelsea Boys Trample Over Sad Liverpool', said Desmond Hackett, adding that: 'Chelsea showed exuberance, skill, determination and glowing fitness.' A few weeks later, we tore Leicester apart 4–1, and one journalist alighted on me and Ossie: 'Cooke, with his bewildering control and instinctive flair, had Leicester bamboozled and the crowd roaring. Osgood, with his thrustful running and ability to read the game, soon found the weak spots in the Leicester defence.' In February, we beat Norwich City at home 1–0 in front of an amazing 58,000 fans, and there were hundreds locked out. It was the FA Cup fourth round, and I scored a goal that even I can remember clearly. Ossie made a square pass to me, and from 25 yards I hit a first-time right-foot drive that went in off the bottom of the post. My performance that day prompted one journalist to hail me as a 'Scottish Stanley Matthews with a shot'. It took a replay to dispose of Sheffield Wednesday in the next round of the Cup, but when we were drawn against Birmingham from the Second Division in the quarter-final, a return visit to Wembley looked to be on the cards. However, we didn't bank on their veteran skipper Ron Wylie marshalling his troops to battle. Nor did we take into account two guys with points to prove, Bert Murray and Barry Bridges, both of whom had been sold by Chelsea and were no longer playing in the top division. Birmingham that day, in front of a full house of 52,000 fans at St Andrew's, were the better side, and a goal from former England player Fred Pickering dispatched us from the competition.

Bobby Brown, the Scotland manager, liked what he saw and he picked me to play against England, the World Cup holders, in February 1968. It was a solid Scotland side with Eddie McCreadie, Tommy Gemmell, Ronnie McKinnon and Billy McNeill of Celtic in defence. Billy Bremner and John Greig were in front of them, and John Hughes, Bobby Lennox and I were up front. Our 1–1 draw was fully deserved against an England team that included many of their Wembley World Cup heroes, with Keith Newton in the place of George Cohen, Brian Labone for Jack Charlton, Alan Mullery replacing Nobby Stiles and Mike Summerbee for Roger Hunt. Bustling 'Yogi' Hughes equalised following a Martin Peters goal, but a draw was enough to ensure that England qualified for the European Championships and we didn't, so we were all bitterly disappointed. Norman Giller in the *Daily Express*

The view of Cowdeknowes Dam from Thom Street, where I grew up.

In digs at Aberdeen in 1960, with Bobby Cummings (left) and Doug Fraser (centre).

The Aberdeen squad during pre-season training.
I am in the front row, third from right.

Early publicity photo, 1963.
(© Aberdeen Journals Ltd)

With The Doc in happy times.
(© R.J. Hayter's Service)

Playing snooker with Peter Bonetti (left) and Tommy Baldwin (centre).

Teeing off. Me with, from left to right: Tommy Baldwin, Tony Hateley,
Bobby Tambling, Peter Osgood and Johnny Boyle.

The great Chelsea squad of the late 1960s and early 1970s. Back row: Hinton, Hutchinson, Webb, Hughes, Bonetti, Dempsey, McCreadie and Hollins. Front row: Birchenall, Cooke, Hudson, Boyle, Harris, Houseman, Osgood, Baldwin and Tambling.

Posing at Chelsea in the early '70s.

Playing at Chelsea in the early '70s.

Jack Charlton apologises for trying to kick me in the 1970 Cup final (© Rod Brewster)

Playing for Palace, 1973.
(© R.H. Wright)

I know who he is, but does he know who I am?
With Ted Heath at Downing Street.
(© Rod Brewster)

WINNERS

1966-67	PETER BONETTI
1967-68	CHARLIE COOKE
1968-69	DAVID WEBB
1969-70	JOHN HOLLINS
1970-71	JOHN HOLLINS
1971-72	DAVID WEBB
1972-73	PETER OSGOOD
1973-74	GARY LOCKE
1974-75	CHARLIE COOKE
1975-76	CHARLIE COOKE
1976-77	RAY WILKINS
1977-78	MICKY DROY
1978-79	TOMMY LANGLEY
1979-80	PETAR BOROTA
1980-81	PETAR BOROTA
1981-82	MIKE FILLERY
1982-83	JOEY JONES
1983-84	PAT NEVIN

This is what I am most proud of:
three Player of the Year awards
at Chelsea to go with one each at
Aberdeen and Dundee.

Me with Bobby Cox, my old
Dundee team mate, at
Dens Park in 2005.

I was honoured to be voted into the Best-ever Chelsea XI along with this man, Gianfranco Zola, in 2005.

With Alfred Galustian, Coerver® Coaching international director.

With my co-author in 2005. Martin Knight is the one with his shirt hanging out.

My son Chas and I at Stamford Bridge with the 2005 Premiership Trophy.

Meeting up with Peter Bonnetti in 2006.

wrote that I had a brilliant 20-minute spell when I 'ran the England defence ragged', and James Craig in *The Scotsman* commented:

> From the draw and their immediate hopes for the future, Scotland can take one small crumb of consolation. In Cooke they had far and away the finest player on the field and long before the finish the huge crowd were chanting an old song – 'Charlie Is my Darling'. Cooke produced every trick in the book to baffle and bewilder England's defenders and he did not tie himself down to an outside right role although he was wearing a jersey marked with a large No.7. Where the ball was, so was Cooke and it was a vast pity that Scotland did not have other forwards capable of taking the chances he made.

Even with all these plaudits and the adoration of the Chelsea crowd, I still suffered from self-doubt and insisted on analysing and re-analysing everything. I always felt I could and should do better, which is no bad thing; but if it becomes obsessive, then it becomes self-destructive. I think an interview I did with Hugh McIlvanney of *The Observer* and his comments make that point perfectly:

> Even the name has a cheeky ring, an alliterative aggressiveness that would be at home on a music hall bill. And as one watches Charlie Cooke on the football field, excited by the sudden grace with which he darts or glides past opponents (leaving efficient defenders looking as ponderous as somnambulists), the overwhelming impression is of a rather solemn impertinence. Here, it seems, is a great technical talent being flourished by a haphazard and egotistical

intelligence. 'I hope my approach becomes sufficiently professional to make me a useful member of the team when the spell of good luck I am having comes to an end. I feel that Dave Sexton may find I am a bit of a luxury. He may have to give me the elbow,' says Cooke. It is an outrageous thought. Very few men in Britain can play football as well as Charlie Cooke, but as a judge of a footballer, especially of Charlie Cooke, he is a hopeless case.

I thank Hugh for the good thoughts, but I can't help wincing when I read my own words and wonder if I really was as stupid as I sounded.

More importantly, I had a cracker of a season and won the Chelsea Player of the Year award at the end of it. This was particularly satisfying bearing in mind the early-season run-in with Dave. All things considered, there couldn't have been a sweeter ending.

It was in that season that the great Chelsea team of the late '60s and early '70s really started to come together. Dave Sexton had signed Alan Birchenall from Sheffield United, David Webb from Southampton and Ian Hutchinson from Cambridge United, and they were all soon making their own unique contributions to our style of play, our qualities and our character. Dave Sexton had managed 'Webby' during his spell at Orient and was obviously a big admirer, and it did not take us long to see why. A game against Coventry City in March 1969 saw Ian Hutchinson score his first home goal for us and Bobby Tambling his 200th overall goal for Chelsea. 'Hutch' was at the start of his courageous Chelsea career, and Bobby was coming towards the end of his. We were all good men, and they were not going to keep us down.

Peter Bonetti in goal was the best keeper I have ever seen or played with, period. He was a model professional who worked hard at his game regardless of how much success or adulation was showered on him. We always argued about who won the most cross-country runs in training, and still do today. Take it from me, I did. 'Catty' would get some wins early in pre-season, when he wasn't carrying an extra ounce of fat (unlike the rest of us who were desperately trying to work off the summer-break lard), but that was it. It is indicative of Catty's absolute competitiveness that he seeks to argue with me about this 40 years later. I've seen him get to balls with such amazing acrobatics that the director of *Superman* would think twice about including the scenes in his films lest they were considered too fanciful. If there was ever a man I would want between the sticks in my dream team, 'the Cat' would be the one.

I can confirm that Ron Harris, our über-practical full-back and captain, was every bit as coldly brutal as he enthusiastically describes to his after-dinner audiences when he recalls the reasons he was known as 'Chopper'. But that should not blind you to his other qualities. Buller (we called him Buller and everyone else called him Chopper, except perhaps his mum and dad) was pretty quick, too, and had great patience and judgement of distance, which kept fast attackers from engaging him and forcing him to hasty tackles or decisions. He was millisecond accurate in the timing of his tackles, which made him one helluva difficult guy to play against. Guys like Tommy Smith at Liverpool and Dave Mackay at Spurs were equally tough, but there were none who were cooler under fire than Buller.

Eddie McCreadie was our thoughtful but possibly half-mad Scottish defender, who started out his career as a centre-forward, which accounts for his excellent control and speed. For a slim man, Eddie was amazingly strong and resilient, with a William Wallace-style over-the-top bravery that was an inspiration to the rest of us. I don't know how many Scotland caps he won, but however many it was not enough.

Somewhere along the line, Paddy Mulligan joined us. His name sounds like an Irish pub, and in many ways Paddy was the epitome of the happy-go-lucky Irishman. Always smiling, always garrulous, he could talk his opponent's ear off if he couldn't handle him. He was another strong tackler, with a great recovery speed, always looking to get forward in attack. He, Eddie and Buller made up a great back line of defence.

In the middle of our defence, David Webb and John Dempsey, an Irishman we purchased from Fulham, could not have been more different. Webby, with his jaw jutting forward, seemed to grow with every roar of encouragement from the crowd as he charged around dispossessing whoever he could (sometimes players on his own side), and he was always up for sailing into the attack when the fancy took him. He could be just as animated in the dressing-room as he told us all about his latest business deal or property purchase. When people talk of utility players, none was a better example than David Webb. He played in goal for Chelsea more than once but most memorably in a match against Ipswich Town in 1971. All of our goalkeepers were unavailable for some reason, and Webby started and finished the game. He made a good save and kept a clean sheet in a 2–0 win. I remember the game well, as I was a substitute and came on for Tommy Baldwin when he got injured, and I managed to put a cross over that Steve Kember scored from for the first goal. John Dempsey was as funny as Dave Webb but in a completely different way, breaking everyone up with his deadpan humour. Where Webby was squat, strong and solid, John was tall, slim and fast. They were a great tandem, complementing each other perfectly, and would both go on to score some vital goals for Chelsea.

Marvin Hinton we called Lou, and I never thought to ask why. He was a classy ball-playing sweeper/stopper. Always understated, he was Mr Composure when all hell was breaking loose, and he was the kind of player that made the rest of us look good. Johnny Boyle was another who sometimes got overshadowed, but he was as dependable a wing-half as you'd find anywhere. He was Mr Fix-It, if you like, who would run and tackle and overlap and cross, then get back and do it again – all day long. I don't like using these clichés, but he was a pro's pro.

Speaking of engines, no one had a better one than John 'Olly' Hollins. John really does have football in his blood: his father kept goal for Stoke and Wolves, and his brother played against us for various teams and was a Welsh international keeper. John was an industrious, disciplined player, and his right and left feet were cannons, scoring us many a fantastic goal that will stay with me for ever. If I was in their flight path, I worried they'd take my head off. He is the perfect example of the kind of goal-scoring threat midfielders have to carry if they are to be a success today. As well as being a great athlete and consummate striker of the ball, Olly was the locker-room prankster. He could mimic Tommy Cooper or my Scottish accent at the drop of a hat and had the knack of keeping the atmosphere light even on the biggest of occasions. Although he won only a single cap for England, his sheer consistency should have ensured many more, and there was a time (years later, when he was playing for Arsenal) when calls for him to play for his country again became very loud.

Unassuming Peter 'Nobby' Houseman had an educated left foot and composure on the ball that were the envy of a league that had a scarcity of wide players in the post-1966 wingless wonders era. Peter made up for any lack of blistering pace with dazzling left-foot wizardry and a savvy appreciation of the game as well as a surprising toughness when necessary. His tragic death in a car crash only a few years after he left Chelsea united us all in grief and a terrible sense of loss, wherever we were in the world. Besides being an accomplished footballer, he was a modest, quiet and industrious man.

At the opposite end of the spectrum in terms of personality was Tommy Baldwin, the Sponge, who, quite seriously, was the most underrated player in our team and possibly the league. Go back and watch the videos, and you'll see a guy putting out like no other and scoring more than his fair share of quicksilver, slashing goals. The lads say that Tommy was nicknamed the Sponge because of his propensity for soaking up alcohol, but it was also because he absorbed the heat around Ossie perfectly, buzzing and stinging and loosening up the tight marking that Ossie invariably drew. Tommy was my best buddy at the Bridge, but don't let that fool you; he was a terrific and important part of that great Chelsea team.

That brings me to big Peter Osgood himself. What can I say that hasn't been said? Tall, slim, great in the air, with the foot skills and body swerve of George Best and the finishing ability of Bobby Charlton. If he hadn't broken his leg when he did, at such a vital point in his career, there is no knowing what more he could have achieved. Alf Ramsey would not have been able to ignore him, that's for sure. I relish the goals he scored, from the towering headers to the 20-yard scorchers, and will never forget his footballing cheek and humour. He was one of the greats.

Ossie's great buddy was Ian Hutchinson, another big lanky man. There was none braver or more honest than Hutch. His selfless commitment led to a career plagued by injury, and this prevented him from reaching his full potential. He will be remembered always by the Chelsea faithful for his important goals, his breathtaking long throw, which caused the viewers at home, with their better view, to rub their eyes and do a double-take – did he really throw the ball that far? – as well as his absolute loyalty to his club and his teammates.

If Hutch was Mr Guts, then the young local boy who forced his way into the team soon after Dave Sexton took over was Mr Smooth. Alan Hudson had tremendous skill and an ability to read the game that was uncanny in a boy of his age. His trick of stepping up a gear at will and leaving the best in the world in his wake made you gasp. If he burst onto the scene today, I cannot even guess at what his transfer value would be.

Last but not least, there was Mr Modesty, Bobby Tambling, Chelsea's record goal-scorer of all time, with 202 goals and the executor of some of the most beautiful left-footed strikes on goal we will ever see. All in all, an eclectic but effective mix of talent, skills and abilities. What's more, a better bunch of lads I could not have wished for as teammates.

The reason I got into Chelsea, and Charlie Cooke in particular, was because of my dad, Crispian. He was a professional photographer and was friends with a couple of journalists called Hugh McIlvanney and John Watt. John knew that my brother Nick and I were into football, and he said that he knew a player called Charlie Cooke. He asked us whether we'd like to go to the training ground to watch them practise. My brother and I met every single one of the players and got all their autographs. Bonetti, Osgood, Webb, Hudson, Houseman – you name them, they signed.

A couple of weeks later, my dad told my brother and me that Charlie Cooke had invited us to a game. On the morning of the match, another friend of my dad's, the actor Eric Idle, together with John and Hugh, all came around to our house, and we all set off in different cars in the direction of Stamford Bridge. However, before we reached the ground, we stopped off at a coffee bar near the Fulham Road to meet Charlie. Although this place had the appearance of a normal café, it was one that had salubrious amounts of alcohol under the bar, and, even though this was before the game, the beverages that the adults were drinking were definitely stronger than tea or coffee!

When it was time for him to go, Charlie asked if my brother and I would like to go to the ground in his Jaguar MK II. We drove through the Shed gates and right up to the players' tunnel at the back of the East Stand. He gave us our tickets and said, 'There you go, boys, go up through there and you'll be looked after.' We went through one entrance and he went in via the players' entrance. He was great, and ever since then Charlie has been one of my all-time heroes. He was like a dribbling demon, he was superb, and his corners were amazing, so accurate! Later on, when Pat Nevin came, people used to say, 'He's the next Charlie Cooke', and even Gianfranco Zola had elements of Charlie's style. For me, anyway, Charlie Cooke was always the best!

Woody, drummer with Madness

12

Mud Fight

The 1968–69 season was for the club one of consolidation under Dave Sexton's leadership. We got off to a stomping start and won most of the first dozen matches, including 4–0 destructions of Manchester United in front of 55,000 at Old Trafford and Queens Park Rangers in front of a full house of 26,400 at Loftus Road. We gained revenge over Birmingham for eliminating us from the FA Cup the previous season by beating them 1–0 in the League Cup at St Andrew's, and in the Fairs Cup we drew the club I'd supported as a child – Greenock Morton. After beating them 5–0 at Stamford Bridge, where I scored, I had to miss the trip back to Greenock and Cappielow Park due to injury. Chelsea won 4–3 for an 8–3 aggregate score. In October, we went to the Baseball Ground to play Second Division Derby County in the second leg of a League Cup third-round tie that should have been a formality. I liked the Baseball Ground because it was the opposite of Stamford Bridge, with the crowd pressed down tightly on you around the perimeter of the pitch, making for a real bubbling cauldron atmosphere. The ex-captain of Spurs' 1967 FA Cup-winning side had been banished up there to play out his dotage, or so the story went. Nobody had told Dave Mackay that, and he inspired his team to beat us that day, and then to win the Second Division championship that season. It was a big deal for County and a blow for us. In the after-match interviews, a confident young manager with Brylcreemed hair was predicting great things for his lads, and, boy, was he correct. His name was Brian Clough.

Disappointingly, we went out of the Fairs Cup in the next round on a coin toss with DWS Amsterdam after two 0–0 ties in Amsterdam and London. Our league form was still strong, however, and we were tucked in nicely among a small pack chasing Leeds United, who were looking unbeatable. On Boxing Day, in an away match with Ipswich Town, David Webb did the almost unbelievable and scored a hat-trick playing defence in our 3–1 win.

Then, just at the beginning of February, there was an episode I think we would all like to forget. After drawing 0–0 the previous Saturday at Deepdale in an FA Cup fourth-round tie with Preston, managed by my old Dundee teammate and coach Bobby Seith, we beat them 2–0 the following Wednesday night at Stamford Bridge in front of 44,000 happy fans. Peter Osgood, Tommy Baldwin, Johnny Boyle and I received knocks, and we had to come in to Stamford Bridge the next morning for treatment. After the first treatments, Ossie, Sponge, Boylers and I went off to Barbarella's restaurant, smack next door to the Bridge on Fulham Road, for lunch. A couple of bottles of wine were proffered by happy fans, before we knew it we were ordering some more and, Bob's your uncle, we were all smashed and having a grand old time to ourselves and had forgotten completely about (or decided to pass on or maybe a bit of both) the second round of treatments. To go on a bender was stupid, but to go on a bender in a bar next door to the club in the middle of the day was complete lunacy. And missing treatment was just looking for trouble.

We soon found it. Dave – who had walked into trainers Norman and Harry Medhurst's 'surgery' and found no patients, while poor Norman and Harry choked on their sandwich lunches – didn't have to be a mind-reader to know where we might be, and a few minutes later he was in the restaurant in a burning rage. He declined our noisy invitation to join us, told us to get our arses out of there pronto and disappeared. We were smashed but not so smashed that we couldn't read the tea leaves and see we were in the crap up to our chins, so we noisily started to get our stuff together and got moving back towards the Bridge. There was a small wall, about 18 in. high, by the pavement outside Barbarella's, and in the noisy dispute about who was to blame – we all figured it was everybody else's fault – I lost my balance and fell backwards over the wall. I lay on my back with my feet in the air, laughing hysterically, with everyone else bent over laughing at me. Passing pedestrians, motorists and bus passengers must have wondered what the heck was going on. Some might have seen the funny side of it, but obviously Dave didn't. Neither did we, of course, once we had sobered up and been given our fines and one-week suspensions. We were even more ashamed when the team went down 5–0 in the next match against Southampton. The only bright point was that our suspension facilitated the debut of the local boy who was turning heads in training – Alan Hudson.

A great deal has been written about the drinking and carousing exploits of our Chelsea team, and I don't want to add too much to that particular canon. I'm not convinced we were much worse than other clubs, certainly not the ones I played at, but the media, then as now, shone their spotlight more intensely on the goings-on at Stamford Bridge. It was because somewhere along the line it was decided that we were part of what was wincingly called 'the in crowd'. It would have been a miracle if young guys and drinkers like my best pal Tommy Baldwin and me, and Ossie, Huddy, Eddie Mac, Hutch and Buller, playing in an exciting team and being the centre of attention, with money in our pockets and next door to the Kings Road, didn't occasionally find ourselves on the wrong side of Dave's rules. On the other hand, that's not to say we were blameless – far from it. Tommy got himself embroiled in a police chase one night during which a bottle, all by itself, took flight at a chasing panda car, narrowly missing it. The Chelsea forward had a night in the nick to reflect on that little escapade. Meanwhile, I got lashed one day during the British Open golf tournament in Troon and totalled my car, resulting in a court appearance and the loss of my driving licence for a year. When Tommy smiled and offered to be my chauffeur for the period, I politely declined.

The idea that half of the Chelsea team was always out together on the booze was nonsense, though. Ossie had his group of pals, as did Alan Hudson, for example, and I was most times with my best mate Mr Baldwin. We had some grand and funny times, no question. But there's a price to pay for it. There's a lot of stuff I can't really remember or that is pretty fuzzy, which sounds awful, but that is what booze does. As the old saying goes, wine is truly a mocker.

We ended that 1968–69 season fifth in the league, with Leeds United the clear champions. West Bromwich Albion, captained by my old Aberdeen teammate and fellow lodger Doug Fraser, put us out of the FA Cup in the quarter-finals.

In the close season, the Home International Championship promised much. England were still world champions and the other home countries were all hoping to knock them off their perch. On Saturday, 4 May 1969, I had arguably my best game in a Scotland shirt. I was only called into the squad at the last minute, when it became clear that some players were not going to be available because of injury, and I was thrown into the match against Wales. The crowd at Wrexham (and the armchair viewers) got their money's worth that day, as we won 5–3 in a thrilling, spilling knockabout game. 'Cast-Off Cooke the Hero', trumpeted the Scottish *Sunday Express*, and Harry Andrew recounted the match thus:

In Wrexham's blazing spring sunshine, Charlie Cooke at last reached his full, glorious international potential. He was our wonder man, our mainspring, the maker of goals – and, frankly, the man who saved our face. It was Charlie's brilliant dribbling and passing that inspired Scotland's thundering start. It was his refusal to be curbed that brought us back three times when the Welsh, fighting like furies, threatened to take command.

That performance excited the media about the match against Northern Ireland two days later, and much was made about me for Scotland and George Best for Northern Ireland raising the game to epic proportions with coruscating displays of individual ball skills. As it happened, the game ended one each, and I do not recall myself, or even George, playing particularly well.

After the home internationals, in May 1969, we went on a post-season tour of Mozambique (whose idea was that?) and I won't easily forget the jape Sponge got me and him into one night. Yes, it was all his fault. We had played the second and last game of the tour, beating the Mozambique Select 2–1 after hammering them 9–3 in the first game of the tour, which maybe showed a decline in our condition and ambition. The whole team went out drinking to celebrate the fact that we had no more games to play and could concentrate on having a real holiday. Unfortunately, I don't recall how Tommy and I came to be on the narrow third-floor ledge of a hotel at three in the morning. That's something only Tommy can fully explain. He claimed he had intelligence of a party in a third-floor room, but why we couldn't travel by the more conventional means of a lift or stairs and corridors still escapes me, and probably Tommy too, I think, if he's honest. So we were balanced precariously three storeys high in the middle of the night, gripping a beer glass each (it was good for balance, we thought), pressed flat against the brick wall and slowly inching along it to the target window when we were confronted by an excitable guard down below in the alley pointing a gun at us, screaming in a foreign language and getting more excited and angry by the second. This wasn't Idi

Amin's Uganda, but we weren't far away, and the guy with the gun sounded like he was about to blow a gasket at any time.

'Tommy, he's got a gun. We better stop and get off here fast,' I shouted at Sponge, who appeared to be laughing.

'It's OK, buddy,' Tommy shouted down. 'Take it easy. We'll soon be off here,' he said, and kept inching onwards.

For those who don't know Tommy, let me tell you that when he gets an idea in his head and he's got a few aboard he's the devil's worst enemy to stop.

'Tommy,' I screamed, 'you've got to be kidding! This geezer's going to shoot the crap out of us if we don't get down. Get a grip, for Chrissakes.

'OK, sir,' I shouted down to the guard, cop, undercover agent, who knew, 'we're just coming. Don't shoot or do anything stupid.'

I stopped on the ledge, wondering what the best move would be and if the guard understood a word I was saying. Just then, another guard came around a corner and joined the first one, and now both guards started screaming unintelligibly and waving their guns at us.

'C'mon, Tom, for Chrissakes, you'll get us killed here!' I shouted.

'Och, he'll be OK. Wontcha, buddy?' Tommy shouts down, 'You're OK, arentcha, eh?'

I started to inch back along the ledge. 'It's OK, sir, we're just coming down,' I shouted again, in what I tried to make a conciliatory tone.

'Ach, OK, we're comin', pal,' Tommy calls down. 'We're not doing anything. Just having a party.'

The guards obviously didn't understand Tommy's Geordie accent, but they calmed down a bit, although not completely, when I started inching back. Slowly but surely, Tom and I made it back to the wall we had climbed, and finally we got down to the alley, our hands in the air but still holding our beers.

The guards were ordering us in sign language to keep our hands up.

'Chelsea,' Tommy said, 'Chelsea Football Club.' He made as if to kick a ball. 'Football, yeah?'

The guards didn't know what to make of him.

'Football,' I repeated. 'Pelé. George Best. Bobby Charlton.'

'Foo'ball, yah,' said one of the guards, nodding his head. I think 'Bobby Charlton' did the trick.

Slowly, we got their confidence, and after we offered them a drink of our beers, which they declined, and some of the paper money we had in our pockets changed hands, they saw us off the premises, no doubt thinking, 'These fool footballers from England are really crazy.'

Back home, we at Chelsea were disappointed not to have won anything yet, but we were bullish as a team and looking forward to the 1969–70 season. We figured that with a bit of tightening up and a tad more consistency, we could have a breakthrough year, and we were right. 1969–70 proved to be our best league performance since 1955. We finished third behind winners Everton and runners-up Leeds. More memorably, though, we won the FA Cup for the first time ever, in an epic two-match battle against Leeds United.

It was billed as a battle of northern steel against southern softies, discipline versus flair; a meeting between hard men Hunter and Harris, the two Eddies – Gray and McCreadie – and the big men, Jack Charlton and Peter Osgood. It promised so much, and this time it did not disappoint.

It does not surprise me that, even to this day, the replay at Old Trafford remains the fourth-most-viewed British television event of all time, with only the moon landing, Princess Diana's funeral and the 1966 World Cup garnering more viewers.

We played Leeds an incredible six times that season. It was like there was a higher magnetic force drawing us together and forcing us to fight it out. In September, they beat us in the league 2–0 at Elland Road, and it was barely worth heading back down the A1 because four days later we faced them again at their place in the third round of the League Cup. We held them to a 1–1 draw, and back at the Bridge 38,000 gathered to see us defeat them in the replay 2–0, with goals from myself and Alan Birchenall.

Bizarrely, after putting Leeds out of the competition, we succumbed away to Third Division Carlisle United at Brunton Park in the fourth round. It was a silly 1–0 defeat up in the northernmost ground in England, but was memorable, especially for Peter Bonetti, because he was knocked unconscious by a rock thrown from the crowd. It wouldn't have happened at the Bridge, of course, where you would need a throw of Ian Hutchinson proportions to propel your missile across the space between the crowd and the Shed End goal.

In January 1970, Leeds were back in west London in front of another sell-out (57,000 fans), and this time they put five past Tommy Hughes, who was deputising for Bonetti. Ossie and Olly netted for us, to make the scoreline slightly less humiliating. Meanwhile, we had embarked on our historic Cup run. After disposing of Birmingham City (who, incidentally, had old boys

Bert Murray and Tony Hateley playing for them) at the Bridge in the third round, it took a replay and extra time to overcome Burnley 3–1 in front of a packed house at Turf Moor after tying 2–2 at Stamford Bridge before 42,000 fans. Crystal Palace, with whom I was soon to become more familiar, were our victims in the fifth round. We took them apart 4–1 at Selhurst Park in front of another bumper sell-out crowd of 49,500. I mention the attendances to give an idea of the excitement we were generating wherever we went and the draw the team had become. A Peter Osgood hat-trick and a David Webb goal saw off Queens Park Rangers in the quarter-finals in a 4–2 win at Loftus Road. They too had two Chelsea old boys on their team, Barry Bridges and Terry Venables. A semi-final against Third Division Watford was our reward for a buccaneering Cup run thus far, and we duly crushed them 5–1 on a muddy White Hart Lane pitch in front of 55,000 fans. All was set for the battle of the century, as Leeds United were to be our opponents at Wembley on 11 April 1970.

I have good soccer reasons to look back at that year through rose-coloured spectacles, but it really was the best and most surreal of times throughout the whole country. Whilst we in Britain were conspicuously consuming, new colour televisions were beaming images of starving Biafran children into our homes. Peter Osgood was in the pop charts with the rest of the England squad, singing 'Back Home', and they soon were, after losing to Pelé's Brazil, who went on to win it, in the group stages. Teenage girls were swooning over Ryan O'Neal in the film *Love Story*, and teenage boys had cropped their hair and taken to wearing steeltoecapped army boots. A procession of pop stars were photographed on courtroom steps after being busted for smoking pot, while the morning-sickness drug thalidomide had been proven to cause deformities in babies. *A Question of Sport* aired for the first time, with Henry Cooper and Cliff Morgan as captains, and a bizarre village-fête-style game show called *It's a Knockout*, hosted by Eddie Waring and Stuart Hall, drew record television audiences. Another Apollo mission to the moon ended in a cock-up, and the British public didn't know it yet, but they were weeks away from replacing Harold Wilson as Prime Minister with Ted Heath. 'Bridge Over Troubled Water' by Simon and Garfunkel was a calming musical influence.

My only disappointment at that time was seeing Scotland fail to make the World Cup finals in 1970. I played in qualifiers against Cyprus, Austria and West Germany. In late 1968, we did OK beating Austria and Cyprus. We drew with the Germans in April 1969, but losing to Austria and West Germany in late 1969 meant we did not get out of our group. It was all a bit of a downer, and I thought perhaps the manager attached some blame to me, for I was not capped again for another two years. Years later, after Bobby was sacked as Scotland manager, I discovered the real reason when he sold his story to a tabloid newspaper. I thought it was a bit cheeky, because the two-page spread was headlined 'Charlie's Night in the Bars', but underneath was the non-story that I had broken my curfew on the eve of the Belgium game in February 1971 and had gone drinking in Liège until 4 a.m. Yes, I had, but it had been two nights before the game, and many other members of the squad had done the same. I should know, because they were on the neighbouring bar stools. But, being Old Firm players, they were neither disciplined by Bobby nor mentioned by name in his newspaper exposé. We players who plied our trade in the English league were known as 'Anglos' in the international side, and there was definitely one law for us and one law for the lads from Celtic and Rangers.

Still, I did not care too much and did not think that Bobby was too bothered (when I say he disciplined me, I got a bollocking) until I read that outpouring years later. I have to admit that the story itself was pretty innocuous compared to the headline, and Bobby, God bless him, made a point of saying that, whatever had happened back then, I was playing well and behaving in an exemplary fashion during the season in which the article appeared. One final point in my defence regarding this shameful transgression: as Bobby Brown as much as admitted in the piece, if you were staying in the kind of dump of a hotel we got put in, in the red-light district of Liège (arranged by penny-pinching SFA wallahs), you would have spent the night in the bars, too.

There have been hundreds of thousands of words written about the 1970 FA Cup final. However, that is unsurprising given that the two matches are indelibly imprinted on the minds of most British citizens over the age of 40, so forgive me for adding my contribution. What most folks could not have appreciated was the poor condition of the famous Wembley turf for the first game of the final. From up in the stands, it looked reasonably green and normal, and with Wembley's reputation for superb surfaces, we were similarly deceived. But when we walked out onto the pitch in our suits to inspect it and soak up the sun-kissed atmosphere, we could feel a squelch underfoot. The Horse of the Year Show, which had been held there a week previously, was also a big television event at the time, and a year later the showjumper Harvey Smith would shock the nation to the core by delivering a V-sign on prime-time television. Man, how times have changed. However, the thing about it from our point of view was that the horse show had almost been washed out, and subsequent heavy rain had transformed the famous turf into a soggy pudding. If you looked carefully, you could see the green areas where the turf had been relaid and dark patches of the old turf where the ball would hardly bounce. One of those black holes enabled Jack Charlton's header from a corner kick to put Leeds 1–0 up in the first half. The ball didn't bounce as Eddie McCreadie and Ron Harris on the goal line expected it to, and it ended up trickling into the goal between them. That had to be one of the softest goals in FA Cup history. But our equaliser, from Nobby Houseman, was equally soft. The turf may have played a role in Gary Sprake's footing or his judgement of the ball's speed, who knows, but he unaccountably dropped the Houseman's 20-yard shot, which he'd looked to have covered all the way.

Meanwhile, Eddie Gray used the underfoot conditions to turn Webby inside out down our right flank, especially in the second half, during which Mick Jones put Leeds ahead again. I think we have to say we were lucky the Leeds forwards didn't make more of the chances Eddie created that day. That said, Hutch's terrific near-post headed equaliser was a beauty, and we could even have nicked the whole thing in the dying minutes, during which we missed another couple of half-chances. A tired overtime was played out on the swamp that was Wembley that day, with neither team able to take advantage.

After the game, we could point to the facts that we had come back twice to snatch the 2–2 draw and that underfoot conditions were poor. But our overwhelming feeling was the same as three years earlier at Wembley against Spurs: dreadful disappointment that we hadn't played our best, not even close. But this time we had squeezed out a draw, a replay and the chance to redeem ourselves, and we couldn't wait to make amends.

The Old Trafford pitch for the replay 18 days later was much firmer. That meant that the ball bounced normally but also that the soggy cushion which had protected you when you fell after a heavy tackle at Wembley was gone. And in that replay, bodies were hitting the ground faster than our post-game drinks kitties used to disappear.

Chelsea and Leeds games were always chippy, mouthy affairs, no matter who won or lost or had the last nasty word. Going into the final, Leeds had recently beaten us 5–2 in the league, which no doubt had them feeling chipper, but they were still nursing their heartbreak over the 1967 FA Cup semi-final defeat to us at Villa Park, when Lorimer's free-kick goal was disallowed. There's no doubt the grudges from it still festered and fuelled Leeds's emotions for the Cup final. So the stage was already set for a stormer, even without the added drama of the FA Cup's first overtime tie and replay, in a competition that Leeds no doubt felt they should have won at Wembley.

There's no question Leeds were a terrific side then.

They were one of the best possession teams in Europe and maybe even the world. Billy Bremner and Johnny Giles worked the ball beautifully and orchestrated everything from midfield. Mick Jones and Allan 'Sniffer' Clarke scored most of the team's goals up front, with a mixture of stealth and brawn on service from Peter Lorimer and Eddie Gray, who were prolific scorers themselves. Big Jack Charlton locked up the middle, with Norman 'Bites Yer Legs' Hunter enforcing things alongside him or up mixing it with Bremner and Giles in midfield. Paul Madeley was an excellent and athletic utility player, either in midfield or in the back four, while Paul Reaney (who was injured for the final) and Terry Cooper at full-back made up a tight and tough defence, making overlapping runs that often kept opposing attackers covering back defensively more than they wanted to. In goal, they had Gary Sprake, who in general was a great goalkeeper but was notoriously prone to the occasional amateur error, as we had seen, to our amazing luck, in the first game. He was backed up by David Harvey, Scotland's first choice at the time. Leeds were world-class, no question.

But we could play with the best, too, and didn't need any phoney gee-ups for this one. We seethed at Leeds's referee intimidation, endless whining and gamesmanship, which they had raised to an art form in the last few years under Don Revie. It would be an exaggeration, but not a big one, to say we definitely felt we had right on our side. Bremner and Giles, both small guys, and Hunter in the middle of the field were involved in just about every stoppage and argument and hissy fit there was. It was like clockwork. The ref would make a decision, it would be disputed, and he would suddenly be surrounded by a bunch of white shirts, almost always including a bleating Bremner, Giles and Hunter, and sometimes, when he thought they needed some assistance, Big Jack Charlton, with his pointy elbows and towering presence, the veins bulging in his long neck. It was understandable that referees got worn down by it. They all did, eventually. It's only human. It would be dishonest to say that Leeds were the only culprits. Every team was up to the same tricks. Maybe not as obviously or vehemently as Leeds, but we were all at it in some shape or form. Call it envy, but Leeds' extra intensity and the success they had at it incensed us and everyone else in the league no end, for years. The replay didn't need any phoney hype to ratchet up the tension or the drama. We were already knee-deep in bad blood.

As it turned out, the game was as tough and exciting as expected, with what I'm sure was some of the craziest tackling ever seen in an FA Cup final. There was one moment in the first half when Eddie McCreadie's boot was scything throat-high on the edge of our penalty area and he caught Billy Bremner on the head with his studs, yet astonishingly the ref let play go on. We won the statistical as well as the psychological battle, coming back to win 2–1 in overtime to make it three times in total we'd come back in the two games.

Dave Sexton deserves credit for the two changes he made for the replay, which probably won us the Cup. He moved Ronnie Harris to right full-back to stop Eddie Gray on our right flank, and he freed Webby to play where he was best suited, in the middle. Both tactics worked like a dream. Buller went in strongly on Eddie Gray in the opening minutes, leaving him slowed for the rest of the game and dramatically less effective than he had been at Wembley; and Webby played like a man inspired back in the middle, adding an exclamation point to his performance by heading the winner off Hutch's long throw in the second half of overtime.

Equally important was Peter Bonetti's gutsy decision to stay in goal despite limping for the remainder of the game after getting a bad thigh knock early in the first half in an aerial challenge with Mick Jones. Goalkeeper substitutions weren't allowed then, and Catty's decision to stay on the field kept our numbers and shape intact.

We also got our equaliser at just the right time, in the 78th minute, and the fact that I provided the cross for Ossie's headed goal, which was a beauty, made it all the sweeter.

I haven't seen the film much over the years, but when I saw it recently, it reminded me what a nice goal it was. As I did a takeover with Ian Hutchinson just inside Leeds's half and was running with the ball right of the middle of the field, I saw Ossie out of the corner of my eye to the left of the Leeds box. In normal circumstances, I would probably have been looking for somebody wide or for overlapping support, or I'd have played to feet at the edge of the box; but we were a goal behind and Leeds were settling into a steady defensive rhythm, and there was a growing feeling that we had to start making something happen soon or the game would get away from us. As I looked up, I thought Ossie might have a chance if I could get it in slowly enough beyond Jack Charlton and the other defenders. I knew it would have to be a sort of feathered, floating cross, almost a chip laid out in front of Ossie if he was to have time to get to it. But I also realised that if I took too long getting it in, he could run offside. I remember thinking, 'That's a nice ball, Cookie,' as it seemed to loop and float just perfectly. As Ossie moved to it, I could see he was going to get there. He laid himself out like an Olympic diver and crashed it home, as he had done so many times before. As he rose, he punched his right fist in the air to salute the ecstatic waves of blue behind the goal, and suddenly we were all over him and back in business. It was a beautiful cross, a great finish and a great moment. I think I'm prouder of it now, almost 40 years later, than I was at the time.

I wish I could recall the post-game celebrations, but I'm afraid they got the better of me. There was the usual champagne-gushing euphoria back at the team hotel, and lots of craziness, but if I told you I remembered it, I'd be lying.

What I do remember, though, are the many Chelsea Pensioners who came out in their bright-red uniforms and full regalia the next day as we took the trophy from Euston to Fulham Broadway in an open-topped bus for all the fans to see. The Pensioners gave the whole occasion a special, sobering significance, and their unaffected happiness made our own celebrations all the more grounded and satisfying.

He's an attractive man is Charlie Cooke. There is a gamin quality about him that is irresistible. The eyes are blue and darting, and his hands and shoulders conduct the jaunty rhythms of his speech. There is also about him an underlying vulnerability and uncertainty that is beguiling. The artist playing the hard man. That he is an artist, and a rare one at that, is undeniable. His control of a ball is uncanny, his ability to beat an opponent remarkable and above all his grace of movement is something to behold. Of all the players in the modern game he is the one that has been crucified most by current dogma that individual artistry takes second place to overall efficiency.

Michael Parkinson, Sunday Times, 1970

13

Chelsea Get Real

That summer of 1970, at the start of the new season, I was still playing some of my best football. I was 28 years of age, and I had experience and maturity without having completely lost my youthful exuberance and enthusiasm. I think a few of the other lads were hitting their personal peaks, and that's what makes for an exceptional team. Ossie and Catty had been with the England squad out in Mexico, Paddy Mulligan and John Dempsey were on regular international duty for the Republic of Ireland, and Eddie McCreadie and I were both appearing for Scotland. David Webb, Tommy Baldwin and John Hollins should all have been used for England, but Alf Ramsey thought different. We were the FA Cup holders, having won it in style, with a dazzling 25 goals scored against 10 conceded in the whole competition, and were considered by the bookmakers to be among the favourites to win the league in the coming season.

We were all in demand for personal appearances, endorsements and business ventures. If the Chelsea team did have a pop-star period, then this time between 1970 and 1972 was it. Alan Hudson, with his long hair, brooding good looks and boutique clothes, picked up all the modelling-type work. Peter Bonetti was involved in a sportswear business, and Ossie even had a personal manager. Yes, it was heady stuff, and it culminated in all of us piling into a studio to record 'Blue is the Colour', which stormed the pop charts. I was heartened to hear the crowd sing it again 30 years later when I visited the Bridge.

The fans were being particularly appreciative of me around this time. It was harder to keep a low profile in everyday life, and at grounds, especially at the Bridge, they were singing my name louder and longer than they had previously. I loved it, and I can remember after one game in which I'd played very, very well I got mobbed on the pitch and as I disappeared down the tunnel back into the changing-rooms. I sat down, and a procession of club people came in, shook my hand and congratulated me on my game. Perhaps I looked like the cat that got the cream, because Ossie pushed up on the bench beside me and said, 'Don't get carried away, Cookie. Never forget there's only one King of Stamford Bridge.' There was a twinkle in his eye. I think. I won't tell you what the wee Scottish barra in me was thinking.

We opened the season by losing the Charity Shield to league champions Everton, but, then as now, the match was a showcase, and nobody took it too seriously, except perhaps Kevin Keegan and Billy Bremner, who got so aerated one season they got to fighting and were both sent off. We remained unbeaten in the league, though, until our seventh match, when Leeds managed to defeat us 1–0 at Elland Road. Some newspapers suggested that this was sweet revenge for their FA Cup final loss. In their dreams.

In September, we flew to Greece to meet Aris Salonika in the first round of our European Cup-Winners' Cup campaign. Salonika were not a world-beating side, but they had a reputation for serving up a hostile reception to visiting teams and supporters. They lived up to the pre-publicity, with the usual niggling and intimidatory twattery followed by the arms-out palms-up shrug and a wounded expression when the ref got involved, like they couldn't believe anybody would even suggest they could do such a thing. Those of us flashing down the flanks had to avoid the flying spit from the crowd, and there were also some ludicrously high tackles and the usual macho posturing so typical of European competition. We did well to come away with a 1–1 draw in front of 50,000 seething home fans.

Back at the Bridge, we were all over them. Hutch and Olly scored twice and Lou Hinton once in our 5–1 victory as I watched, injured, from the touchline. After the game, Milovan Ciric, the Aris manager, said:

> Chelsea will win the Cup-Winners' Cup. They are a family. Every man plays forward, they all play back. They work for each other and run their hearts out. And they employ first-rate tactics. They are a credit to British soccer. In Alan Hudson, they have one of the most promising players in the world. He works so hard. How I wish he were Greek. Peter Osgood and John Hollins were also terrific and complete masters of their trade. I have no doubt they will be the Champions.

Good call.

Next up was CSKA Sofia from Bulgaria who were also

a physical side, especially in front of 45,000 of their own fans in Sofia. One bittersweet memory I have of that away game is of some fool going over the top on Buller and giving it the big one in front of their fans thinking no doubt that Chopper wouldn't dare react. The next thing we see when the geezer gets the ball is a crunching tackle from Buller, the Bulgarian whining like a stuck pig as he's stretchered off, and Mr Harris doing the old 'Who me, ref?' better than any of the European con merchants ever could. We beat them 1–0 in Sofia and 1–0 again at the Bridge to ensure our quarter-final spot. Possibly the most notable statistic about the home tie was the fact that this was the only time a club has fielded a team at Stamford Bridge in which every single member's name ended with the letter V. Our man on target in the second leg was Dave Webb, who seemed to store his goals up for important cup ties. He headed the post first from my cross, before drilling in a goal from a Keith Weller headed pass. The Bulgarians became increasingly desperate as the game proceeded, and one of their players was sent off for throwing a haymaker at John Boyle. Afterwards, their manager, Manol Manolov, illustrated the way we all see things differently:

> My players are furious. I do not think Chelsea will win the European Cup-Winners' Cup because they are not a good footballing side. Chelsea are a very rough side, especially Osgood and Hutchinson. In my opinion, five players should have been sent off.

He must have had amnesia about the first game. Bum call.

Before we got to play Club Brugge in the quarter-finals, the two Manchesters put us out the domestic cups, United removing us from the League Cup in the fourth round and City putting us out of the FA Cup at the same stage. In the United game, George Best scored a goal that has been replayed on television a great deal since his death, and I had forgotten how good it was. He collects the ball in his own half and shrugs off various of our defenders before Ronnie Harris steams up behind and lunges at him, but George stumbles, regains his composure and leaves Chopper thrashing around on the deck. Catty, realising it's all down to him, rushes out, but Best simply walks around him and casually puts the ball into the net. After the game, Peter Bonetti said of the goal:

> It was superb, the kind that few others besides Best could hope to score. I saw it coming all the way, almost from the halfway line, but there was nothing I could do about it. A lesser player would have tried to chip it in when he got to shooting range, but Best kept his head and brought it right up to me. He dragged it around me and pushed it in.

Manchester City's fourth-round FA Cup win two weeks after the United loss was even more emphatic, City seeming to get all their many talents to play perfectly together that day and whipping us 3–0 in front of 50,000 at Stamford Bridge on two goals from Colin Bell and one from Ian Bowyer. We played City five times that season, and that was their only win. We would get revenge of sorts by knocking them out of the Cup-Winners' Cup later in the season.

Our league form was pretty good, but by the time the Brugge matches came around, it was clear that not only were our FA Cup and League Cup hopes dashed but we would not be able to catch Leeds or Arsenal in the league. All our hopes for silverware in that season would have to be pinned on European Cup-Winners' Cup success. If we failed, 1971 would go down as a massive anticlimax. Imagine our despair, then, when we fell behind 2–0 in Belgium in the first leg. Then, in the two league games before the second leg, we lost 2–1 to Spurs and tied Huddersfield 0–0 at Stamford Bridge. In Belgium, I think we were slightly shocked by the 17,000 crowd that somehow contrived to make as much noise as 70,000. The parade of worried-looking policeman patrolling the sidelines with guard dogs was disconcerting, too.

The second match turned out to be a nail-chewing barnstormer, with Ossie, just returned from a harsh two-month disciplinary ban, getting the follow-up goal to Peter Houseman's opener to make the aggregate score 2–2 and force extra time. Sponge and Ossie put away two more in the added minutes to ensure our semi-final spot. Our opponents were to be Manchester City, the holders.

City were in their golden period and were enjoying the unusually reversed position of being on the up while Manchester United were on the down. Whilst the United side that had won the European Cup in 1968 were beginning to age, and George Best was skipping training and the occasional game, Manchester City had a tight, youngish team, which had flourished under the joint management of Joe 'Experience' Mercer and Malcolm 'Flamboyance' Allison. Joe was a former England forward and a wise old owl in the management game, later to be

England caretaker manager. Malcolm was a product of the so-called West Ham Academy whose career had been cut short by illness and who had then channelled his energies into coaching. They made an interesting partnership before manager-and-assistant or manager-and-coach teams were particularly common. In 1969, they won the FA Cup, beating Leicester City 1–0 on a Neil Young goal, and in 1970, they took the European Cup-Winners' Cup, defeating Gornik Zagreb and completing a Double by also winning the domestic League Cup. In Colin Bell, they had a world-class midfield player; he was nicknamed Nijinsky (after the horse, not the ballet dancer) for his all-round athleticism, working behind a formidable forward line of Francis Lee, Mike Summerbee and Neil Young. Mike Doyle, Tommy Booth and Alan Oakes formed the core of the defence, with full-back Tony Book their captain. We felt sure we would beat them, although I'm not sure why, because we had failed to do so in the league that season. By that point, though, there was a strong feeling among all the players that the Cup-Winners' Cup was our destiny that year.

To be fair to Manchester City, they were depleted by injury when we played them in the first leg, and Bell, Doyle and Summerbee were missing; but to be fair to us, Ossie was injured. As Victor Railton, writing in the London *Evening News*, helpfully pointed out, 'Charlie Cooke and Alan Hudson may be the brains of this Chelsea side but Ossie is their heart,' and, worryingly, 'Chelsea without Osgood are like a man without his trousers – embarrassed.'

Trouserless or not, we managed to squeeze out a 1–0 win, with Derek Smethurst scoring the goal. I remember it was one of the first matches Micky Droy played for us. At 19 years old, he stood 6 ft 4 in. tall and was built to match; frighteningly, he was still growing. We battled to scrape another 1–0 win up at Maine Road, courtesy of an own goal, and the scene was set for a classic Cup-Winners' Cup final, to be held in the birth place of Olympians, Athens, Greece, against none other than Real Madrid, the magical descendants of that great team of Di Stéfano, Puskás and company which had thrilled me back at Hampden in 1960 and who had turned winning European trophies into an art form.

Incredibly, Francisco Gento, who had played in that legendary 1960 game, was still in the side. He had made the number 11 shirt his own, and the Spaniards dubbed him 'la Galerna del Cantábrico' (the Storm of Cantabrico). He was now nearing the end of his career and closer to forty years old than thirty, but any man who had played in eight European Cup finals, winning six, and won the Spanish league twelve times was a legend in my eyes. I remembered the awestruck kid I was in 1960 watching that historic match, and I marvelled at how gobsmacked I had been going back to Greenock on the train that night and how I could never have imagined in my wildest dreams that one day I would be facing one of those Real Madrid heroes in a European cup final. Dreams sometimes do become reality, it seems. In 1971, Real were no longer the force they had been, and four of their players – Zoco, Amancio, Velázquez and Gento – were over thirty, but they remained soccer royalty and had won the European Cup itself as recently as 1966.

We had some injury worries before the game: Eddie McCreadie broke his nose in a training-ground clash with David Webb; Hutch was out following a cartilage operation; and there were for a while some doubts over Ossie and John Hollins. On the night, though, we managed to field a good-strength side of Bonetti, Boyle, Harris (capt), Hollins, Dempsey, Webb, Weller, Hudson, Osgood, Cooke, Houseman. When we came out onto the pitch, my eyes immediately went to Gento. He was slightly thicker in body than I remembered, but then he was 39 years old. I had read that he smoked 70 cigarettes a day, which, if true, was remarkable, as most of the Continental players were admired for taking good care of themselves. It was as tough a game as I remember, and when we broke the deadlock, we were mightily relieved. I put a ball through to Johnny Boyle, who sent in a cross that Ossie managed to get his head to, but there was no power. Luckily, the ball bounced back to him, and Ossie spun around and stabbed in a lovely left-peg shot low to the right of the goalkeeper. That goal kept us ahead until the dying seconds of the match, and we all saw the trophy itself being placed on the sidelines for its imminent presentation. We just waited for the whistle, but the next one we heard was for a goal, not full-time. John Dempsey fluffed a clearance and Zoco sprung on it, shot and scored. We were stunned. A real smack on the chops. The Cup was scooped up and whisked away, and we faced half an hour of exhausted and tense extra time. Ossie and Olly had been replaced by Tommy Baldwin and Paddy Mulligan respectively as their injuries got the better of them, and we were really on the back foot in those added minutes. Webby made two fantastic off-the-line clearances, which kept us in business, and the 120 minutes ended a goal apiece. Yet another cup final replay for us was scheduled for the Friday night. We, and as many of the Chelsea faithful as could afford it and beg time off their jobs, were staying for a couple more days than we'd envisaged.

Tommy Baldwin and I rose that Thursday morning after the first tie and wondered how we could fill this bonus day in one of the world's most beautiful and sun-splashed cities. We figured we'd take in some sights and that the Hilton Hotel might be a good place to start. We got a taxi from our hotel outside of the city and arrived a bit after noon, and, noticing the empty cocktail bar, we decided to get ourselves a little snifter. Half an hour later, Ossie came by and joined us, and Alan Hudson, God bless him, seeing what was shaping up and still upset at having missed the 1970 FA Cup final against Leeds through an ankle injury, decided against it and left. Needless to say, we hung one on together all the way through until we had to catch a taxi to get back to our hotel by 9 p.m. We were stumbling drunk by then, but I made it just in time to miss Dave and get to my room. Meanwhile, Tommy, for some reason, lost contact with me on our return and ran into Dave at the team dinner, where Dave told him to get a grip. OK, these maybe weren't his exact words. This session has gone down in Chelsea folklore, it seems, but I have to say it was unplanned, one of those things that creep up on you. A couple of snifters, and the hours can flash by, and it did not occur to us at the time that we were being irresponsible. Fans were dropping by every now and then and having a banter, and it was a terrific, relaxed afternoon. We never intended it to be what it turned out to be. I don't recall going to bed, but I can remember waking up with the sort of hangover I would have paid silly money to relieve. It wasn't till after noon that we started feeling close to normal, but no hangover could have stopped us for that game.

Booze and sun can be a lethal combination, and I well remember the state I was in after an all-day sun session in Sitges, Spain, once when we had a day to kill before catching the plane back to London that night. We overdid it big-time, trying to develop deep tans. We kidded ourselves that by boating and swimming we'd protect ourselves from burning. Wrong. By the time I was back in London and staying at the Kensington Park Hotel, I was one huge blister and as sick as a dog. I lay there in the dark for a day and a half with a 'Do Not Disturb' sign hanging on the door, cursing my stupidity. I camped out up there, barely able to move or eat, with blisters popping and weeping all over, puking up every couple of hours. If I had died, nobody would have known for days, as there was no training after the trip and nobody would have missed me. I finally surfaced with skin peeling all over my body, to just about manage a cool tea and a couple of biscuits. I was a sorry state, and, needless to say, I have not been a sun worshipper since.

Back in Athens, on the day of the replay Dave Sexton did a good job of rallying and readying us for the battle ahead. We heard that Pirri, possibly Real's most effective player, had broken his hand in the first match and would not be playing. That lifted us. As it happened, he did appear, but his arm was in plaster.

'That was Real's chance. We will do them today. We have survived their great moment, and we are going to win the Cup,' Dave declared. However, his opposite number was making similar noises. Miguel Muñoz told the press: 'I am more confident now than before the first match. And we are ready for Cooke, who was their one great player.'

Much as I'd have liked to, I didn't agree with Muñoz's assessment, as I did not feel I had a great game, or that the match was particularly exciting. I still had a level of expectation of myself and the occasion because of my boyhood experiences of European football that perhaps was hard to meet. In my eyes, we were in a European final and the occasion was graced by Amancio (widely believed to be Spain's finest-ever winger), Zoco, Pirri (a very great player), and the legendary Gento. And, of course, we had some marvellous players. It should have been a stage and a performance fit for kings, and I don't think it was quite that.

Dave changed the team formation to 4-2-4, with me and Huddy in midfield, and Tommy Baldwin coming in for the injured John Hollins. It worked a treat. From the off, we were on them and far more threatening than we had been in the first game. Wonderfully compensating for his defensive error in the first leg, John Dempsey screamed a shot into the net fairly early on, and soon after, Tommy Baldwin made a short, piercing run and slipped the ball to Ossie, who let rip with a scorcher that stretched the back of the net to its extreme. Two goals up at half-time, we were super-confident, but Dave sensibly grounded us, saying that when we went back out it was 0–0 and we were to start all over again. But Real's manager had done a good job in inspiring them, too. They came at us with a vengeance in the second half, and we found it harder to settle. When Fleitas scored for them, visions of the first leg descended on us, but we kept them at bay, especially when Peter Bonetti made a magnificent save from danger man Zoco. This time, when they brought the Cup out we were truly the victors, and we savoured the moment.

At Heathrow Airport on the Saturday morning, we knew we'd done well and we knew there would be a welcome, but we honestly did not conceive that the reception would be of the magnitude it was. We boarded a yellow-painted coach and pulled out into the west London traffic to head back to Fulham. Crowds were already lining the streets and embankments, and banners and bunting were draped over road signs and structures. A cavalcade of vehicles followed behind the coach along the route, people hooting and hollering, with scarves and colours dangling from the windows. The nearer to Fulham we got, the thicker the lines of supporters became, until we reached Earls Court Road, Fulham Road and Kings Road. As the coach shuddered forward, we finally had to come to a halt at World's End, where the fans completely enveloped us, and we all smiled and basked together in an ocean of triumph and joy.

If we can stop Charlie Cooke, we will win the Cup.

Amancio, Real Madrid and Spain, 1971

14

Out of the Blue

None of us knew it that close season of 1971, but we were at the top looking down. We were being fêted by the great and the good. Celebrities (or 'famous people' as we knew them then) jostled for seats at the Bridge. All sorts of characters came out of the woodwork claiming to be Chelsea supporters, echoing more recent times. We players were in demand for magazine spreads and television appearances. I can remember guesting on the Mike and Bernie Winters television show and appearing on *Blue Peter* to perform juggling tricks. They didn't even give me a badge. As a cultural icon, Chelsea Football Club became interchangeable with the Kings Road, where miniskirts and Chelsea boots ruled the roost; the scribes and commentators conveniently omitted the fact that the ground actually stood on the less well-heeled Fulham Road, where Dr Marten boots and braces were the dominant fashion. Still, mustn't spoil a good story, and I played my part in the whole swinging sixties thing, driving around in a Mini Minor with blacked-out windows and going out with my future wife, who ran a boutique called the Sign of the Times near the Kings Road. At one point, I even landed columns with the *Evening News*, interviewing leading personalities of the period, and with the *Daily Express*, commenting on football issues. What the likes of Edward Heath and Elton John thought when I turned up with my tape recorder heaven knows.

During those post-Athens celebrations, I think we knew it couldn't get much better than this, and as it turned out, it didn't. The unravelling of Dave Sexton's great Chelsea side happened disturbingly quickly. In the summer of 1971, we were super-confident European champions and all-round footballing buccaneers. One short year later, we only had a disappointing League Cup final defeat to show for the season, and after the team's sputtering start to the 1972–73 season, Paddy Mulligan and I were being moved on to pastures new. The seeds of discontent that to this point had been kept under wraps grew apace with Chelsea's growing financial and ground-reconstruction problems. After we left, the decline accelerated (I am not claiming there was any connection), and two years on, when Peter Osgood and Alan Hudson famously fell out with Dave Sexton and were shipped out also, Chelsea Football Club entered a period of regression that would take nearly a quarter of a century to reverse.

The deterioration at Chelsea over the coming few years mirrored that in Britain as a whole for a while. The 1960s optimism lasted into 1971, but soon Prime Minister Edward Heath found himself grappling with a failing, inflationary economy and an increasingly belligerent workforce. The news was full of strikes, and new words like 'demarcation', 'solidarity' and 'downing tools' entered the everyday vocabulary. A miners' dispute led to nine-hour electricity shutdowns and an upsurge in the sales of candles. Eventually, the entire country was put on a three-day working week. The newspapers asked who ran the country – the Government or the miners – and an election was forced. For a while, as in Britain generally, they were dim days at Chelsea Football Club, and it was difficult to see the light at the end of the Stamford Bridge tunnel.

But in those first heady days after the Athens victory, we were all walking on air. Within days, Manchester United went public saying that they wanted Dave Sexton to succeed Sir Matt Busby as manager at Old Trafford. Brian Mears, who had succeeded Pratt as chairman in 1969, stepped in quickly and offered Dave a five-year contract and a salary that was reputed to be one of the highest in the game. 'He is the greatest manager Chelsea have ever had,' stated Mears. That may well have been statistically true, but it seemed as if the Chelsea board had been hustled into action by the Manchester bid rather than as part of some long-term strategy for the club. This would become increasingly clear in the next couple of years, as Chelsea's financial and on-field woes multiplied.

Any ideas we might have had that European success had bestowed some level of infallibility on the team were shattered on the first day of the 1971–72 season, when the stark reality of a London derby and 49,500 expectant fans at Highbury confronted us. Arsenal slammed three past us, and I spent the game on the sidelines. Peter Batt in *The Sun* wrote:

Saving Cooke was like putting money in the bank for a rainy day when you are standing ankle deep in floodwater. Only three months ago in Athens, Charlie had played the game of his life to give Chelsea midfield mastery in the European Cup-Winners' Cup Final. Yet it was precisely in his department that Arsenal outplayed Chelsea almost to the point of humiliation.

It was a sign of things to come, as Dave began juggling positions. Old faces like Paddy Mulligan, Marvin Hinton, Sponge, Alan Hudson, Johnny Boyle and myself competed with new ones like Steve Kember, Keith Weller, Chris Garland and Derek Smethurst for meaningful and consistent roles. It seemed like Dave was trying to fit too many square pegs into the proverbial round holes as he switched the squad around to make things work or, some might unkindly say, to justify his buys. I was still playing the role of the good pro and not complaining, no matter how Dave used me or didn't, which I can see in retrospect didn't do me or Dave any good. I think I should have spoken up, declared my unhappiness about where I was being played and let the chips fall where they might. I think it might have been good for my state of mind, and maybe it would have helped Dave to understand the situation better and to make up his mind exactly what he wanted to do with the team.

As it was, it was unsettling for everyone, with no obvious pattern, no consistency to it all, just changes for changes' sake with fingers crossed, or so it seemed. New players like Stevie Kember and Keith Weller, who had been stars at their old clubs, were often playing no more than back-up roles, or when they took the places of established players like Alan Hudson, Johnny Boyle or myself, we were left nursing our egos. Big squads and player rotations may be the way of the Premiership clubs, and players today have to accept the situation, although the jury is still out on how well it works; but back then, in the early 1970s, if you weren't playing you were dropped, and there was no suggestion of resting specialists or rotating midfielders even when the clubs had the personnel to do it. If the true art of management is managing change, I don't think this was a stellar time for Dave. You can always lay part of the blame on egotistical players, and I suppose we're all guilty to varying degrees, but I also think this was a time when Dave's natural reticence and lack of communication, as well as his steady accumulation of similar players, worked against him.

Manchester United beat us at the Bridge next in an exciting 2–3 game, during which I came on as substitute, and we did not record our first victory until we defeated relegation-doomed Huddersfield Town in our fifth league game, by which time I was back in the starting line-up. In September, we easily disposed of Luxembourg side Jeunesse Hautcharage 21–0 over two legs in the first match of our defence of the Cup-Winners' Cup. I have the dubious honour of not having scored even one of those 21 goals – a stunning example of how my lack of focus on finishing had infiltrated my game.

The second round produced a shock that shattered us all. We were drawn against a team of Swedish part-timers named Atvidaberg, and although they held us to a goalless draw at their ground, we fully expected to hammer them back at the Bridge – not so emphatically as we had the Luxembourg boys, perhaps, but we believed it would be an easy game. When Alan Hudson finally broke the deadlock 15 seconds into the second half, we thought the floodgates would surely open, although Atvidaberg were giving a pretty good impression of the Alamo, with every man to the defence. Lots of chances came for all of us – but we could not convert. Ossie missed a few, John Hollins hit the outside of the post with a penalty, and John Dempsey struck the bar. But, to our horror, the Swedes pulled one back, and as the final minutes ticked by without us having scored again, the full reality of the away goals counting double rule hit us like a sledgehammer. At the end, as we traipsed off the pitch – not only defeated but humiliated – the sound of slow handclapping from the seats and booing from the Shed was a first at Stamford Bridge that I did not savour.

Our league form had improved, though, and we were soon in touch with the leading pack; there were also the League and FA cups to focus on. We pummelled Bolton Wanderers in the League Cup fourth-round replay at Burnden Park, and I did manage to get on the score sheet that day. Days later, we nipped through the quarter-final against Norwich at a packed Carrow Road courtesy of an Ossie goal, which set us up for a juicy two-legged semi-final against arch-enemies Spurs. We'd beaten them a few weeks before in the league at Stamford Bridge – I had scored the only goal of the match – so we fancied our chances of a welcome return to Wembley and our third final in succession.

The first match, played two days before Christmas, was the perfect present to our fans, packed in at the Bridge. Midway through the first half, as Ossie raced to get on the end of a through pass from John Hollins, Pat Jennings, the great Spurs goalkeeper, came out to the edge of his box to meet him but collided with pursuing Tottenham defender Terry Naylor. Ossie took full advantage and cheekily curled the ball into the net. Naylor made up for his part in the error by equalising in the second half, and then Martin Chivers added a second to leave us trailing. Chris Garland, a blond, fresh-faced youngster we had signed from Bristol City a couple of months earlier, rose to a Peter Houseman corner and headed his first goal for the club to put us back even. But then that man Terry Naylor again handled in the area, and John Hollins stepped forward and rammed the penalty home. The Chelsea fans invaded the pitch to celebrate the win, happily ignoring, at least for that moment, the fact that there was still a tough away leg to play and only a 3–2 lead to take with us.

Spurs came at us from the off at a heaving White Hart Lane, and their efforts paid off shortly before half-time when Ralph Coates centred and Alan Gilzean rose and executed one of his trademark back headers, setting up Chivers to power home. We were now drawing overall, and it was a relief when I put Chris Garland through to score a scorcher past Jennings halfway through the second half and our advantage was restored. We just needed to hold on for 20 minutes, but when Alan Hudson handled the ball in the area and Martin Peters converted the penalty, it was looking like extra time would be needed. It was unusual for Huddy to make such a mistake, and he corrected it in his own inimitable style. (OK, we were lottery-winning lucky.) We were awarded a free kick on the edge of the Spurs penalty box, and Huddy took it. The kick was poorly struck on the ground and seemed to carry no hint of danger, but it was like watching the bunny

from the Duracell advert – it just kept going . . . and going
. . . until finally it trickled over to the post where Cyril
Knowles had it covered – or he thought he did, everyone
at White Hart Lane thought he did – but he seemed to step
over it, and the ball was in the net. Alan said afterwards
he intended the kick to be a near-post cross and was as
surprised as anyone when it went in. Poor Knowles. He
sank to his knees and put his head into his hands, the full
burden of missing the League Cup final resting on his
shoulders. You can imagine the Chelsea fans' glee. It's
weird. I could have sworn that at this point the Chelsea
contingent began to sing, 'Nice one, Cyril, nice one, son,
nice one, Cyril, let's have another one,' but I'm told that
that particular song, recorded by the Cockerel Chorus, as
the Spurs supporters titled themselves, wasn't released
until a year later. Interestingly, Hunter Davies, during the
writing of his acclaimed book *The Glory Game*, was in the
Spurs dressing-room that day, and his description brings
home how devastating it was for the Tottenham players:
'They sat like shipwrecked hulks, naked, with their faces
in their hands, unable to move. Knowles seemed to be
crying. His eyes were red and swollen. His arms were
shaking. No one could look at anyone else.'

The Spurs result maybe didn't make up for our
elimination from the Cup-Winners' Cup by Atvidaberg,
but it gave us and the fans a League Cup final at Wembley,
our third final in three years, to look forward to, and we
were still in the FA Cup. We had put out Blackpool and
Bolton in the third and fourth rounds respectively, and
a fifth-round tie against Second Division Leyton Orient
suggested that our passage to the quarter-finals was
assured. Our own song 'Blue Is the Colour' was taking the

charts by storm, and the Shed had adapted a number-one single, 'Son of my Father', by the long-forgotten Chicory Tip, to:

> Oh, Charlie, Charlie,
> Charlie, Charlie, Charlie, Charlie,
> Charlie Cooke

If a week is a long time in politics, it is an aeon in football. On 26 February, we trotted confidently out onto the pitch at Brisbane Road only to slouch back into the dressing-room 90 minutes later defeated, the Second Division side having dumped us out the Cup in a 3–2 victory. We (and the fans) hardly had the time to recover from the shock before the next Saturday we sought to put things back on track, against Stoke City in the League Cup final. We underrated them, too, I reckon.

There was a perception that Stoke was populated by old-timers past their peaks, but this was not really the case. George Eastham and Peter Dobing up front were in their 30s, but younger players like Mike Pejic, Mike Bernard, Denis Smith, Terry Conroy and Jimmy Greenhoff were all very talented and energetic. And, of course, they had Gordon Banks in goal, who was still in his prime. Stoke took an unexpected lead through flame-haired Terry Conroy, and Ossie poked in a goal to level us at half-time. In the second half, in a lovely (for him) swansong to his fine career, George Eastham picked up on a shot that Catty had parried from Jimmy Greenhoff and drove in the winner. Although we did not play as badly as we perhaps thought, Stoke were deserved victors. Their appetite had been stronger and their heads in the right place.

With the Stoke result following hard on the FA Cup and Cup-Winner's Cup disappointments, our season had gone pear-shaped fast. We got some consolation by beating Stoke 2–0 at Stamford Bridge in the league six weeks later, and winning six of our last fourteen games for a seventh-place finish, which wasn't too shabby considering our terrible start to the campaign. But we finished the season with crushing 4–0 and 2–0 losses away to West Bromwich and Leeds to end on a downbeat, and perhaps ominous, note.

We started the 1972–73 season in great form, smashing Leeds 4–0 at the Bridge on opening day in front of 54,000. I scored one, and there was one from Ossie plus two from Chris Garland. We couldn't have asked for a better start considering the end of the previous season. But we were flattering to deceive. The only consistent thing about us after that was our inconsistency. We had only 10 points from a possible 22 by the end of September, and Dave had been changing the starting line-up with admirable consistency of his own when he approached Paddy Mulligan and me with the opportunity of speaking with Bert Head at Crystal Palace with a view to us moving there. Paddy and I had been starting, but Dave's apparent willingness to let us go wasn't a ringing endorsement or reason to be optimistic about our futures at the Bridge. We were both deeply disappointed, and after a short period of deliberation, we both chose to take our chances at Selhurst Park, no matter how bad a career move some might have thought it to be.

Our final game in Chelsea blue was on 23 September 1972. We beat Ipswich Town 2–0 at home. Paddy played at full-back, partnering Eddie McCreadie, who had taken over the captaincy from Ronnie Harris in another of Dave's shake-ups; Micky Droy played at stopper for the injured David Webb; Chris Garland, a striker, played in midfield alongside Johnny Hollins and Steve Kember; and I played wide on the left, with new boy Peter Feely partnering Ossie up front while Bill Garner sat on the bench. At least it was a winning farewell as Ossie scored our first and Steve Feeley got the winner, but I mention the game because it was typical of our constantly changing line-up at the time. Dave didn't seem to know what he wanted, and was changing players and positions at a rate of knots. I think that lack of a set line-up was a big reason for the team's twelfth-place finish that year, the club's worst position in ten years. As for Paddy and me leaving, I would guess that the Palace offer probably came as a relief to Dave, as it would have eased his selection problems and put some sorely needed cash in the club's coffers.

It was sad to be one of the first to peel off and leave what had been such a special team, but I was happy to go. I had grown tired of playing wide and, just turning 31, wanted to operate in the middle, where I believed I was best suited to playing. I felt I had proved myself there in the 1970 and 1971 finals at Old Trafford and Athens, many times for Scotland, indeed during the whole of my early career in Scotland, as well as a bunch of other times for Chelsea in the league. It was the position Tommy Doc bought me to fill, yet Dave would use me there only in emergencies. I felt he used me wide because he had been unable to find a younger player to fill the position either through the youth team or in the transfer market, and he used me to mask that failure because I was more versatile than most of the other players. Instead of looking for younger legs, he had been loading up on midfielders and forwards only to have them sit on the bench or give them games in midfield in order to keep them happy. I hadn't been banging on Dave's door about it, which in retrospect was a mistake, but I had won Chelsea's Player of the Year award in 1968 for playing wide and I had several cup final medals to show for it, so I figured I didn't have too much to complain about. But the older I got, the more a move made sense, and with Dave's willingness to entertain the Palace offer, the writing seemed to be on the wall. Besides, Dave wasn't going to give me a chance in the middle of the field even if I stayed. I would get the opportunity at Selhurst Park, so my answer was easy.

Little did I know, as all this was going on, that the Ipswich game would not be my last in a Chelsea shirt and that Dave's, Eddie Mac's and my paths had a few more twists and turns yet to come. But I held no bitterness about the split at all. It's all in the game, as they say, and not liking to look back too much (which is a bit rich coming from a person presenting an autobiography), I bade my farewells, flung my boots over my shoulder and headed across south London to Selhurst Park.

Charlie Cooke was one of those players who looked the part. He would not have looked out of place blowing a trumpet in Ronnie Scott's or understudying Charles Bronson in The Great Escape. *He looked like a really cool guy, and he was a player with a style all of his own. He was a flair player, who could make the hairs on the back of your neck stand up when he waltzed down the wing. He always looked so cool and unhurried when he was on the ball, holding it up in front of the defender, feinting one way before pushing it another and bursting past his opponent with a turn of pace. He was one of those players who you could say played as though the ball was glued to his feet. In those days, Chelsea had a great side, with the likes of Peter Osgood, Ian Hutchinson, Peter Bonetti, David Webb and the rest of them. They were brilliant on their own, but having Charlie Cooke in the side made Chelsea something special. When Woody first joined the band, we discovered that we had a mutual love of Chelsea and in particular Charlie Cooke. Like Woody, I think that Charlie's contribution to that great side of the 1970s was immense. He gave Chelsea that 'something else' which undoubtedly helped them win the FA Cup in 1970 and the European Cup-Winners' Cup in 1971. Charlie's claimed his place in history with one of the most famous goals ever scored by a Chelsea side, that being Peter Osgood's FA Cup final replay equaliser against Leeds. It was that brilliant ball pushed forward by Charlie that Ossie ran onto and headed past David Harvey. It was a defining moment, not just for Chelsea, but also for me as a Chelsea supporter.*

Suggs, lead singer with Madness

15

Palace – My Part in their Downfall

The origins of Crystal Palace Football Club lie in the Great Exhibition of 1851. Britain was at the forefront of the Industrial Revolution and still the ruler of an empire that spanned the world. The powers that be decided that a massive exhibition should be held just to remind everyone of the fact. Prince Albert, consort to the monarch, Queen Victoria, apparently had the idea of constructing a building of glass as the centrepiece of the Exhibition, and therefore the first Crystal Palace was erected in Hyde Park in central London. After a few years, when people tired of this massive construction in one of central London's most beautiful open spaces, it was moved down to Sydenham in south London, and there it remained until it burned down in 1936.

In 1861, the employees of Crystal Palace formed their own works football team, and in 1871, the club became one of the founding entrants to the new FA Cup competition. Ties to that competition were strengthened as FA Cup finals were played at the Crystal Palace's sports ground between 1895 and 1905. In that latter year, Palace applied to join the Football League, as did Chelsea. While Chelsea were accepted, Palace were rejected and had to settle for a place in the Second Division of the Southern League. In 1915, the Admiralty requisitioned their ground to help with the war effort, and they played for a couple of years at Herne Hill before settling into another ground, cosily named 'the Nest', at Selhurst near Croydon. In 1920–21, Palace became a founder member of the new Division Three formed by the Football League, and they promptly became champions, gaining promotion to Division Two. They were destined to float around those lower divisions for the next half-century.

In 1924, Crystal Palace moved into what was then the newest football stadium in London at Selhurst Park, where they remained. Their nadir came in the 1955–56 season when they were forced to apply for re-election to the Football League after finishing 23rd in Division Three (South). But the following year, they edged upwards to 20th, and a local boy called Johnny Byrne made his debut. He was to become Palace's most famous player for many a year. They formed part of the new Fourth Division when it was set up, and they crept up to gain promotion in 1960–61, with 30 goals from Johnny Byrne, who would soon be capped by England and, inevitably, transferred. Progress was made throughout the 1960s, first under manager Arthur Rowe, who had shaken up British football in the 1950s with his revolutionary 'push and run' Tottenham Hotspur side, and then with Dick Graham, who took the club into the Second Division in 1964. Although they had no big honours to their name, Palace always did have the potential to pull in big crowds, and in 1964–65 a record-breaking 45,000 turned up to see them lose to Leeds United in an FA Cup sixth-round tie.

The seeds of Palace's most successful side to date were sown when Dick Graham was sacked as manager and replaced by Bert Head, who was in charge at Bury and had enjoyed some success at Swindon Town. John Jackson had already established himself in goal following the unpopular sale of Bill Glazier to Coventry City, and a slip of a kid called Stevie Kember had made his debut and showed exceptional promise. With these players and some shrewd signings by Bert, a new team was fashioned, and they finished seventh in Division Two in 1966–67, Head's first full season as manager. In 1969, he took them into the First Division for the first time in their history. Life in the top flight was difficult to say the least, and in that 1969–70 campaign, relegation was avoided by a hair's breadth. At Christmas 1969, a new record was made when 49,498 people crammed into Selhurst to see their heroes crash 1–5 to a rampant Chelsea. A guy called Charlie Cooke was playing for the winners, but the man the Palace fans have cause to remember most was Peter Osgood, who found the net four times that chilly afternoon and sent them home crestfallen to eat their cold turkey dinners.

There was a small improvement in 1970–71 with an 18th-place finish, which nonetheless meant another relegation struggle. They did put together an impressive League Cup run, however, and went out to Manchester United in the quarter-finals, having ejected Arsenal on the way, in a year when the Gunners famously went on to win the Double. By this time, Bert Head had signed

Alan Birchenall and Bobby Tambling from Chelsea, and the defence had been shored up by the arrival of the dependable Mel Blyth from Scunthorpe United. The 1971–72 season was a familiar story, with a 20th-place finish and the dreaded relegation only just avoided once more. A successful businessman, Raymond Bloye, had taken control of the club, determined to change things, and the purse strings were opened before and during the 1972–73 season.

As well as paying £75,000 for Paddy and £85,000 for me, Palace had also forked out around £100,000 for Ian Philip, a young defender from Dundee, who were continuing the Dens Park modus operandi of selling at least one top player a season, as they had done with me seven years earlier. Bert Head announced that he'd also just missed out on bagging Ted McDougall, a goal-scoring sensation down at Bournemouth, when Manchester United beat him to the punch with a £200,000 offer. Bert said he was still looking for another outstanding forward, and this turned out to be Don Rogers, who, remarkably, was still playing for Bert's old club, Swindon Town, in the Second Division. I say 'remarkably' because Don, for £147,000 at his flying best, was one of the finest talents I have ever seen, and I don't say that lightly; yet he was playing his football at lowly Swindon even after the whole country had seen what he could do when they had beaten Arsenal in the League Cup final three years earlier. His career was a mystery to me. He set Crystal Palace alight like nobody had since 1936 and delighted television audiences with his terrific pace and mind-boggling finishing, yet he never played for England and never established himself anywhere else in the same way he did at Palace.

Shortly after getting Don, Bert Head returned from Everton with a blond, curly-haired forward named Alan Whittle. Alan was only a little guy, but he made himself busy up front, and the crowd soon took to him, singing:

> Five foot two,
> Eyes of blue,
> Alan Whittle's after you,
> La la la la la la

The spending spree continued with Derek Possee, another diminutive striker, from Millwall. All these forays into the transfer market gave me heart, for Bert Head was a wily buyer (I heard him described, not unkindly, as a great horse-trader), and it seemed clear to me that the club had ambition in spades. The way I saw it was that we had the talent now not only to stay up but also to secure a healthy mid-table position. The battered and bruised Palace faithful felt the same way.

I knew many of the players at Palace already. Paddy, of course, was a Chelsea teammate; John 'Yogi' Hughes had played alongside me for Scotland, and had a 1967 European Cup-Winners' medal with Celtic to his credit; John McCormick had joined Aberdeen as I was leaving; and I knew Tony Taylor, whom Bert had signed from my boyhood idols Greenock Morton, from having played against him so often. My old mate and Chelsea's leading scorer even today, Bobby Tambling, was still there, although he moved on in 1973, to Cork Hibernians. I already admired goalie John Jackson as a result of previous games against him, as I did Mel Blyth, a terrific athlete in the middle of the defence, and David

255

Payne at right full-back, who was the epitome to me of an honest and dependable pro. We also had a good stable of youngsters, including Bill Roffey; the Hinshelwood brothers, Paul and Martin; Nicky Chatterton; and the powerful central defender Jim Cannon, who would make his debut that season and still be playing for the club 15 years later in 1988.

My first game in a Crystal Palace shirt was at home to Coventry City on 7 October 1972. A fair old crowd of 22,000 turned up, but we lost 0–1 in a scrappy and uninspiring game. Jeff Powell in the *Daily Mail* detected promise, though:

> If it was possible to prove anything amid the misery of Palace's result, Cooke and Mulligan established themselves as the most positive, inventive, lucid and composed men I have seen in Palace shirts. The stunned reaction of some of their teammates to what they were trying to achieve had me quietly humming that tune about passing strangers.

I had to wait until my fifth match to savour the experience of a Palace victory (a rare taste, I'm afraid). This was against Everton and marked Don Rogers' debut. He scored the only goal of the game, and the manner of it was to become his trademark. Picking up the ball near the halfway line, he streaked away, leaving defenders in his wake, then drew out the goalkeeper before neatly tucking the ball into the corner of the net just beyond the keeper's reach. He did it time and time again. I thought this could be a turning point, and it nearly was.

Our next home win was an emphatic 5–0 trouncing of Manchester United. The TV cameras had rolled into

Selhurst Park – perhaps sensing an upset, as United were suffering in the lower reaches of the First Division – and the whole country saw Palace's frustrations explode all over the Red Devils. We did look good that day, and we showed that there was quality there and that we could play as a team. Don Rogers confirmed his hero status with two goals, and Paddy Mulligan puzzled us all and probably even himself by netting a brace, too. The other was scored by Alan Whittle on his debut. Bert Head must have felt he was starting to get a return on his money. A by-product of this headline-grabbing result was that Frank O'Farrell was relieved of his post as United manager and my old boss at Chelsea Tommy Docherty was appointed to football's hottest seat.

But the turnaround in our fortunes that we'd thought we could see on the horizon was not to be, and despite some good wins over Southampton, West Brom, Manchester City and even Chelsea, we lost too many games, finished second to bottom and were relegated. It was a unique experience for me. I didn't play particularly well and accept my share of the blame. I scored only one goal in all my time at Palace, and that was in our 1973–74 FA Cup run, against Southampton. It wasn't really what you'd call a Cup run, but it felt like one. We played three fourth-round draws and two lots of extra time against Sheffield Wednesday before we got knocked out.

Before we were relegated, though, there was a significant development. The chairman decided that Bert Head should be moved upstairs and that someone younger and more dynamic should be brought in – and they did not come much more dynamic than Malcolm Allison. The official line was that Bert was moving to serve the club in an advisory capacity, but he was soon gone completely. Before leaving, however, he proved he was a gentleman of the old school by taking the man who was replacing him onto the pitch to introduce him to the crowd before his first game in charge. As I watched it, I thought it was sad, brave and honourable all at the same time.

I don't know whether Mr Bloye was expecting an immediate turnaround or was looking to the long term, probably both, but Malcolm's arrival with his assistant Frank Lord so late in the season, with the club already in relegation trouble, seemed like strange timing. Some saw it as a smart win-win move for the club and Malcolm. If Palace stayed up, it would be credited to Malcolm, and if we went down, then it would be seen as Bert Head's legacy – not a very charitable view if you were a Bert Head fan and knew what he'd put into the club those past few years to get it where it was. In the event, our run-in was dire, and we won only one game of our last seven under Malcolm's management, which, looking back, should have been a wake-up call for everybody. But the relegation was spun as Bert's legacy, and Malcolm's reputation survived unsullied.

Malcolm had enjoyed success with Manchester City as assistant coach/manager under Joe Mercer, with players like Mike Summerbee, Colin Bell, Mike Doyle and Tony Book. But when Joe Mercer left, Malcolm appeared to lose the confidence of his players, and this was his next post after those problems. Malcolm, however, was nothing if not media-friendly, and the Palace fans and the newspapers ate up his flamboyance. They had no doubts in their minds about hailing him from the off as the Second Coming, the Messiah and the Selhurst

Saviour. Malcolm revelled in the adulation, and that day when Bert introduced him to the fans, he strolled past the Arthur Wait Stand with his fedora hat on and his overcoat round his shoulders, smoking a six-inch cigar. This showbiz side reached its apotheosis when he invited Fiona Richmond, a well-known nude model, to share a bath with him and the players, but that was later, after I had gone. It was Hollywood come to good old Selhurst Park, and everyone was loving it.

Hollywood or not, relegation was official after a defeat to Norwich in the penultimate game. A drunken wake at our Norwich hotel that night and a frank outpouring of many of my dammed-up frustrations, much of it not complimentary to Malcolm and Frank, contributed, I'm sure, to my move away from Palace and out of Malcolm's hair nine months later.

So what went wrong? Ask every one of the staff who was there then, and I'd bet you'd get different answers and plenty of finger-pointing. So first let me own up to my own failings. I didn't do the very thing that could have done more than anything else to help Palace in the critical situation we were in: I didn't score goals. I worked hard always and was never given to letting my head go down. No matter what was said about my ball-playing style or what people may have thought about Chelsea players being dilettantes, I worked tirelessly in training and in games – it was who I was and who I still am. But industry wasn't in short supply at Selhurst. Guys like Tony Taylor, David Payne and Paddy Mulligan had it in spades. What Palace needed was goals, and, along with too many of my teammates, I didn't score any. This had been a weakness in my game for years. Since I'd started off as second-top scorer at Aberdeen as a 17 year old in 1960 my tallies had steadily declined. Back then, I'd allowed the headlines about my being the team schemer and midfield general to get into my head, with the result that I ignored finishing. Now, at Palace, that attitude came home to roost with a vengeance. My lack of goals had been masked when I was playing in a successful team at Chelsea, where we had guys like Ossie and Tommy B who could put them away, and all they needed was service. I was voted Chelsea's Player of the Year in 1968 for providing that service, but it was clear at Selhurst, where we had no high-profile scorers, that we needed more than service from me and the rest of the midfield – we needed goals, and we weren't getting them.

That I didn't find the net was bad enough; but even worse, I think, for someone with my experience, was that I didn't see the need to do it. I figured that what I had to do was work harder and run more to support others and fill in wherever I could, without even recognising how much more valuable it would have been to the team if I had got my name on the score sheet even occasionally. Just an extra three, four or five goals a season could have made a huge difference to our points total, and, who knows, even have saved us from relegation. But I couldn't see it, and for that I'll always be teed off at myself. Not to mention the depressing memories I have of those games and the fatigue of all that running that was getting me nowhere. Too often, I'd work my butt off running all over the field, then get the ball and be too tired to do a thing with it except to shovel it onto a teammate to do any finishing there was to be done. To say it was an unproductive and unsatisfying time is an understatement, and I know it had to be the same for the fans and for my teammates, too. It felt like I was throwing all my effort and ability down a black hole and getting no return on it. And the stupidest thing of all was that it was my own fault for not seeing what was to be done.

I worked hard and played very well in some games, but I didn't carry a scoring threat for Palace, and it was a huge and damning weakness that nothing I did could make up for. It's been a lesson well learned, for it's my mantra to young midfielders in the US today. There are zillions of kids here who are excellent technicians and who work hard, with a great attitude. If they want to keep progressing, I tell them, they have to be able to finish from midfield.

This isn't to point a finger at our Palace strikers. We had good finishers like Alan Whittle, Derek Possee and Yogi Hughes. But neither Alan nor Derek was taller than 5 ft 6 in., which isn't a problem if you're a Maradona, but they were front men. They were unlikely to get a lot of joy in the air, although they were both excellent near-post guys, and did better in the air than you would credit for their sizes. But in the box, where size and heft are just as important as skills, especially late in games when you are chasing a goal and the ball is being humped in at every opportunity, they were at a distinct disadvantage without a big guy to play off. Yogi Hughes was a much bigger fella, but he was a converted winger who liked having the ball at his feet and who created chances for himself and his teammates with fantastic foot skills, facing and running at opponents. He wasn't the kind of robust and patient front man, good with his back to goal, who might have been a real help to Derek and Alan. If we had had such a player, he would have enabled Yogi to play wide, where he worked best, and would have helped Derek and Alan to fulfil their potential. Don Rogers, to whom I will always take off my hat, was an excellent scorer, but he too played wide, where he had space to use his speed, and was never a traditional front man. So scoring was a big problem.

Things were no better in defence, as, like most teams in relegation trouble, we made some horrendous mistakes that led to unnecessary defeats. For a while, Malcolm wanted us playing an offside trap, something that the Palace veterans and even some of us new boys had never done at our old clubs. Certainly at Chelsea we relied on each player's smarts to see when a high early line was on and when it wasn't, and there was no consistent tactic or plan to play that way. Tony Taylor reminded me of a time when he had been slow to get up with the line after a corner against and Malcolm had given him a roasting for it at half-time. So thereafter Tony made a point of always being out early and often out first. This can have good results: in Tony's case it made him think and react quickly, sometimes clearing and sometimes holding. But the offside trap is a tricky tactic to fool with, and for relegation strugglers it's a high-risk strategy. As sure as a gun is a pistol, we got caught out several times with it and conceded the kind of goals that make managers eat their fedoras. Many a game, we'd be giving as good as we were getting, even against the best teams, only to see all our efforts unravel with a sloppy goal because a defender had misread the trap and not cleared our lines or, alternatively, had cleared unthinkingly. These were goals you could perhaps afford in mid-table, but not when you're in the bottom three fighting for every point you can nick. Every 'bad' goal we gave away then was like a knife in the chest.

Malcolm (or 'Big Mal', as the press dubbed him) has to share some of the rap. His flamboyant arrival generated a lot of ink, and sometimes it almost seemed like he thought controversy and column inches were enough in themselves. We opened the 1973–74 season with a 4–1 home defeat by Notts County, who thumped us royally, and Malcolm astonished the media, and, I think, everyone else, by claiming after the game, 'We won't just get promotion, we'll win the Second Division championship.' Being at least part American now and a boxing fan, too, I think I've seen and heard as much pre-fight and pre-game hot air as anybody I know. The smoke and mirrors can take you only so far. Eventually, you have to put up or shut up, and I don't believe Malcolm ever did either (except, some might say, in getting rid of me). He busily put Palace on the media map with japes like giving us players nicknames. (I was 'the Card Shuffler', I think, Alan Whittle 'the Hustler' and Tony Taylor 'the Road Runner', and so on, and he even had the nicknames printed alongside the players' names on the match programmes – a short-lived gimmick, thank heavens.) He also replaced the old claret-and-blue uniform with new scarlet-and-royal-blue stripes and dropped the old 'Glaziers' nickname to rebrand the club as 'the Eagles'. It all fitted nicely, I suppose, with his modern renaissance man, playboy image, but none of it helped one iota to tighten our defence or solve our goal-scoring problems, the tasks he was really there to achieve.

As the 1973–74 season opened, Malcolm, it seemed, wanted to make the club over in his own image and cut all connections with the old regime. There were legitimate opinions for and against concerning the new club identity as well as the management changes, but perhaps one of the most polarising moves of all was dropping veteran Palace goalkeeper John Jackson in favour of young Paul Hammond. Most savvy observers inside and outside the club agreed that Jacko had saved the team's bacon on many a bad day, that he deserved as much credit as anybody on the staff for the club reaching the top flight and staying there as long as it had and that he was still doing sterling work despite the relegation. Paul Hammond was a tall and promising young keeper, who was knocking on the first-team door and looked to have a bright future, and Malcolm preferred him to Jacko for a spell. Unfortunately, sections of the Selhurst crowd didn't take to the move, and after a couple of games during which young Paul was constantly harangued, Jacko was reinstated. He played five games, but, after taking the blame for two of the opposition's goals in a 3–3 draw with Cardiff, he lost his place again. Shortly afterwards, he was traded to Orient, managed by George Petchey, who was assisted by Terry Long, both former Palace head coaches. Long had left Selhurst shortly after Malcolm's arrival. Jacko would go on to several more seasons of top-class net-minding, and Orient, with five former Palace players in the side – Jacko, defenders Bill Roffey and David Payne, Phil Hoadley and front man Gerry Queen – nearly made it up a division that season. Embarrassingly, Palace's season, in contrast, continued to spiral downwards towards relegation to the Third Division (without me, I hasten to add). The symbolic break with the past that Malcolm had made by first dropping then letting go Jacko, a long-time fan favourite, seemed more and more to be egotistical nose-thumbing, directed at the old regime, which had cost the club dearly.

Whether or not this interpretation of events was correct, the results at the start of that 1973–74 season were a disaster, and we had to wait until the 16th game to record our first win. Monday-morning team meetings after a defeat were the pits: rounds of Malcolm pontificating and Frank Lord opinionating and player responses that ranged all over the map, from pointing out a specific mistake that had led to a goal against in the last game to lame theoretical stuff about 4-2-4 versus 4-3-3 and how we should play.

After one home defeat when I was injured and had been in the stands and, on a whim, taken some statistics, we had the inevitable Monday-morning meeting, out on the field by the Holmesdale Road end. Malcolm and Frank had their say and as usual asked for comments.

'Yes,' I said, 'I took some statistics Saturday. They surprised me. How many times, for example, did John Jackson have the ball, either from a goal kick, from the ground or from his hands?'

'Ten, twelve, maybe?' someone threw in.

'No, higher. Any other estimates? Frank?'

'Fifteen,' said Frank, just guessing.

'No, higher. I'm not trying to trick anyone, but I was astonished myself at the number. What about you, Malcolm, how many do you think?'

'Oh, eighteen, twenty, maybe a couple more,' he replied, not sure where this was going.

'John had the ball forty-six times,' I said. 'He kicked it out of his hands thirty-two times. And we got possession from those forty-six three times, not including throw-ins that went either way.'

265

'So what's your point?' somebody asked.

'None, really,' I said. 'Although, if I wanted to be snide, I could suggest that we could maybe look at the forty-three times we just turned the ball over from Jacko's kicks. That maybe we could start thinking about him throwing the ball, or ways to keep possession better. But that's something else. My point is that we have these meetings every week, and everybody has his opinion, and none of us are anywhere close to the truth even on some simple facts.'

Everything went quiet, and I realised I was contributing to the very thing I hated, these interminable team meetings in which nothing got resolved. I wasn't interested in statistics in the normal run of things and sure didn't think they were the way to solve our problems. All I wanted to see was Malcolm get a grip of the whole thing, take the lead and say how it was going to be, then rule with an iron fist and tell anyone who didn't like it to take a hike. With strong leadership, I thought, we would have a chance. We needed a leader, and what we were getting was a media maven and pseudo-renaissance man holding open forums. The old adage about talk being cheap never fitted better.

I thought Malcolm smiled, but it might have been a smirk, as he turned to Frank, clapped his hands together and said, 'Let's go.' Frank did his usual noisy jolly-up to get us moving around the field.

And that was that. As we changed back into our clothes after training, I could have sworn we could hear a tapping coming from Malcolm's room. I reckon it was the sound of another nail being hammered into my Palace coffin.

When I was a teenager in the 1970s, the walls of my bedroom were decorated with pictures of my heroes. Pride of place went to my two favourite footballers: Jim Baxter and Charlie Cooke. Although they were nearing the ends of their careers, to me they embodied what a Scottish footballer should be. They did not score many goals, but they were skilful and crowd-pleasing entertainers.

The Rev. Peter Macdonald,
St George's West Church, Edinburgh

16

Steady Eddie

If anyone still believed Malcolm Allison's spin that we were headed straight back up to the top flight, they must have been having their doubts by this stage. In 15 games without a win at the beginning of season 1973–74, we'd conceded 25 goals and scored only 11. At this rate we would be relegated to the Third Division by Christmas! Yet Malcolm showed few signs of stress. Palace remained headline news, and this seemed to sustain him. Don Rogers scored most of those 11 goals, some of which were blinders, and his brilliance tended to divert attention from the dire situation we were in.

On 16 November 1973, we beat Bristol City 1–0 with a goal from Alan Whittle and recorded our first victory of the season. It was to be my last game for the Crystal Palace first team as Malcolm dropped me and I spent my last couple of months as a Palace footballer in the reserves. As a professional footballer I had hit my lowest point, and I thought seriously about retiring, although what I'd do for a living in the future was a complete mystery to me. I was past 30 and floundering at a failing club, and for the first time my thoughts turned to America. Ever since those Saturday-morning pictures days, I had loved the Westerns and cowboys and all things American. To me it was the Promised Land, and I promised myself I would go there. By now, I had married Diane, my American girlfriend whom I had met in Los Angeles after the World Cup in Mexico, and British football was being kick-started over there in the States. All the ingredients were in place to make it the right time to take the plunge.

But, as they say, life is what happens to you when you are busy making other plans, and one day Malcolm asked me if I would like to talk to Dave Sexton. Yes, I certainly would. There had been no hard feelings between me and Dave, and it was a real boost to be asked if I wanted to return to Chelsea. I'm sure Malcolm was also glad to get rid of me, especially as a fee of £17,000 was agreed, which represented a good 15-month profit for Chelsea. I had kept myself fit and was determined now to make the most of this lifeline. Chelsea's offer couldn't have come at a better time for me. It had been a real shock when I read that Charlton Athletic had shown an interest in signing me but had decided against it, apparently over wages and because of my carousing reputation. Seeing that in the press was sobering in itself. When you drink during your 20s you are 'full of high spirits' and 'boisterous'; carry on into your 30s and you become a 'drinker'. In your 40s, it is then seen as a 'drink problem' and by the time you get to your 50s, if you make it that far, you are an 'alcoholic'. Around the same time, I filled in one of those magazine questionnaires asking 'Are You An Alcoholic?'

There were 15 questions, such as, 'Do you forget things?' – I can't remember the others. Yes, that was meant to be a joke. Anyway, they said if you answered three out of the fifteen in the affirmative, you were an alcoholic. I stopped at number five. A penny started to drop, but there was still some time before it landed.

I worked hard and played hard but ineffectively at Crystal Palace, and my stay coincided with a dark time in their history, so from that point of view I have to say my Palace days were disappointing. Nevertheless, I look back if not on the time, certainly on the club with great fondness. I still think Palace are a sleeping giant. They always pull in good crowds, and if they were in the top half of the Premiership they would certainly be able to match the patronage of all the big boys. The fans are a good-humoured, affectionate bunch, and in my time there the club, staff, players and fans bonded well despite the disappointing results. And even though I had my run-ins with Malcolm Allison and felt sad at Bert Head's fate and frustrated at my own inability to help much to bring success, I have to admit that Malcolm did many good things for the club, too.

He brought Palace a new profile, a new kit and a whole new identity. In a way, he did for Palace what Ted Drake had done for Chelsea all those years ago when he banished the 'Pensioners' nickname and all that went with it. But success under Malcolm was a long time coming, and his time at the club coincided with two successive relegation seasons and three painful years in the Third Division. He did, however, introduce some memorable players. When I was there, we played some breathtaking football in small bursts, and that was the nub of my frustration: we were so near but yet so far. In one of my last games, he introduced one of these terrific players, a new signing from Southend United. His name was Peter Taylor, and it was clear from that first day that he was a great prospect. He was a strong, barrel-chested and industrious winger who could run at bunches of players and come out the other side with the ball. With him on one flank and Don Rogers on the other, I thought if Malcolm could find a big guy for the middle, Palace would have the most exciting and effective forward line in the league.

Palace were relegated that 1973–74 season, despite winning nine games in the second half of the term compared to two in the first, and Malcolm, Don, Peter and the rest endured three seasons in the Third Division, which included the highlights of making the FA Cup semi-final in 1976 and seeing Peter Taylor capped for England. It was unheard of for a Third Division footballer to receive a full England cap. Terry Venables joined the club as a player, and when Malcolm left, he took over. By 1979–80, Palace were back in Division One. Yet, to this day, I am approached by Palace fans who say the most gracious things and claim that the period when Don, Malcolm and I all arrived was the greatest of times. Strange, but some proof that results and success (in the eyes of the supporters, at least) are only part of the overall footballing experience.

Between the time I had left Chelsea and the lifeline that Dave was now offering, a lot of water had flowed under Stamford Bridge. The construction of the East Stand was presenting all sorts of financial challenges and rumours of possible bankruptcy abounded. The previous season, 1972–73, the one full season I had been away, Chelsea had finished 12th in the league – their lowest placing for many a year – and despite making the semi-finals of the League Cup and the quarter-finals of the FA Cup, there was a perception that the team was in decline. These feelings of crisis boiled over just before my return, when Dave's strained relations with Peter Osgood and Alan Hudson finally snapped. For all the parties it became, I gather, a 'this club ain't big enough for the both of us' scenario. Both sides had power: Dave was the manager, with standing in the game, who not so long ago had brought silverware to the club, while Ossie and Huddy were star players, adored by the fans. A training-ground bust-up was the trigger, and a transfer to Stoke City for Alan and a little later a move to Southampton for Peter was the result.

The Shed roared their displeasure, because on the surface not only were Chelsea underperforming but the manager had now fallen out with their two most popular players and dumped them. To many, it looked like career suicide by Dave. The pressure on him must have been huge, and it was suggested that this was why he came in for me, to placate the fans and ease the pressure. But the Shed gave me a great reception for my first game back, and my return may have absorbed some flak. However, I think even the hardcore fans were getting a bit tired of the whole Ossie and Huddy drama by that stage. The more likely reason for my signing was that money was short at the Bridge. Most of the cash from Ossie and Huddy would have been chucked down the black hole of debt that the club was in, and Dave couldn't have had much to spend. I was cheap. He knew I could do a job, and I'd played with most of the lads before. It made football and financial sense, and, knowing Dave and how he tended to get white-knuckled and dig in his heels when the pressure was on, I reckon that would have been the real explanation. As well as a bit of good old PR, of course. Dave may have been stubborn, but he wasn't stupid.

I don't recall any dressing-room dissent against Dave when I arrived or any positive or negative feelings about Ossie and Huddy following the bust-up, except perhaps that the two of them had played their media connections to the hilt. I think the players were just tired of the media brouhaha and felt relieved that it was now over and they could concentrate on the job at hand. Tommy Baldwin may have felt vulnerable as, especially after I had left, he was closely identified with Peter and Alan, but, in usual Baldwin style, he kept his head down and got on with it. There is this idea that us Chelsea players all went out on the razzle as a group, but the reality was that you could count on the fingers of one hand the number of times there were more than three of us in a bar together other than on tours or with the team in hotels or at club functions. Tommy and I were always drinking buddies and usually went our own way. We went out together regularly, often down Fulham and Chelsea way and to other central London haunts. Huddy had his crowd and so did Ossie and Hutch in their neck of the woods, just as Eddie had his friends far from the Bridge. We six were maybe the heavier drinkers at Chelsea, but rarely did we all drink together.

Had I still been at the club when the row blew up, I doubt I'd have got embroiled in it. One upside of my arm's-length relationship with managers was that while I never had close relationships with any of them I didn't fall out with them either. If I had anything to say, I would say it, but I was never one for cliques or dressing-room piques or press campaigns. I think it was the Greenock in me. And I wouldn't moan about where I was played. For example, I was never ever happy about Dave playing me on the wing, but I wouldn't have felt right rapping on his door to whine about it. To my way of thinking, real players shut up and got on with it. I'd had success playing there, and I figured I didn't have too much to complain about. I always knew the wee Greenock barra in me would have told anybody else in a similar situation to shut up and get on with the job.

The press made a big fuss about my return to the Bridge, and most of them were very supportive. The *Daily Mirror* devoted their whole back page to the move, announcing: 'Back from the Dead – Palace Reserve Cooke Joins Chelsea and Is Given Key Role'. My first game back was against Derby County at home and we drew 1–1. 'Cut-Price Charlie Proves his Worth', was the *Daily Express* headline. Below, James Lawton wrote: 'Charlie Cooke explained the wisdom of Dave Sexton's £17,000 buy through giving Chelsea width, poise and that quality so priceless on the production line of modern soccer . . . an unpredictable touch of pure skill.'

The papers also reported that for some reason Malcolm Allison had attended the game and said that, knowing his luck, I would score a hat-trick, adding that he had only ever seen me score on television. It was fair comment, I was quoted as saying afterwards. How's that for diplomacy?

The only real newcomers to the Chelsea team since I had left were Gary Locke and Ian Britton. Gary was a classy, pacey full-back who ended up serving Chelsea for many years, and if it had not been for nagging injuries he would surely have been an England regular. Ian was a little Scottish terrier of a guy who had energy to burn and did great for us up front. When Ian, a slightly built 5 ft 6 in., and Micky Droy, a mountainous 6 ft 4 in., were together for set pieces, it could look quite comical.

As the season progressed, more youngsters started to push through, including John Sparrow at left-back and Ray Wilkins in the middle of the field. Ray had been at the club as a boy before I left, and I hadn't really noticed him, but once he established himself in the first team, a blind man could see he had talent to spare. He truly was an old head on young shoulders, and his ability to read the game and see openings for teammates and deliver pinpoint accurate passes was jaw dropping. He didn't have Clive Walker speed, but he saw things early and always seemed to have a step on his opponent. I marvelled at his field generalship and clinical finishing with both feet and followed his career with interest when he later played for Manchester United, AC Milan and England.

It was while watching him play for England years later that I wondered if the same thing had happened to his game as seems to happen to most England midfielders, and myself, where playing safe becomes almost the point of the exercise, and the player seems to lose his true identity and ability to take risks. Ray was still delivering pinpoint passes, but too many were only ten yards long and horizontal or even backwards. Those measured defence-splitting balls that used to shock you with their accuracy and cleverness weren't even looked for it seemed, and his shooting from any range, which had been such a feature of his game, seemed to have been mothballed. In fairness, this neutering of England midfielders happens all too often. Paul Scholes and Bobby Charlton before him are the only ones I can remember who actually seemed to carry the same attacking edge on to the field for England as they did for Manchester United, and whether Steven Gerrard and Frank Lampard can really produce their club form in an England shirt remains to be seen. Playing safe and keeping the ball for the sake of it aren't new concepts, but they're insidious, and once you get into the habit of playing square and backwards it's the devil's own job to get out of it. It looked for all the world as though this had happened to Ray, and it was a real shame.

We ended the season in 17th place, having been dumped out of the League and FA cups before I got there, but I was very happy now playing a measured midfield role that suited my time of life, and, even for the cynical judge in me, I was playing well, I thought. I had been rescued from the wastelands of reserve football for a Third Division-bound club and transported back to centre stage – it was for me a marvellous turnaround and testament to the utter unpredictability of life and the game. The young players coming up looked good, and, even though it was clear there were no funds for transfers, I thought we could consolidate and hold our own for the time being.

I was wrong. The next season started disastrously with a defeat by Carlisle United at home on the opening day of 1974–75. Carlisle had come all the way up from the Fourth Division and were strong favourites for relegation, but for a few heady days they were top of the league. Our form did not radically improve even though we had signed David Hay, an excellent midfielder, from Celtic. David was powerful in the tackle and on the ball and was one of the finest young players in Scotland when Dave Sexton imported him, but, unluckily for us and most of all for him, an eye injury plagued his career from almost the day he arrived. I scored goals in each of the two games after Carlisle, which was the same tally as I had managed throughout the previous two seasons. Indeed, the six goals I scored in 1974–75 was the highest number I ever managed in one season at Chelsea.

In September 1974, three defeats on the trot to Ipswich, Derby Country and Wolverhampton Wanderers were enough to make Chelsea chairman Brian Mears sack Dave Sexton. I felt bad for Dave, but he quickly picked up the job at Queens Park Rangers and went on to further success with Manchester United and later within the England team set-up. Dave's assistant, Ron Suart, took temporary charge whilst everyone and his uncle were being linked with the vacant position. I don't think Brian Mears or anyone else on the board had a clear idea of who they wanted to succeed Dave, and although under Ron Suart things did not get much worse, they also did not get much better, and it was clear he did not have a firm mandate from the board. Motivated chiefly by self-interest (and perhaps a buried fear that Malcolm Allison might get offered the job – lighten up, that's a joke), I urged Eddie McCreadie, who by now had stopped playing and was coaching at the club, to go for it. I could be wrong, but I don't think Eddie had considered applying for it at that time. I told him he was crazy not to, or to have any doubts about his abilities or qualifications, as in my opinion he was as ready and suited for the job as anyone inside or outside the club. He was a straight shooter who knew the players by heart and the board as well. To this day I have no idea if what I said played any part in his decision, but in April the Chelsea board gave Eddie the job, unfortunately just too late to save us from relegation.

The drop was a big shock to the Chelsea fans, especially those who had been converted as kids during the halcyon days of 1970 and 1971 and had not experienced the badlands of the Second Division. I was more realistic and less spooked, I think, having already played in Division Two with Palace. On a personal level, Chelsea fans had honoured me by voting me their Player of the Year for the second time, and I was so very pleased and honoured by this show of appreciation in such bad times. Contrary to thinking that relegation put any shadow or doubt on it, I felt that to play well in bad times was perhaps even more laudable than to do so in good. I knew I had played well, despite the relegation; I was proud of my contribution and felt we had the players to get things done. Ron Harris, Johnny Hollins, Peter Bonetti, Peter Houseman, Hutch, Marvin and Tommy were all still around the place and providing valuable knowledge and experience to the young bucks, who were coming on a ton.

My return to form had not only been marked by the Chelsea fans, as in February 1975 I got the shock of my life when Scotland, now being managed by Willie Ormond, recalled me for the away match against Spain in a European Championship qualifier. It was my first cap in four years. Only Billy Bremner remained from my previous forays into international life, and we drew 1–1 with a goal from Joe Jordan in the first minute that followed a free kick of mine. It wasn't a bad Scottish side at all, with the likes of Kenny Dalglish, Danny McGrain, Martin Buchan, Gordon McQueen and Kenny Burns all playing. The result, however, was a huge disappointment for Scotland, as it was commonly acknowledged that we played well and deserved to win, but the draw meant that we would not qualify for the European Championships the following year. Chelsea withdrew me from the international squad against Sweden, worried that I might get injured, but I played again and for the last time a few months later against Portugal, when I was substituted for Lou Macari and we won 1–0. The substitution part didn't disappoint me at all, as I was chuffed just to have been considered again for Scotland at 33 years old, especially with the Bobby Brown episode behind me, and was proud that I hadn't let anybody down. I was on the bench for the England versus Scotland match at Wembley in May 1975, and that was my last time in Scottish colours. After jumping off the cliff at Palace, I was happy to have proved a few points and to have climbed back to make a real contribution at the Bridge and in a small way for Scotland, too. This second career of mine was turning out to be great fun.

Eddie's leadership qualities soon became apparent. He signalled his confidence in the youngsters at the beginning of 1975–76 by boldly appointing the teenage Ray 'Butch' Wilkins captain. It was a shock to everyone but a masterstroke by Eddie. Butch has since intimated it was a nerve-wracking time for him at the start, but you would never have guessed it by his demeanour, as he played the role brilliantly on and off the field. More youngsters were blooded, including Gary Stanley, who possessed a wood-splitting shot, Steve Wicks, who ranks among the best young defenders I had played with to that point, and Steve Finnieston, a sharp, hard-running centre-forward who just got better and better while I was around. Although there was the not so attractive novelty of playing in smaller stadiums often in front of crowds of less than 10,000, that 1975–76 season and the one that followed were actually great times. Eddie had united and inspired the team and the club as a whole. The fans were calling themselves Eddie McCreadie's Blue-and-White Army, travelling away in greater numbers than before and making away games noisier than home ones, while the players were learning fast and often performing very well.

Our best gate of the season was a bumper 54,000 when we took on my ex-club Crystal Palace and Malcolm Allison at Stamford Bridge in the fifth round of the FA Cup. We lost 2–3 in an action-packed match, with two of Palace's goals coming from the impressive Peter Taylor. How did I feel about it? Ticked off that we lost but no more so than against any other team or in any other losing game. As I've said before, I always had a soft spot for all the clubs I played with and always rooted for them and genuinely wished them well no matter how my time with them had been, and Palace were no different.

We finished halfway in the Second Division and, to my amazement, after being out for much of the first half of the season with injuries, I was awarded the Player of the Year title again. This made it three in total at Chelsea, something I'm immensely proud of, as it has been equalled only by Gianfranco Zola. What exalted company for the wee barra frae Greenock! Zola always reminded me of Zorro: flashing around the pitch, beating opponents with speed and skill and finishing with deadly accuracy. Watching him, I was like every other fan: on the edge of my seat, wondering what he was going to do next. In an age of players recoiling from invisible blows in attempts to get opponents red-carded or crumpling on contact (and sometimes no contact) anywhere near the box, Gianfranco was and remains a beacon of dignity, discipline and sportsmanship.

I don't want to harp on about the Player of the Year awards I won at Aberdeen, Dundee and Chelsea, but they really are the most important things I've ever won in the game, including my European Cup-Winners' Cup and FA Cup medals and international caps for Scotland. Coming as they do from the fans, I feel they're the ultimate recognition. Without goal-scoring statistics to make my case, I felt they were for the intangibles: the hard-to-measure things that often as fans and players we can only respond to intuitively and from our guts, weighing the importance of different qualities that we value in players. In my case, I think I got the vote for fitness, competitiveness, team spirit, skill, flair and entertainment. These were the qualities I admired in others, and I was proud beyond words to be recognised for them.

Eddie Mac's wise leadership was a revelation, and I think he was becoming more confident by the game that we'd go up the next season. We could all feel it. Ray Wilkins had not only captained the side stylishly and with aplomb but he was the top scorer with 11 goals. Impressive as this was, it also signified a weakness among our forwards, but towards the end of the season Steve Finnieston had started putting them away, and we were sure he'd be a star in 1976–77. As for me, I was nearly 35 years old and although Eddie and I never discussed it we both accepted that I would play a smaller and smaller part in this young side.

That summer was the hottest in Britain that anyone could remember; it was all anybody talked about. Lester Piggott won his seventh Derby on Empery and teenage girls swooned over handsome Swedish tennis player Björn Borg, who won his first Wimbledon. I missed it all, for at the end of the 1975–76 season I boarded a plane to America and played for Los Angeles Aztecs for the summer. The pull of America was becoming ever stronger.

The next season, 1976–77, proved to be a humdinger, with 'Jock' Finnieston's 24 league goals being the most by a Chelsea player since Bobby Tambling in the early 1960s. It was a remarkable bag, especially as Ian Britton and Kenny Swain also made double figures. The defence had much to be proud of, too, remaining unbeaten at home throughout the season, and Micky Droy was an unsung star. Although I spent a lot of time in the reserves during the season, I enjoyed myself immensely. Playing with the youngsters kept me on my toes and knowing that we were all pulling together for the Chelsea good again was a great feeling. I loved watching and encouraging these boys, and it was exciting to see them then plunged into the first team – boys like Clive Walker, who on his day was capable of tearing the place apart.

I played in only eight first-team games during the campaign, but these were all in the run-in, with the most memorable being a 1–1 draw with Wolverhampton Wanderers at Molineux. The draw ensured that both clubs were promoted, with Wolves as champions, and at a time when hooliganism was a real threat to the game, it was heartening to see the Wolves and Chelsea fans thronging the pitch afterwards, singing together, 'We all agree, Wolves and Chelsea are magic.'

But fate stepped in again. Eddie had a disagreement with Brian Mears, supposedly over asking for a company car, though I have heard different versions since, and he resigned. Sure, the financial situation at Chelsea remained tough, but whatever the finer detail of the dispute was, it must rank among the dumbest decisions ever made by a board of directors at a football club to allow Eddie McCreadie to leave Chelsea. With the petulant rubber-stamping of a board minute, another Chelsea golden age was flushed down the toilet.

I had been dreading and delaying making the telephone call. Each time my fingers strayed to the dial, my courage failed me, and I knew that if I lifted the receiver I would be lost for words. For it is hard to find the right words for a friend, a professional footballer in his mid-30s, who has been told by his club that he is no longer wanted and that he may go whither he pleases on a free transfer. In the end, I need not have been so timorous. I had screwed up my will, but Charlie Cooke's voice was not that of a broken man. Far from it. In fact, he sounded positively cheerful.

'To tell you the truth I'm glad the hanging on is over and the decision has been made,' he told me. 'Now it's up to me to sort out my own future.'

I reflected that Chelsea's Stamford Bridge ground will be a duller place without him, but he added, 'I suppose my only regret is that the decision was taken for me. But that's how it is in football. Right from the day you sign professional forms, there is always someone else making the decisions for you.'

The odd thing is that Chas always impressed me as a better player on the days he made his own decisions on the park and ignored the theories drummed into him by the coach. So many magical moments. Remember the Wembley Cup final of 1970 when the best Leeds team ever ran Chelsea ragged? Charlie must have covered every inch of that heavy turf keeping his all but shattered team in the game and finally earning the replay which Chelsea won. A year later in Athens for the Cup-Winners' Cup, he again unfolded the full pattern of his genius and earned homage from the great Ferenc Puskás.

To me, Charlie's uniqueness lies in his ability to beat his man. I must have seen him do it a thousand times, yet I am no nearer knowing his secret. There would be Charlie and the ball moving as if tied together towards the full-back. At the last moment, without apparently touching the ball, Chas would dip his left shoulder and the defender would be left kicking air and gazing at green grass where a moment earlier there had been a man and a ball. Jim Baxter, the greatest of all post-war Scottish footballers, summed it up perfectly when he said, 'When Charlie sold you a dummy, you needed a ticket to get back into the ground.'

Tantalising, mercurial, frustrating Charlie Cooke. Sometimes it was all too obvious why managers would occasionally despair of him. There would be afternoons when his talent would retire into a private shell and he would give a fair impression of a man with a club foot playing with a square ball. Well, you wouldn't hire Michelangelo to paint the bathroom wall. Charlie's spirit bloomed best in the packed arena; he craved the big occasion. Managers must live in the present. That is their misfortune. We football fans are able to luxuriate in the memories that give football its true beauty. Charlie has provided a cupboard full of memories that I will cherish. My sons have the No. 4 shirt he wore in the last promotion-winning game of last season. The certainty is that the achievements will grow in the retelling, and that is how it should be.

Llew Gardner, journalist and broadcaster,
'The Wonderful Wizard that Was',
Evening News, 1978

17

The American Dream

It was with some bewilderment that 18,000 Chelsea faithful assembled on the steps of the Shed for the first home game, against Birmingham, of the 1977–78 season. It was good to be back in the First Division while the country basked in sunshine and the warm and fuzzy nostalgia the Queen's Jubilee celebrations engendered, but many were still wondering what the heck had happened at the Bridge since the end of the last, so successful, season. Eddie Mac had taken on the task of rebuilding the club without a cent to spend. He had done the job brilliantly and fashioned this young side with so much promise, then, almost as if he had never been there, he was gone. Gone to America and not coming back. Ken Shellito, the former Chelsea and England full-back, stepped into Eddie's shoes, and whilst he commanded respect among older Chelsea fans as a great player forced into premature retirement because of injury, he had no track record as a manager. The crowd had quite rightly hoped for a signing or two to strengthen the squad, not the disappearance of their leader. I had just returned from my second close-season stint with Los Angeles Aztecs, playing in the North American Soccer League (NASL) with the likes of George Best and Ron Davies, and was brimming with energy. I hoped the new manager would make use of me but had no high expectations, and by and large that's how it turned out.

Still, the boys did well in stepping up a flight, especially considering that Steve Finnieston, who had such a good season the previous year, was dogged by injury and that they had to adapt to a new manager. There was a sweet 1–0 win at Old Trafford, with a goal from young Tommy Langley, and I got my first run on against Bristol City in the October. It was almost my swansong. We won 1–0 and the *Sunday Mirror*'s headline of 'Well Cooke-ed' may have reminded some I was still around. 'Charlie Cooke at 35, playing his first match of the season, was man of the match,' wrote Tony Roche. 'The former Scottish international displayed all his weaving, bemusing skills and completed a fine individual performance by laying on Trevor Aylott's goal.' We went on a little run, beating top-of-the-table Nottingham Forest and drawing with Norwich and Aston Villa. My final goal in a Chelsea shirt was in a friendly against Chelmsford City, and my final, final game for Chelsea was when Ken played me in a cameo in the third round of the FA Cup on 3 January 1978 against Liverpool. It was a cracking good game against a world-conquering Liverpool side that included Alan Hansen, Kenny Dalglish, Phil Neal and Phil Thompson. In front of 45,000 appreciative fans, we thumped them in a 4–2 thriller, with two strikes from our great white hope Clive Walker and one each from Jock Finnieston and Tommy Langley.

We finished a reasonable 16th that season, but by that time I had taken a free transfer in order to make a new life and career for myself in America. The twists and turns at Chelsea would continue. Ken Shellito was sacked the following season and replaced by Danny Blanchflower, who was coming back into front-line football after having written a newspaper column for years, and the club was relegated. Peter Osgood returned to the Bridge, but, as with Dave Sexton, he did not see eye to eye with the next manager, Geoff Hurst, and he left having made little impact. Even Alan Hudson came back but to no avail. The good times could not be rekindled. The next five or six years were played out in the Second Division wilderness. Indeed, in 1982–83, a Clive Walker goal was all that kept Chelsea from the Third Division.

There were many reasons why America seemed attractive to me besides my infatuation with Westerns as a kid. My wife, Diane, was from southern California, and we had spent the last two summers out there while I played for the LA Aztecs, so we knew the country and the lifestyle, and I had a club to go to. Football in America was taking off, although it had taken a long time and many millions of dollars to get to this point. In 1966, the World Cup final between England and West Germany had been shown live on the NBC television network and had captured the public's imagination to such an extent that business interests decided to start a professional league, headed by former Welsh international footballer Phil Woosnam. It must have also occurred to the powers that be that here was a sport with which almost the entire world was obsessed; yet they, the most powerful and influential country on the globe, had no real chips on that particular table. Someone, somewhere must have thought, 'Hmmm, we'll get this moon-landing business out of the way and then take a look at how we go about winning this World Cup . . .'

The following year, two rival leagues were formed: the FIFA-approved United Soccer Association and the National Professional Soccer League. In 1968, common sense dictated they combine to form the North American Soccer League (NASL). However, it remained a struggle to survive, and it wasn't until the early 1970s that attendances started to build and there was genuine ground-level interest. But this was not enough to financially sustain the clubs, and every season teams folded to be replaced with others supported by rich benefactors. In 1975, things changed dramatically when New York Cosmos figured that the key to generating national interest was to sign one of the few footballers that the American man on the sidewalk had heard of – Pelé. Backed by money from film company Warner Bros., they made the Brazilian legend an offer even he could not refuse to come out of retirement. Lazio hero Giorgio Chinaglia followed, and gates shot up, with the Cosmos now attracting 50,000 or more for their games. Suddenly America was where it was at. Then the second most famous footballer in the world – George Best – touched down on American soil and signed up for Los Angeles Aztecs, where I was playing my second summer. America's first serious assault on planet football had begun in earnest.

A word here about George Best. I didn't really know him too well when we played football in England. We were ships that passed on the wing. He was in Manchester; I was in London. He was Irish and I was Scottish, so except in competitive matches we never really met, but when he arrived at the Aztecs, although we did not become best buddies, we were pals. I can honestly say I never saw him the worse for drink and could only admire his commitment to training and his efforts on the field. I can remember him and me at the Hollywood race track, both in our mid-30s and both with drinking reputations, putting many of the younger players to shame with our appetite for hard running and training. At the Aztecs he was still a great player, and many of those US crowds were treated to some of his wonderful moments. I've sat in bars with him, including his own one, and never saw him work his way through more than two or three drinks, and indeed I have a cringing memory of being at dinner with my wife Diane and his wife Angie, and it was me drunkenly running off at the mouth that George was the standard-bearer of our generation of footballers that he had to . . . he had to . . . he had to . . . I'm not sure what I was blabbering about. George just sat quietly, smiling wisely. Years later, I did not recognise the character portrayed in the media and could hardly believe the stories, many of them from his own book. Sadly, I was wrong, and I was deeply upset by his premature death in 2005. Diane and I were on a boat trip down the Danube when each evening we would read on the crawl below the CNN News 'British footballer weakening', 'Irish football star stable', 'George Best, Irish footballer, in serious condition', 'George Best dead'. It was a shock, even though we had been expecting the worst while hoping for the best.

As clips of George's career flickered across the screen,

Diane said, 'It's so sad. He was so gifted. And such a handsome man.'

That's how I'll always remember George: as a handsome man and a phenomenal footballer. It was a privilege and a pleasure to have trained, played and socialised with him.

It was during my early days in the US and while playing for the LA Aztecs that one of the weirdest things in my life happened to me. I was at training on a beautiful Los Angeles morning – maybe a tad hot at around 85 degrees and with a light breeze, but absolutely beautiful, a perfect workout morning. We trained hard, contrary to what you may have heard, and we had already done some physical work and running and now split up for a nine-a-side game. I was charging around as I always did and, recently arrived from the UK, was drinking numerous cups of Gatorade, a sports drink that's on almost every sports team's bench here in the States. There was nothing different about that session that I can recall, but when I went to drive Terry Mancini, Phil Beal and Bobby Sibbald home to our apartment complex, I started to feel dizzy. Terry and the guys immediately got me out of the driver's seat, and by the time Terry had driven us home, I was hopelessly out of it and they had to carry me up the stairs to my bed. Diane was panicking, wondering what had happened to me. I slept through the afternoon and night, and next day discovered or at least heard the whisper that somebody had spiked the Gatorade with angel dust. I believe that's PCP, but I could be wrong. I was to discover that another player, John Mason, a Scottish midfielder, had gone out and purchased size twelve shoes when he only wore size eight, while Steve David, our Trinidadian centre-forward and top scorer, lay shivering and shaking in his bed all afternoon. Even today, 40-odd years later, I'm still shocked that anybody could be so stupid as to lace anything that might be taken by people who are going to drive. Everybody was surprisingly tight-lipped about the whole thing next day, the management no doubt covering their arses in case of lawsuits. But there was no comeback. Without any proof, who're ya gonna call, as they say, and it became a subject of some levity. But it surely goes to prove the old saying that there's one born every minute. And how did it feel to be on an angel-dust high, you ask? I don't know. I fell asleep.

In LA, we were getting 6,000 fans on average for the Aztecs games in the 100,000-seat LA Coliseum – nothing like the 50,000-plus attendances the New York Cosmos were pulling in at the Giants Stadium. And of course there was little in the way of away support, as you had to fly 3,000 miles to New York to watch the Aztecs play the Cosmos if you were an Aztecs fan and vice versa. But clubs other than the Cosmos and the Aztecs were doing well at drawing in the crowds. Minnesota, featuring the great South African star Jomo Sono, were pulling in 28–30,000 fans every week; the Fort Lauderdale Strikers, with Peruvian World Cup forward star Nene Cubillas and Englishman Ray Hudson running the midfield, averaged 15,000 or so; and in South Florida, the Gordon Jago-managed Tampa Bay Rowdies, with Rodney Marsh and Roy Wegerle, were pulling 20,000 and more for big games. Up in Seattle, the Sounders were drawing good attendances in the old AstroTurfed Kingdome, one such occasion being the semi-final of the NASL Championship in 1977 when they beat us 3–2 in front of 52,000 fans.

Over the following few years, it was hard to think of

well-known English League pros who did *not* come out for an NASL stint. Rodney Marsh was particularly popular at Tampa Bay Rowdies, Peter Osgood joined Philadelphia Fury, Alan Hudson was a Seattle Sounder, Johan Cruyff joined the Aztecs, and the likes of Gerd Müller, Bobby Moore, Peter Lorimer, Alan Ball, Mark Hateley, Peter Beardsley, Johan Neeskens, Franz Beckenbauer and Eusébio all turned out for various sides at various times. It was the ageing European footballer's Indian summer, although some might unkindly say it was the ageing European footballer's Indian summer holiday. That's definitely not what I saw and experienced. I compared notes when I ran into Terry Mancini back in the UK recently, and he agreed with me that nobody, no matter what league they had come from, could come over and dominate in the NASL without being in top shape and prepared to work hard. Some 'stars' fell flat on their faces, which may account for some of the more facile put-downs, no pun intended, while other lesser-known players became bigger stars in the States than they were at home: ex-Newcastle man Ray Hudson, who became a team lynchpin in Fort Lauderdale, was a perfect example; Dennis Tueart, ex-Manchester City, enjoyed a huge following alongside Pelé and Chinaglia for the Cosmos; and Mike Flanagan, formerly of Charlton but out here with the New England Tea Men, vied with the likes of Pelé to win the coveted Most Valuable Player (MVP) award.

It irks me a little how many British players from that era put down the American game and those NASL days as a circus sideshow. They have allowed the razzmatazz that accompanied US soccer at the time to overshadow the fact that good competitive football was played, hard training schedules adhered to and crowds royally entertained, even when the game wasn't the best, which we all know can be quite often. In their memoirs and newspaper articles, they treat their time in America as a joke, but I didn't see too many of them stroll through it like it was a breeze and pick up cup-winner's medals or Player of the Year awards, and, more to the point, there were plenty who didn't do well at all. Sure, you get dancing girls before a game, and at Fort Lauderdale, for example, there was a horse-drawn hearse, driven by their English boss, Ron Newman, which pulled up before the stand in order for the team to come jumping out of the coffin while the band played on. The coffin wheeze was maybe a bit overdone for our stodgy Brit tastes, but it's funny how you get used to it all and how much you miss it when it's not there. And who would suggest that all the pre-game razzmatazz before NBA or college basketball games or NFL and college football games takes anything away from the world-class players and teams on show or the highest-quality competition they offer. So I would caution you, although I doubt it's needed today, not to let your prejudices blind you to the real quality that's out there on the American playing fields and in their state-of-the-art stadiums.

In 1978, rising attendances and the influx of players from abroad gave the NASL the confidence to expand the league to 24 clubs. One of these new clubs was Memphis Rogues, and Malcolm Allison was installed as their manager. When a short time later he was sacked, having failed to sign any players before their first-ever game, Eddie McCreadie replaced him. Eddie traded for me from the Aztecs mid-season, as the new American contract allowed, and so Eddie Mac and I were together once again, albeit 4,000 miles from Stamford Bridge. Talk about déjà vu. We had some good players, including English striker Tony Field from the Cosmos, forward Jimmy Husband of Everton fame, ex-Chelsea defender David Stride and flying winger Neil Smillie who had played at Palace. What none of us knew was that 1978, the year I threw my lot in fully in America, was the beginning of the end for the NASL. Like all bubbles, it had to burst, and when the revenues did not catch up with the expenses, the gravy train started to stutter. Memphis Rogues itself lasted only four years, but we had a lot of fun during that time and some pretty good games, too. Eddie parted ways with the club, and I took over as interim coach. I didn't know about Eddie's situation until the news was dropped on me and the offer to take over was made. I wasn't looking for such a position at the time, but when approached by the club it seemed like a better solution from my own and the rest of the players' standpoints than a new coach altogether. It all hardly mattered, however, because although we went to the NASL indoor finals, where we lost to Gordon Jago's Tampa Bay, the club was living on borrowed time. The franchise was sold to a local owner and not long after to a group based in Calgary, Canada, and it folded for good in 1980.

The league was shrinking now as franchises succumbed to financial reality. Like most of the other players who had hoped to make a new life in the States, I was a football gypsy forced to go where the teams located themselves. In 1982, I went to play with the California Surf in Anaheim – home of the Angels baseball team – managed by Peter Wall, who left Palace shortly after I arrived, and at the end of that season I hooked up again with who else but Eddie

Mac, now coaching the Cleveland Crunch in the MISL, the Major Indoor Soccer League. (In US soccer, you have to get used to the alphabet soup nomenclature: for example, the old NASL is now MLS – Major League Soccer.) He invited me to come and play there through the winter, the outdoor close season in the States. The idea was to go up to Cleveland as an assistant coach, but a call a few days later from Eddie changed the role to player with no explanation.

By now the once powerful NASL outdoor league that had boasted the likes of Pelé, Cruyff, Neeskins and Beckenbauer on its masthead and Warner Bros. among its ownership groups was now scrambling unsuccessfully just to stay solvent, while the fledgling MISL indoor league, fighting for its own existence, was bleeding its outdoor competitor dry of players and front-office personnel, hastening its demise. MISL crowds were healthy, especially in hotbed cities like Baltimore, where the Blast were playing to 17,000 sell-out crowds, and Cleveland's Force were regularly pulling in 15,000 fans. Players like Clyde Best, the big Bermudan striker who had made his name at West Ham, and Steve Zungul, who had starred for Hajduk Split in Yugoslavia, were banging in the goals and making what was in some ways a new career for themselves in a new game, at least for as long as the league was going to last, which at that point was anybody's guess. However, guesswork or not, at the age of 39, with outdoor franchises sinking all around us, I was willing to give it a go, at least until any other opportunities cropped up.

I had been in Cleveland for three months and was playing only sporadically when Mick Hoban, a former

English professional who had played for Portland Timbers in the NASL but was now head of Nike soccer promotions, approached me in the middle of the season about coming to work for Nike. I sensed an exit opportunity and jumped at it in principle, pending Eddie's and the club's OK. Eddie could see that it was a way out for me, and, on agreeing I would be paid only what I was due to the date of leaving and no more, I had Eddie's and the club's blessing, we shook hands on my contract and that was it. With the shake of Eddie's hand and a last parting look at the team, I closed the door on my playing career. I had no regrets whatsoever, and in fact I was excited to be out in the wide world facing a whole new challenge. It was an unplanned and yet much welcomed ending for both Diane and myself, as she had stayed back in southern California while I was in Cleveland. We had become tired of failing franchises and the upheavals that moving home entailed for the children Gail and Claire and our son Chas. The new Nike opportunity was exactly what I'd been looking for, and to this day I am eternally grateful to my friend Mick Hoban for giving me the chance at what was a pivotal time in my life.

Nike today is a worldwide household name, but in 1983, despite being movers and shakers in the NBA and college basketball and the NFL and college football, sponsors of some of the biggest names in tennis and dominant in the running shoe market, they were babes in the woods in the soccer footwear market. They had yet to introduce their fabled air technology and their Air Jordan line of basketball shoes, which added over $100 million in sales in its first year alone in addition to their existing basketball footwear line, already a market leader. In contrast, Nike's soccer line was in its infancy, and it was our job to get as much exposure as possible for the fledgling product among the market influencers and trendsetters, the top pro players and teams indoors and outdoors and the leading youth coaches and grass-roots organisations. Children today cannot conceive of an age before trainers, but when I was a child all we had for PE classes were canvas plimsolls with rubber soles. There were none of the state-of-the-art designs and moonshot materials catering to every nuance and need that confront the buyer today. Our shoes came in black or white, they smelled a lot, and you played in them until you scuffed them down and they virtually fell off your feet. Today, of course, kids have different shoes for different sports, and Nike, having penetrated athletics, basketball and tennis (their ability to spot talented youngsters at a ridiculously early age and sponsor them was uncanny), turned their eyes to soccer and have since risen to become market leaders in football boot design and distribution, with a stable of superstar players and teams to compete with their prime competitor and traditional market leader Adidas.

Most company people go straight into their corporate job from school or college, but I was nearing 40, and, after nearly a quarter of a century in full-time football, I found it hard to adapt to having an office, desk, telephone and somewhat regimented hours. It was a huge change reading sales reports and boning up on Nike's and our competitors' product lines and promotional efforts. It was made a bit easier because I was constantly around other sports promotions departments and teams and players we had on contract, but there was always the nagging concern in the back of my mind that I really wasn't a corporate man in my bones. I did my best and toughed it out for almost three years, with Mick Hoban always helping and supporting me, but in the end I had to be honest and admit to myself that I really wasn't cut out for the corporate lifestyle.

It was while at Nike that I made two decisions that changed my life. The first and the one that had by far the most profound and lasting effect was my decision to give up drinking. The fact is, my drinking worried others more than me, although by the time I stopped that was changing and I was beginning to see the light. I always trained hard and gave 100 per cent, and I figured that as long as I trained and played hard, then everything was fine. But, of course, I wasn't playing now and I wasn't keeping fit with rigorous training schedules. Like many at Nike, and afterwards when I went to Dallas and then Wichita, I ran at least three or four times a week, but it was a casual commitment and my conditioning was nowhere near what it had been. Maybe that was the final prompt I needed, as I have to report there was no holy moment, no falling on my knees or terrible incident that caused the change. The simple truth is that for several days I had had two or three glasses of wine in the evening and the following day I woke up with an excruciating headache. It seemed like far too much following too little. 'I'm poisoning myself,' I thought, and on about the fourth morning of these terrible head pains, I decided that was it. I stopped and have never touched another drop or felt the inclination to ever since. That was a quarter of a century ago. I don't mean to belittle anyone else's efforts and problems or make it sound easy, but it was for me – if you can call waiting 30 years for the penny to drop easy. I can't even say whether I was an alcoholic or not. I had drunk regularly and often since I was 15 or 16 years old, so I guess maybe I was. And when it came to writing this book, I was provided with evidence enough of the damage done. Whilst my memories of my childhood, youth and Greenock are fairly clear, ordered and fresh (at least I hope they read so), they are less crisp when I get to Aberdeen and Dundee and positively blurred at Chelsea and Crystal Palace onwards until I stopped drinking. I have no doubt that that pattern isn't coincidental.

The biggest downer for me about the drinking years, and there were many, believe me, is not the memory loss or any bad behaviour on my part (fortunately, I have forgotten most of it, although that doesn't make it any less stupid or occasionally reprehensible) but the fact that the drinking prevented or at least contributed to me not seeing or acknowledging the glaring fault in my game, which was my failure to score goals. This is especially galling because I had excellent speed and good tight skills to create shooting opportunities, and I had a cracking good shot in both feet when I chose to use it, which wasn't often. If I hadn't been drinking and pursuing that lifestyle, I am sure that I would have seen clearly what was happening to my game and would easily have figured out not only how to get myself into more finishing positions every match but how to make it a passion and maybe even an obsession like the one I had with juggling as a kid. There were simple things I could have done, like spending time working on my shooting and becoming one of those players who are dangerous with a shooting opportunity anywhere within 30 yards of goal, like the Gerrards and Lampards today.

I should have known the exact number of times I was getting into the opponents' box and why, and found ways to increase that number. Simple strategies such as getting in the box for free kicks and corners instead of taking them and generally turning my attention to that most vital skill – scoring goals. Looking back, it all seems so straightforward, but at the time my addled mind couldn't see the wood for the trees.

The second decision was the one that launched me back into the game, this time as a coach, and the one that would lead me to the Coerver® Coaching directorship that has been my life these past 25 years. While on my Nike travels, I met Gordon Jago, president and head coach of the Dallas Sidekicks in the MISL, at an indoor game and did something that I never imagined myself doing – I asked him if he needed an assistant coach. I almost fell over when Gordon said he did, and I told him I would be interested and just like that I was back in the game. Gordon had been a very successful young manager in England with Millwall and Queens Park Rangers in the 1970s, and I can remember him being touted as a successor to Alf Ramsey for the England job. He had moved to the States to manage/coach the very successful Tampa Bay Rowdies in the NASL outdoors, which by now had folded and become a fading memory along with the glory days of Pelé and Beckenbauer. Gordon had brought Tatu, the diminutive Brazilian striker, from Tampa. He led the indoor league in scoring and was MVP almost every year. Incredibly, Tatu was still playing football for Dallas as recently as 2003.

I spent a very happy year and a bit with Gordon and the Sidekicks before I was offered the post of head coach at

Wichita Wings, another MISL club. Wichita was one of the league's smallest markets, but it had one of the top teams and several of the best and, perhaps more importantly, highest-paid stars. Among those players were Erik Rasmussen from Denmark, a truly brilliant indoor scorer, and Kim Roentved, another powerful, high-scoring and hard-working Dane. I mention their salaries not because I thought they weren't deserved or anything like that but because, having experienced several clubs folding under my feet not so long before, I felt that somewhere down the road there wouldn't be a happy ending for clubs with a bleeding bottom line, no matter how well heeled, generous and patient their investors might be. Memphis and California were two good examples, and the recently demised New York Cosmos were a classic case, having had Warner Bros. footing their bills. Like many in the league then, I think, I held my breath and hoped for the best. The MISL did get into trouble and saw many franchise deaths and resurrections, but it was a longer time coming than expected and it's been a stubborn league that survives today, albeit in a much reduced form with only eight current indoor teams.

Wichita wasn't a particularly successful or satisfying experience for me as a head coach, although I think it taught me several hard but enlightening lessons. While being almost unbeaten at home, we had problems getting results away from home, which pissed me off no end and led me to say some things I'm not so proud of today. I was sacked midway through my second season, and I took that dismissal hard, for although I knew I had plenty to answer for, I felt hugely let down and perhaps by nobody more so than myself for not seeing things as they were rather than as I would have liked them to be. In the end, however, it worked out well, because by this time I had met another coach, an Englishman from Wimbledon called Alfred Galustian, at the NSCAA (National Soccer Coaches Association of America) convention in Philadelphia. After the two of us had heard and been mightily impressed by the coaching philosophy and methodologies of Wiel Coerver, a former player and manager of the Dutch side Feyenoord, we set about getting permission and formed a new trademarked coaching entity that is known around the world today as Coerver® Coaching.

There was a boy a few years older than me who used to go from back door to back door swapping comics. 'Any swaps?' he'd say. He did it every week, like the insurance man or the milkman. He was a Spurs supporter. When he was asked what he wanted to be when he grew up the answer was always the same: 'Pat Jennings.' He didn't want to be like Pat Jennings, the goalkeeper from Newry with the foot-long hands. He wanted to be Pat Jennings.

We laughed, but I understood. When I was 11 I wanted to be Charlie Cooke.

Charlie Cooke played for Chelsea. My team. I'd chosen them because everyone else followed Leeds or Manchester United and because my best friend followed them. I went through a lot of best friends then: the Chelsea supporter lasted two weeks and four days. I stayed loyal to Chelsea after I'd dumped him and he'd dumped me. We didn't support teams; we followed them. 'Who do you follow?' 'Chelsea.' 'Crap.'

In fact, I followed them nowhere. I'd never been to London; I'd never been anywhere, except Wexford and Kerry. I'd never been inside a football stadium. I hadn't even walked past one. But I had a Chelsea scarf. My mother'd knitted it for me. The blue wasn't quite right, but it didn't matter; it was a Chelsea scarf, the only one in Kilbarrack. Someone in the schoolyard tried to pull it off me. It scorched the back of my neck; the skin was crispy back there for days after. All for Chelsea. I could name the team and the subs. I knew their dates of birth. I knew how much they'd cost. I knew the names of their wives and children. I could put my hand over the top of the team photograph on the bedroom wall and tell all the names by the shape of their legs. Ian Hutchinson cost £5,000. Peter Bonetti was born in Putney. Charlie Cooke was 5 ft 8 in.

Charlie Cooke.

Charlie Cooke was a winger. He was brilliant. He was a genius. He was as good as Georgie Best, and he didn't mess around with women. He was 5 ft 8 in., 12 st. 2 lb. He was from Fife. He was born there on 14 October 1942. 'He was a wonderful dribbler,' it says in Chelsea: A Complete Record *by Scott Cheshire, 'often leaving a series of bemused opponents in his wake.' It's true; it was like that. Often, the opponents were bemused before he even got to them. They just let him trot by.*

'Osgood. Now Hutchinson. Cooke!'

He was 5 ft 8 in. He made himself look smaller: modesty and cunning. It was the height I wanted to be; I'd be happy if I reached it. I was 11 and just over 5 ft. I thought I could make it. His hair was long but not that long; it was a length mothers didn't object to, my mother didn't object to. He was Scottish, I was Irish; both of us weren't English. He'd be 32 by the time I was 16, and I'd sign apprentice forms for Chelsea. He'd be a big brother to me. I'd clean his boots.

305

We'd share digs. My mother would like him. He'd come to our house for Christmas because his parents were dead. I'd save his life. He'd come to my funeral.

One of my friends commentated on matches while we were playing them on the road. He was very good, very fair – considering he was playing as well. We had to tell him who we were before the start. 'Best.' 'No, I'm Best.' 'You're not; I am.' 'Charlie Cooke,' I'd say, always. No one minded. He was mine. I was him. I missed a sitter. 'Oh, no!' I said it with a Scottish accent. 'And, my word,' said the commentator. 'Charlie Cooke holds his head in despair.' I missed a lot of sitters. That was the difference between me and Charlie Cooke: he was brilliant and I was shite. I was good at holding my head in despair. I practised it.

Chelsea played Leeds in the 1970 FA Cup final. The first match was a two-all draw. The replay was eighteen days – ages – later, on a Wednesday night. I prayed for bad weather. Good weather meant high pressure and bad television reception. The day stayed cloudy and mucky for me. I got my homework out of the way. I couldn't eat my dinner. I sat in front of the telly with my scarf ready, a one-man terrace. For most of the game, Chelsea were 1–0 down. It was going to stay that way; I felt it crawling through me. I was very tired and cold. Then . . .

'Osgood. Now Hutchinson. Cooke! . . . And OSGOOD . . .'

Hutchinson stepped over the ball. Osgood kept running. Cooke took the ball and chipped – it took for ever – and Osgood dived and headed, and they'd scored. I ran out into the garden; the house wasn't big enough for me. They were going to win; they were going to win.

They won.

My father shook my hand. 'Well done, old son.' I'd won the FA Cup. It was one of the great moments of my life. I still think that.

Charlie Cooke ended his career playing for American teams called Los Angeles Aztecs, Memphis Rogues and – this one really upsets me – California Surf. I hate to think of him playing on the beach, watched by the cast of Baywatch.

'Yo, Charlie!' 'Way to go, Charlie-ie-ie!'

Jesus.

I don't know where Charlie Cooke is now. I hope he's well. I hope he's 12 st. 2 lb. I hope he's still leaving bemused opponents in his wake.

Roddy Doyle, writer

18

Coerver

In some respects, that meeting in Philly 25 years ago was a historic one for Alfred's future and my own, although we had no way of seeing that fully then. In fact, it couldn't have begun less auspiciously. On the first night there, on walking out of the downtown Philadelphia convention hotel, Alfred slipped and fell on the snow and ice and broke his collarbone.

As if that wasn't bad enough, after getting him by cab to the local hospital emergency room, and while Alfred constantly adjusted his posture to ease the pain, we had to convince the hospital administration people to finally accept Alfred's American Express card in lieu of payment, as they wouldn't accept the excellent private insurance coverage he already had for just such emergencies. In the end, Alfred was attended to, but not before a long and painful wait into the night and an eye-opener regarding some of the cases that a downtown Philly hospital cares for on a Friday evening. There was everything from auto-accident cuts and grazes and broken limbs to a gunshot wound and a long-haired flea-infested down-and-out who was being cleaned up after a mishap. In the end, we got Alfred fixed up, and we always joke about that emergency room and the amount of bag-toting and suitcase-hefting I had to do on his behalf for the rest of that weekend.

That said, it was that weekend that set our future courses for directorships in Coerver® Coaching. We arranged to meet later in the summer at Manhattanville College, NY, where we also met up with Mercer Reynolds and Werner Kummerle, two prominent Cincinnati businessmen who headed a group that underwrote the Cincinnati Classics youth soccer club and a new fitness and indoor soccer facility, the Cincinnati Sports Mall in Fairfax, Ohio. And so it was that Diane, Chas and I came to live and make our home here in Cincinnati, where we still live today. The Reynolds and Kummerle families have been great friends and staunch supporters all these years. They introduced us to a whole new life, and they have my eternal thanks for the opportunities they have provided and for all their many kindnesses to Diane, Chas and me.

For Alfred and me, our interest in Wiel Coerver's philosophies had begun much earlier than the Philadelphia convention. In fact, it was in the late 1970s and early 1980s that Weil had originally come to prominence. Due to poor health, he had left a successful coaching position as a UEFA Cup-winner with Feyenoord to work on his youth-development initiative. He travelled the world looking for a skill-development programme but found none and so started to look at films of old games and break down the moves of some of the great players of the game: Cruyff,

Beckenbauer, Pelé, Matthews, *et al.* He then experimented in teaching the moves step by step, and today it is a widely accepted way to teach what are, to some, complicated skills. Up to that point, technique and quickness and cleverness with the ball were seen as innate abilities. You either had them or you didn't, depending on how blessed you were, and that was that.

When we first came across Weil's work, Alfred and I knew instinctively that he was on to something important. Whilst in the years since we have developed our own curricula and content to include all facets of the game, we have stayed true to Weil's original vision that technique is the foundation of the game, on which all other parts of it are built.

Today, due to Alfred's international efforts, there are Coerver® Coaching player camps, schools, academies and coaching clinics in seventeen countries and on all six continents. Alfred, in his role as global ambassador and presenter, has accumulated dozens of testimonials as to the excellence of our programmes from numerous national coaching federations, internationally renowned coaches such as Sir Alex Ferguson, Carlos Alberto Parreira (Brazil) and Gérard Houllier (France) and many international players, including Jürgen Klinsmann (now Germany coach), Roberto Rivelino, Sir Geoff Hurst and John Collins. I don't think it's too fanciful to say that Coerver® Coaching has changed the way football is taught in many parts of the world today and helped many teachers, parents and players to coach and play better football, and no less importantly, to have more fun and satisfaction while doing so.

What then is Coerver® Coaching, you might ask.

It is two things:

1. <u>A Soccer Skills Training Method</u> suited to players aged 5 to 17, especially in the 8 to 12 year golden years of learning, and their parents, teachers and coaches.
2. <u>A Global Business Network</u> with schools, camps, coaches, clinics and educational products in Europe, Asia and North America.

Our vision back in the day seemed so lofty, and yet it doesn't today. It was to make: 'Coerver® Coaching a leading soccer education provider in key markets around the world by means of coaching products and services that contribute to the improvement and enjoyment of young players and their coaches and teachers'.

I'll still go along with that.

Philosophically, Coerver® Coaching sees the game not as an eleven versus eleven contest but as constantly changing sequences of play between two, three and sometimes four players in different parts of the field. We posit that a team's success is dependent on its players' performances in these exchanges.

We understand that coaches of young players are always working towards playing games, often at weekends, so they frequently concentrate on team tactics. But in Coerver® Coaching, we work on individual and small-group skills. Then we encourage the player to express him or herself through these skills within the team's tactical plan.

Our goals are to develop happy, healthy and responsible players and effective parent/teachers and coaches by:

- Promoting skilful play.
- Empowering students through individual skill development and self-improvement.
- Teaching sportsmanship and respect for all.
- Valuing competition and the desire to win but not at the expense of good sportsmanship or performance.
- Constantly updating and refining the curriculum to maintain leadership in the field and adapt to our customers' needs.

That doesn't sound too bad at all to me either.

In 1997, we developed our six-block Coerver® Coaching Pyramid of Player Development©, which plays a key role in all of our programmes.

Coerver® Coaching Pyramid of Player Development©

THE BUILDING BLOCKS

Ball mastery – Ball exercises of increasing difficulty using both feet to improve touch, flexibility and control.

Receiving and passing – Exercises to improve first touch and develop accurate and creative passing.

Moves (1 v. 1) – Exercises and games that teach game-winning individual moves that can create space.

Speed – Exercises and games that improve acceleration, speed with and without the ball and change of pace.

Finishing – Exercises and games that teach technique and encourage instinctive play around the box against packed defences.

Group play – Exercises and games to improve small-group combination play with an emphasis on attack.

At Coerver® Coaching player camps and schools, we train hundreds of thousands of boys and girls of between 15 and 17 years of age all over the world in individual and small-group skills and encourage them to express themselves. We believe that it's the players and their abilities and not the team systems that are important. That between two teams playing similar systems, as is the usual scenario in most professional, amateur and youth leagues around the world, it's the individual players' qualities that make the difference. As Alfred likes to put it:

English players in the Premiership today don't lack nutritional or physical conditioning guidance. They are as big and strong and usually just as quick as the imported superstars. The differences lie in their abilities with the ball, their skill to be deceptive and work the ball at speed, pass

314

and receive perfectly under pressure, and above all their comfort and confidence in taking on opponents. These are the things Coerver® Coaching helps develop.

As for the game in America, it is going gangbusters, and I think you'd have to have been in a coma these last ten years not to know it. The US youth game is huge and ever growing, equally represented by boys and girls. At the pro level, several feeder leagues are already competing under the leadership of the MLS outdoor league, and while the Women's Soccer League has temporarily closed shop, the US women have already won the World Championship and will continue to go close every time they compete.

As for the future of the youth game here in the US, I think it is beyond most countries' wildest dreams. America is a huge and diverse country with dramatically varying climates and demographics, and there are a couple of things that spring immediately to mind when I think of the soccer situation here compared to many other parts of the world.

First off, the weather. In Scotland, for example, it's iffy at best during the football season. Summers can be nice, but that's when most youth football closes down along with the school systems. The bottom line is that there are no really long periods of good weather for youngsters to play in really good outdoor conditions.

This isn't so different to other parts of the world, including some parts of the US. But one of the reasons football is growing so fast and effectively here is that they have so many purpose-built indoor facilities in addition to school gymnasiums and all-weather school fields where kids and adults can play at any time. In Cincinnati alone, a city of 500,000 and maybe 1.5 million in the greater urban area, we have at least 12 soccer-specific indoor facilities, not counting multisports indoor and outdoor fields at local schools and colleges, which are in popular demand. In the fall and winter, these facilities are packed with youth leagues and club practices that, with the coming of good weather in the spring, go outdoors for the summertime leagues, not to mention summer tournaments, which in themselves are huge and everywhere. So kids in the US, no matter where they live or whatever climate they have, can train and play in competitive leagues and tournaments with their team almost year long if they wish. I don't think that's as much the case in many other countries, although I'm sure that's changing just as it continues to change and develop here. But leaving aside the affluent American parents' drive to provide the best opportunities for their children and the natural American instinct to compete and win, I believe it's this easy access to training and competition that will in the long run prove a terrific advantage to the US.

There's also been a change in perception of Coerver® Coaching over the years. Skilled attackers are hugely valued these days, as the constant importing of mind-bogglingly expensive foreign stars into the Premiership demonstrates. Centres of Excellence directors who maybe previously suffered the Brit superiority disease – like we did before Puskás and Hungary showed us better in 1953 at Wembley, Real and Eintracht showed us at Hampden in 1960 and the rest of the world has been showing us ever since 1966 – are now waking up to the enormous benefits they can reap by developing skilled players along Coerver® Coaching programme lines.

But irrespective of the British game waking up to some hard realities about what the country is producing through the youth system, Coerver® Coaching will continue to do good things for its students around the world whatever level they play at. It doesn't matter whether they go on to become professional players or just play the game for fun, they'll learn some top-class soccer skills, build self-esteem and have bunches of fun doing it. Take a child who's maybe not fast but gets interested in developing his skills. He pays attention, asks questions and applies himself. He develops excellent ball skills to make up for his lack of pace and becomes an outstanding shooter or an important playmaker, or maybe just an efficient cog in his team, no matter what level he may be playing at. That child can feel good about himself and his game. He can be proud of what he's achieved and carry the lessons he's learned about discipline and perseverance and the importance of practice and technique into every other part of his life. Sounds a bit corny maybe, but it's the youth-development vision Alfred and I began with and why we're still so passionate about Coerver® Coaching.

Today, Coerver® Coaching continues apace throughout the world. It is firmly established in Europe, Asia and Australia, and here in the US we have licensees in 41 states. We hope to continue that growth both here in the US and throughout Mexico and South America in the coming years.

Alfred and I produce soccer-training DVDs and books that are sold around the world and were lauded as 'The world's number-one soccer skills teaching method' by none other than the great Sir Stanley Matthews. This should prove to be an exciting part of our business development as we start the twenty-first century and enter the new and ever developing digital world.

Since those days in the early 1980s, Coerver® Coaching events have taken our families to diverse locations throughout the world: the Houses of Parliament for a press demonstration; several NSCAA conventions throughout America for my son Chas and his teammates at the Classics to show off their skills; tournaments all over the US; an unforgettable team trip to Werner Kummerle's home town of Reutlingen, near the Black Forest in Germany, when the boys were only 12, a trip that all the players and parents still remember fondly and reminisce about nearly 20 years later; trips to coach and spread the Coerver® gospel back in my old stomping ground of Aberdeen, as well as to Tokyo, Coogee Beach in Australia and the playing fields of Eton, no less.

The year before the 1994 World Cup here in the US, we hosted Roberto Rivelino, Sir Geoff Hurst and Sir Stanley Matthews for a nationwide tour on behalf of consumer giant Procter & Gamble who have their world headquarters here in Cincinatti.

We were also honoured to have Karl-Heinz Rummenigge work out with Chas's team during that time, and he very kindly participated in a visit of Coerver® kids to Munich and a video we made for German TV.

Coerver® Coaching also enabled us to attend the 1998 World Cup in France and present a Coerver® Coaching clinic in the mini-stadium under the Eiffel Tower, not far from the crowded lawns and gardens where international groups of fans collected to mingle and celebrate and play each other in sometimes nothing less than full-blooded five-a-side games. My brightest memories of that trip are the Scottish fans in kilts and sporrans on the lawns leading to the Eiffel Tower sharing their beers and whisky with anybody and everybody, and the fun they had playing the foreign opposition from all parts of the globe. It showed so clearly the game's ability to draw peoples together.

In recent years, there's obviously been a sea change in Chelsea's finances and performances and the way the club is now run and perceived around the world, and I have to confess it's been a welcome and flattering change for me. Chas and I had the opportunity to watch the 2005 Premiership trophy presentation from the Sky TV booth, and in the recent Chelsea Centenary Year celebrations Diane and I had the chance to attend several terrific functions put on by Chelsea Pitch Owners in conjunction with the club, and marvellous affairs they were. This was especially true of the Century of Chelsea celebration held at the Bridge under the West stands, at which the greatest-ever Chelsea XI, as voted for by the fans, was revealed. Not only was I humbled to be voted into such exalted company, alongside Desailly, Terry and Lampard, as well as my old teammates Eddie Mac, Peter Bonetti and Ossie, but it was also a chance to appreciate just what lengths the powers that be at the club have gone to to make us 'old 'uns' feel welcome again and to promote the history of the club, of which, of course, we are a part.

During those recent visits, I also had the chance to make a couple of appearances on Chelsea TV, hosted by Neil Barnett, and I want to take this opportunity to thank him for having me on and reminding the world that, yes, I am indeed still alive and kicking. The experience was truly appreciated.

It is exhilarating for Chelsea fans to be supporting a club that knows where it is going but has not forgotten its past and its heritage. I am personally gratified that in their pursuit of world domination, Chelsea have not forsaken their culture of playing entertaining football and attracting and developing flair players. Petr Cech is astonishing in goal, John Terry stops us all biting our nails, Frank Lampard is the sweetest midfielder for many a year and Joe Cole – well, Joe makes my heart flutter, and that's not good at my age.

I was over again when Chelsea won their second consecutive Premiership in 2006 and was truly honoured and touched when Ronnie Harris and I were asked to go out onto the pitch and hand over the trophy to be presented. A marvellous gesture towards us, I thought, and indicative of the inclusiveness and kinship that is thriving again at the club. Long may it last.

The saddest event of the last couple of years was undoubtedly Peter Osgood's passing. It was more poignant because we had been together with most of the guys having a grand old time of it just a couple of weeks before, and he was looking pretty good, I thought. He had lost a few pounds since I had last seen him, and I figured that had to be a good thing, as it would be for any of us. Ossie had gone on to a successful after-dinner speaking career, and I envied that skill and was happy to tell him so that evening after our reunion event at the London Hilton.

'Anybody could do it, Cookie,' he said. 'It's all a matter of practice, of getting up there and doing it. I was terrible my first couple of times, but after a bit I got it down, and now I can do it no problem. But anybody can do it.'

These were some of the last words I remember hearing Ossie say as he was going to his room. We were leaving early from the hotel to catch our plane the next morning and wouldn't get a chance to say cheerio.

'Good night, Cookie, lovely to see you, old mate, and have a safe trip home,' he said as he got in the escalator.

'You too, big fella,' I smiled, and those were the last words we spoke.

Final Word

I couldn't end this book on a sad note. It wouldn't be right. It's a great blow for all us guys when we start to drop off our perches – not only do we lose great friends like Ossie, Hutch and Nobby Houseman, and thoughts about our own mortality then jab us in the ribs, but we are transported back to the days when we were young, fit and carefree. When every day just got better. We were lauded and applauded. Fans hung on to our shirts and our every word. We were doing what we wanted to do more than anything in the world, and we were getting paid handsomely for it. It was beyond our wildest dreams, so no wonder none of us wanted it to end.

My overwhelming emotion having finished this book is one of gratitude. I am thankful to everyone that contributed to my career in whatever way. In these pages, I may have taken a few swipes at managers and boards at some of the clubs I played at, but I hope I was providing my perspective on certain situations. When all is done,

I am eternally grateful to all the owners, directors and managers who employed me in whatever capacity during my career and life. You see, I am still that little boy in my back yard juggling with a ball till the sun went down.

I am grateful to my family, my friends, my colleagues and, of course, to the fans of all the clubs I played for. Without you, as they say, none of this would have been possible. I thank you all for helping me to make a living and enjoy an eventful life in the finest game in the world.

Appendix

A Statistical Record
by Paul Collier

PLAYING CAREER –
BRITISH PROFESSIONAL CLUBS

	League		FA Cup		Lge Cup		Europe	
	A	G	A	G	A	G	A	G

Aberdeen (June 1960 to December 1964)

1960–61	32	10	2	0	5	0	–	–
1961–62	29	5	5	0	5	2	–	–
1962–63	27	8	3	0	6	0	–	–
1963–64	22	3	4	0	4	2	–	–
1964–65	15	1	0	0	6	1	–	–

Dundee (December 1964 to April 1966)

1964–65	18	7	1	0	0	0	0	0
1965–66	29	4	2	0	6	0	–	–

Chelsea (April 1966 to October 1972)

1966–67	33	3	5+1	0	3	0	–	–
1967–68	41	3	5	1	1	1	–	–
1968–69	25+1	0	5	1	2	0	3	1
1969–70	35	4	6	0	2	1	–	–
1970–71	28+3	1	3	0	3	0	8	0
1971–72	35+3	2	3	1	7	1	4	0
1972–73	7+1	2	0	0	0	0	–	–

Crystal Palace (October 1972 to January 1974)

1972–73	29	0	3	1	0	0	–	–
1973–74	13+2	0	0+1	0	0+1	0	–	–

Chelsea (January 1974 to March 1978)

1973–74	17	1	0	0	0	0	–	–
1974–75	38+1	5	1	0	4	1	–	–
1975–76	16+1	1	2+1	0	0	0	–	–
1976–77	8	0	0	0	0	0	–	–
1977–78	6	0	1	0	0	0	–	–

RECORD

	League		FA Cup		Lge Cup		Europe	
Team	**A**	**G**	**A**	**G**	**A**	**G**	**A**	**G**
Aberdeen	125	27	14	0	26	5	–	–
Dundee	47	11	3	0	6	0	0	0
Chelsea	204+8	15	27+1	3	18	3	15	1
Crystal Palace	42+2	0	3+1	1	0+1	0	–	–
Chelsea	85+2	7	4+1	0	4	1	–	–
TOTALS	503+12	60	51+3	4	54+1	9	15	1

EUROPEAN APPEARANCES (ALL WITH CHELSEA)

Date	Opponents	Round	Venue	Result	Goals
1968–69					
18/9	Greenock Morton	ICFC 1R 1L	Home	5–0	1
23/10	DWS Amsterdam	ICFC 2R 1L	Home	0–0	–
30/10	DWS Amsterdam	ICFC 2R 2L	Away	0–0	–
1970–71					
17/9	Aris Salonika	ECWC 1R 1L	Away	1–1	–
4/11	CSKA Sofia	ECWC 2R 2L	Home	1–0	–
10/3	Brugge	ECWC 3R 1L	Away	0–2	–
24/3	Brugge	ECWC 3R 2L	Home	4–0	–
14/4	Manchester City	ECWC SF 1L	Home	1–0	–
28/4	Manchester City	ECWC SF 2L	Away	1–0	–
19/5	Real Madrid	ECWC Final	Neutral	1–1	–
21/5	Real Madrid (replay)	ECWC Final	Neutral	2–1	–
1971–72					
15/9	Jeunesse Hautcharage	ECWC 1R 1L	Away	8–0	–
29/9	Jeunesse Hautcharage	ECWC 1R 2L	Home	13–0	–
20/10	Atvidaberg	ECWC 2R 1L	Away	0–0	–
3/11	Atvidaberg	ECWC 2R 2L	Home	1–1	–

Appearances	Won	Drawn	Lost	Goals
15	8	6	1	1

Key
ICFC = Inter-Cities Fairs Cup
ECWC = European Cup-Winners' Cup

MAJOR HONOURS

FA Cup winner's medal (1970)

FA Cup runners-up medal (1967)

League Cup runners-up medal (1972)

European Cup-Winners' Cup winner's medal (1971)

16 caps for Scotland

TRANSFERS

Aberdeen to Dundee (December 1964, £40,000)

Dundee to Chelsea (April 1966, £72,000)

Chelsea to Crystal Palace (October 1972, £85,000)

Crystal Palace to Chelsea (January 1974, £17,000)

MANAGERS

Tommy Pearson (December 1960 to December 1964)

Bob Shankly (December 1964 to February 1965)

Sammy Keane (February 1965 to April 1965)

Bobby Ancell (April 1965 to April 1966)

Tommy Docherty (April 1966 to October 1967)

Dave Sexton (October 1967 to October 1972)

Bert Head (October 1972 to March 1973)

Malcolm Allison (March 1973 to January 1974)

Dave Sexton (January 1974 to October 1974)

Ron Suart (October 1974 to April 1975)

Eddie McCreadie (April 1975 to July 1977)

Ken Shellito (July 1977 to March 1978)

NB Dates above indicate the period that Charlie Cooke played for each manager

PLAYING CAREER – NASL

	Regular Season				Play-offs		
	A	G	As	P	A	G	As	P

Los Angeles Aztecs (June 1976 to July 1978)

	A	G	As	P	A	G	As	P
1976	12	2	6	10	1	0	0	0
1977	20	2	15	19	5	1	1	3
1978	16	2	5	9	–	–	–	–
Total	48	6	26	38	6	1	1	3

Memphis Rogues (July 1978 to August 1980)

	A	G	As	P	A	G	As	P
1978	7	0	0	0	–	–	–	–
1979	22	2	3	7	–	–	–	–
1980	25	1	8	10	–	–	–	–
Total	54	3	11	17	–	–	–	–

California Surf (March 1981 to August 1981)

	A	G	As	P	A	G	As	P
1981	29	3	10	16	–	–	–	–
Total	29	3	10	16	–	–	–	–
Overall Total	131	12	47	71	6	1	1	3

Key
A = appearances
G = goals (2 points)
As = assists (1 point)
P = points

SCOTLAND INTERNATIONAL CAREER

App.	Date	Opponents	Competition	Venue	Result	Goals
1965						
1.	24/11	Wales	HIC	Glasgow	4–1	–
2.	7/12	Italy	WCQ	Naples	0–3	–
1966						
3.	18/6	Portugal	Friendly	Glasgow	0–1	–
4.	25/6	Brazil	Friendly	Glasgow	1–1	–
1968						
5.	24/2	England	HIC/ECQ	Glasgow	1–1	–
6.	30/5	Netherlands	Friendly	Amsterdam	0–0	–
7.	6/11	Austria	WCQ	Glasgow	2–1	–
8.	11/12	Cyprus	WCQ	Nicosia	5–0	–
1969						
9.	16/4	W. Germany	WCQ	Glasgow	1–1	–*
10.	3/5	Wales	HIC	Wrexham	5–3	–
11.	6/5	N. Ireland	HIC	Glasgow	1–1	–
12.	17/5	Cyprus	WCQ	Glasgow	8–0	–
13.	5/11	Austria	WCQ	Vienna	0–2	–
1971						
14.	3/2	Belgium	ECQ	Liège	0–3	–
1975						
15.	5/2	Spain	ECQ	Valencia	1–1	–
16.	13/5	Portugal	Friendly	Glasgow	1–0	–

Appearances	Won	Drawn	Lost	Goals
16	6	6	4	0

Key
HIC = Home International Championship
WCQ = World Cup qualifier
ECQ = European Championships qualifier
* appeared as second-half substitute

MANAGERS

Jock Stein (apps 1–2)

John Prentice (apps 3–4)

Bobby Brown (apps 5–14)

Willie Ormond (apps 15–16)

OTHER REPRESENTATIVE GAMES

Scotland Under-23s

Date	Opponents	Venue	Result	Goals
1962				
5/12	Wales	Aberdeen	2–0	–
1963				
4/12	Wales	Wrexham	1–3	–
1964				
2/12	Wales	Kilmarnock	3–0	–
1965				
24/2	England	Aberdeen	0–0	–

Appearances	Won	Drawn	Lost	Goals
4	2	1	1	0

Scottish League Representative Team

Date	Opponents	Venue	Result	Goals
1962				
14/11	Italian League	Rome	3–4	1
28/11	Irish League	Celtic Park	11–0	2
1965				
17/3	Football League	Hampden Park	2–2	–
8/9	Irish League	Hampden Park	6–2	–

Appearances	Won	Drawn	Lost	Goals
4	2	1	1	3